EXPORTING REVOLUTION

EXPORTING REVOLUTION

CUBA'S GLOBAL SOLIDARITY

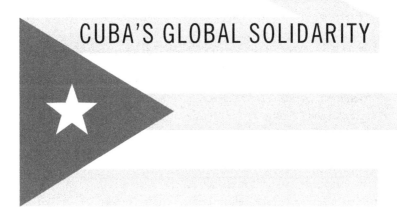

MARGARET RANDALL

DUKE UNIVERSITY PRESS
Durham and London | 2017

© 2017 Duke University Press
All rights reserved
Printed in the United States of America on acid-free paper ∞
Text designed by Jennifer Hill
Cover designed by David Drummond
Typeset in Minion Pro by Westchester Publishing Services

Library of Congress Cataloging-in-Publication Data
Names: Randall, Margaret, [date] author.
Title: Exporting revolution : Cuba's global solidarity / Margaret Randall.
Description: Durham : Duke University Press, 2017. | Includes bibliographical
references and index.
Identifiers:
LCCN 2016044712 (print)
LCCN 2016047428 (ebook)
ISBN 9780822363842 (hardcover : alk. paper)
ISBN 9780822369042 (pbk. : alk. paper)
ISBN 9780822372967 (ebook)
Subjects: LCSH: Cuba—History—Revolution, 1959—Influence. |
Political culture—Cuba. | Cuba—Foreign relations. | Cuba—Relations—
United States. | United States—Relations—Cuba.
Classification: LCC F1788.R254 2017 (print) | LCC F1788 (ebook) |
DDC 972.9106/4—dc23
LC record available at https://lccn.loc.gov/2016044712

For Mark Behr

    1963–2015

wise and courageous friend,

brilliant thinker, writer,

and teacher

CONTENTS

ACKNOWLEDGMENTS

This inquiry has been a journey. For decades I witnessed the Cuban Revolution's extraordinary internationalism, so familiar it seemed hardly out of the ordinary. When I lived in the country it was a daily presence in the moral stance of individuals as well as on the part of the population as a whole. After I left, its profile began to stand out against an increasingly mean-spirited backdrop of global greed, violence, and plunder. Why was no one writing about the phenomenon?

When I decided to do so, many friends and others offered their ideas, experiences, questions, and support. My beloved life partner, Barbara Byers, made room for the new inhabitant in our lives and helped make my work possible with her clarity and feedback. Gisela Fosado, my editor at Duke University Press, was an inspiration: enthusiastic, critical, and as encouraging as she has been with the earlier books we've done together; her assistant, Lydia Rose Rappoport-Hankins, was knowledgeable and helpful. As always, Duke assigned a patient and capable production editor to the project; thank you, Liz Smith. The two anonymous reviewers who read my original proposal offered suggestions that encouraged me to ask the hard questions, and I am grateful to them as well.

My profound gratitude also goes to the numerous people, inside and outside Cuba, who contributed in one way or another. Anya Achtenberg read an early draft, challenged me on a number of important points, and made suggestions that enormously enriched the final manuscript. John Randall read a draft and gave me valuable feedback. My son, Gregory Randall, read the manuscript while we were vacationing together in Uruguay. He and I have shared our thoughts on Cuba and the state of our world for many years, and his input this time around was especially meaningful. Nancy Alonso, Arturo Arango, Teresa Blankmeyer Burke, Luisa Campuzano, Norberto

Codina, Emilio Comas Paret, Laidi Fernández de Juan, Jorge Fornet, Michele Frank, Silvia Gil, Julio César Guanche, Juan Luis Martín, Christina Mills, Laura Ruiz Montes, Jane Norling, Mary Louise Pratt, Rini Price, V. B. Price, Víctor Rodríguez Núñez, Renato Rosaldo, Maruja Santos, Robert Schweitzer, and Mirta Yáñez listened to one section or another, answered questions, discussed specific issues, or helped in other ways. I am also grateful to William P. Kinney at the University of New Mexico's Zimmerman Library for some much appreciated last-minute detective work. Angelita Arenal provided a welcoming home away from home while I did my final fieldwork in Cuba. I am, of course, indebted as well to the many others who have written about areas covered here and whose work I have consulted.

One with whom I expected to have particularly insightful conversations about internationalism was Mark Behr, my dear friend and South African novelist who died suddenly before we could explore the issue in the context of this writing. As a young Afrikaner, Mark fought on the wrong side of the war in Angola. Later he became one of the strongest defenders I've known of the principles he had betrayed in his youth. I can only imagine the stories and wisdom he might have shared. Mark was deeply thoughtful about the meanings and implications our actions have for ourselves, our various communities, and national policies. Thanks to interviews and to other texts he left behind, I have been able to draw on his brilliant contributions to the subject.

My conclusions, as always, are my own.

Thank you all, and may the conversations continue.

1

HOW THESE IDEAS
TOOK SHAPE

Exporting revolution: that was the accusation the United States launched at Cuba for years, the one it used to justify all manner of subterfuge and attack. Exaggerating the threat of "communism at our doorstep" and creating an aura of fear toward the tiny island nation were part of U.S. governmental strategy from the beginning and continued to be for more than half a century—even when many in the corporate community began pleading for policy changes that would facilitate doing business on the island. Yet even with the reestablished relations between our two countries, regime change and nation building clearly remain part of the U.S. agenda.

It's time we claim the old phrase *exporting revolution*, free it from its cold war aura, and acknowledge its legitimate meaning.

Exporting revolutionary aid—not imposing its way of life on other countries but lending military support to movements fighting for independence in Africa or aiding insurgent groups attempting to defeat cruel dictatorships in Latin America—has always been Cuban revolutionary policy. Unlike powerful nations occupying weaker ones at will for geopolitical gain or in order to take possession of their natural resources, Cuba's international outreach constituted a new and far-reaching model of solidarity. That solidarity continues to be seen in the Revolution's extraordinary humanitarian aid and disaster relief.

The Uruguayan poet and public intellectual Mario Benedetti, writing in 1973, addressed the U.S. accusation that Cuba was exporting revolution by going to the grain: "The truth is . . . the revolution has ceased to be an abstract possibility and become a real transformation,

a believable image. The imperialists have never tired of accusing Cuba of exporting revolution. But of course the real and unforgivable export for which
Cuba is responsible (just like Vietnam) is the example of a small country far
from the great powers, that is capable of defeating the empire and even hu-
miliating it in the eyes of the world."[1]

During the Cuban Revolution's first months a group of Nicaraguan rebels were already undergoing rudimentary military training on the island,
and a Guatemalan group planned to set sail from its coast and establish
a base on home soil. Cuba's leadership denied having anything to do with
either (failed) effort, although we now know that wasn't true. It was important to establish a political identity that would ensure the country a respected place in the community of nations, which meant going slowly with
both Washington and the Kremlin. At the same time Cuba's increased isolation as well as its rapidly consolidating ideology made its government eager
to support guerrilla warfare, especially in Latin America. As U.S. covert and
overt attacks intensified, the Revolution also felt justified in defending itself
and in countering a policy of ongoing attack with a strategy of supporting
liberation struggles throughout the world.

It was logical that a small island nation that had successfully defeated a
dictatorial government would be eager to help others do the same. Cuba was
the last Latin American or Caribbean country to liberate itself from colonialism and the first to free itself from imperialist control. As such it had
tremendous moral support from its neighbors in the region, all of whom
endured some degree of exploitation and humiliation from decades of U.S.
interference in their internal affairs, unfair economic and trade policies, and
their own governments' brutal treatment of dissidents. Domestic national
security forces learned many of the techniques employed in that brutal
treatment (among them extreme interrogation methods, often tantamount
to torture) at U.S. academies in Panama and Georgia.[2]

Following its own victory the Cuban Revolution naturally began to see
itself as part of a worldwide movement to extend freedom and the promise
of social justice to a number of Third World countries where liberation
struggles were under way. Its military aid to these insurgencies took place
in the 1970s and 1980s and had pretty much run its course by the end of the
latter decade.

But Cuba's internationalism is not limited to battlefield assistance. It includes helping others out of poverty and backwardness, shaping new ideas
about the causes of underdevelopment, teaching adult literacy, coming to
the aid of nations suffering dramatic natural disasters, and sending teachers

and medical personnel to dozens of poor countries. It involves lending its experts in fields ranging from agriculture to fishing and biotechnology. It encompasses bringing tens of thousands of young people to study in Cuba, including hundreds to obtain medical degrees—all tuition-free. This internationalism is ongoing and spectacular.

In fact Cuba's aid to those mired in poverty and underdevelopment has evolved as one of the Revolution's most profound and emblematic characteristics, a quality consciously cultivated in the new human being who emerged *opposite Bunck* in the throes of such profound social change. The Cuban internationalist is the New Man (and Woman) of whom Ernesto "Che" Guevara spoke.[3] As a revolutionary virtue, then, Cuba's internationalism is more complex and multifaceted than simply going elsewhere to fight or heal or teach. It is a quality the Revolution has consciously and systematically instilled in its citizens. *Internationalism = rev. virtue*

The accusation that Cuba was exporting revolution surged immediately following Fidel Castro's victory at the beginning of 1959. In the Soviet Union in January of that year Khrushchev and others in the Kremlin already had their eyes on Che Guevara and Raul Castro, who, they believed, had Marxist tendencies. Cuba did not yet have diplomatic relations with the Soviet Union, so the Soviets tried sending a security agent disguised as a journalist to the Caribbean island to find out what kind of a revolution had taken place.[4] They attempted to get information from their embassy in Mexico as well. No one really knew who those bearded rebels were.

In the United States the questions struck closer to home and were even more urgent, and plenty of undercover investigation was also going on. In April 1959 Fidel Castro made his first trip to Cuba's neighbor to the north. Much has been written about his meeting with Vice President Richard Nixon (neither man impressed the other) and his unsuccessful attempts to get the United States to increase its sugar quota or otherwise invest in the new Cuba. In all his U.S. venues Fidel denied that he was a communist. Pride in victory was high, popular participation the name of the game, and free elections were promised.

In fact Fidel may not have been a Marxist at the time, in the strictly academic sense, and he did not belong to his country's Communist Party (the People's Socialist Party, PSP), but this had little effect on what others thought, or on the direction his revolution would take. He certainly believed in the egalitarian nature of socialism, an egalitarianism long suspect in the United States. Despite discussions within his administration about whether to try to control or eliminate Cuba's new leader, President Dwight D. Eisenhower soon authorized the first of many covert programs aimed at destroying the Revolution and bringing the island back into the U.S. fold.

In Cuba Che was also being questioned by representatives of a number of nations and their security agents. He too denied communist affiliation and described a revolution intent upon serving the needs of the Cuban people. As was true of Fidel, Che had never been a member of the Communist Party. It seemed important to emphasize the movement's originality and not make pronouncements of concern to governments whose recognition and support were needed.

The Soviets were courting Cuba's revolutionaries, who just might have pulled off the first socialist revolution in the Western Hemisphere. The United States was becoming ever more alarmed. Today, when it is possible to read some of the intelligence from those years, what we find seems uniformly inept when not frankly out of synch with reality (although clues can be gleaned to support several different hypotheses). The relationships of powerful countries with those that suddenly become players and must be taken into account are always beset with intrigue.

Raul and Che had read Marx and Lenin, and Fidel was well read in all the philosophical classics. There were also a number of high-level members of the PSP—Carlos Rafael Rodríguez, Juan Marinello, and Blas Roca among them—who possessed a profound knowledge of Marxism-Leninism and were fully integrated into the new government. Like most communist parties of the era, the PSP had opposed armed struggle and had come on board only toward the end of the war, when the July 26 Movement's victory seemed inevitable.[5] In postwar Cuba some of its members began to occupy positions of power. Over the next several decades their influence led the country into more than one economic error. It also did harm in the cultural arena, although this eventually proved easier to reverse. The Revolution's leadership, finally fully concentrated in the men and women who had come to political maturity through the recent struggle, was developing a uniquely Cuban ideological identity. For the first time Cubans themselves were deciding their future and devising ways to bring hundreds of thousands of men and women—most of whom were brought up on a discourse of virulent anticommunism—to understand what socialism could mean for them.

These positions radiated outward. Following the 1959 Revolution, the small Caribbean island country exerted an influence far beyond its size or population and in areas in which it might not have been expected to do so. This is a book about that influence and solidarity. Much of it is a product of the Revolution, though some of its roots can be traced to earlier times. My association with Cuba has been long and close, but my realization of its influence and exceptional world presence in so many different areas came about in an unexpected way.

Throughout the spring and summer of 2015 I was putting the finishing touches on a bilingual anthology of Cuban poetry.[6] The volume covers eight decades and includes the work of fifty-six poets, from the diaspora as well as the island. The selection process wasn't easy. My exploration led me from one poet to another, and I read poems by Nicolás Guillén, Dulce María Loynaz, Virgilio Piñera, José Lezama Lima, Gastón Baquero, Fayad Jamís, Roberto Fernández Retamar, Fina García Marruz, Antón Arrufat, Nancy Morejón, and Reina María Rodríguez, among others. Although I had known many of these poets and their work for years, I can only describe as breathtaking the experience of reading with an eye to translating for this collection.

As I worked I realized that more than a few Cubans had influenced Latin American poetry far beyond the country's borders. I discerned a transition from modernism to conversational mode earlier than when that transition occurred elsewhere, and a leading-edge vernacular. I found an engagement with humanity emblematic of the socially conscious but not bogged down by clichéd or propagandistic images of worker-owned factories or farms. I listened to powerful voices reinventing language and leading in directions not yet explored in Spanish elsewhere—or in English. Younger poets less well known internationally were just as impressive. Other Spanish-speaking countries have had their brilliant voices: Spain's Lorca, Peru's Vallejo, Chile's Neruda, Uruguay's Benedetti, Mexico's Paz.[7] But for its size and population Cuba has produced poets with an inordinate impact.

I immediately intuited that I was looking at a sociocultural phenomenon, and needed to explore it more closely. At any given time intellectuals and artists, perhaps especially poets, are a nation's social conscience. In the most propitious circumstances they are a chorus of its diverse voices, reflecting character and circumstance. In the least their silence speaks for cultures that have been stifled, forced underground, or even decimated by the numbing mentality that so often results from endless war, an impoverished socioeconomic climate, or heavy-handed political control (although when poets strive to escape their suffocating effects such situations themselves have also generated great poetry). Throughout history and across the globe poems smuggled out of prisons have borne truths rarely plumbed in the history books or on what passes for the nightly news.

All revolutions, in the creative convulsions of their immediate aftermath, have given birth to exciting art. In the Soviet Union the years 1917 to 1925 were marked by artistic innovation. The filmmaker Sergei Eisenstein, poet Osip Mandelstam, and painter Wassily Kandinsky were but three among an explosion of artists who emerged in that place and time.[8] As the Russian Revolution struggled to survive, the work of such luminaries fell victim to a politics of bureaucratic rigidity and censorship. This happened in Cuba as well, but the most powerful voices were eventually able to prevail. I wanted to understand why creativity and freedom of expression survived in Cuba when it suffered more definitive repression in other twentieth-century revolutions.

Poets also create and project a nation's imaginary: glimpses of a future unique to its history and culture and, when endowed with a profound understanding of the intersections of chance, ideas, collective feeling, and praxis, trace fragments of the roadmap by which a people may claim that future. Centuries later we often look to an era's major poets for clues to that era's significance and complexities. The poetic genre, so little appreciated here in the United States, mirrors who we have been and are in ways that invite exploration (think Whitman, Ginsberg, Rich, di Prima, Harjo).[9] So when one nation's poets exert an influence on others, it is noteworthy, especially when that nation is a small and beleaguered island struggling to survive.

Cuba's rich intellectual and artistic history goes back centuries, issuing from diverse cultures even as its people came up against class and racial barriers. In poetry one need think only of José María de Heredia, Gertrudis Gómez de Avellaneda, or Nicolás Guillén. The U.S. poet, translator, publisher, and editor Mark Weiss writes, "Cuba has had an active literary culture for four hundred years, which since the late nineteenth century has had a disproportionate influence on the literatures of all the Spanish speaking Americas."[10]

Other artistic genres also offer important figures. In music there were such greats as Ernesto Lucuona, Bola de Nieve, Sindo Garay, and those other old men now most commonly referred to as the *vieja trova* (veteran troubadours). In the visual arts were Víctor Manuel, Wilfredo Lam, René Portocarero, Mariano Rodríguez, and Antonia Eiriz.[11] The work of Amelia Peláez still reflects the island's colors and light, and one can see the luminous *media lunas* that inspired her unique vision in some of the country's older buildings.[12] Crossover genres unique to the country, such as those in which artists have reproduced those half-moon stained glass windows or preserved the Santería signatures or symbols, also feed a rich ambience.

That so much of this ambience has gone to ruin during recent decades of privation makes these glimpses of art all the more precious and magical.

A nineteenth-century novel translated into dozens of languages, which has always remained in print in Spanish, has been reproduced in several genres both before and since the Revolution of 1959. It is *Cecilia Valdés* by Cirillo Villaverde. The book was first published in Havana in 1839 and, demonstrating its cross-border appeal, came out in an expanded version in New York in 1882. Gonzalo Roig composed a two-act zarzuela based on the novel, which had its Havana premier in 1932 and was staged by New York's Metropolitan Opera Company in 1965. In 1981 the Cuban filmmaker Humberto Solás made *Cecilia*, the most expensive production launched by Cuba's film industry to that moment.[13] The domestic version was four hours long; the one for international release ran two hours. A six-hour television miniseries of the novel was launched in Spain around the same time.

I mention *Cecilia* because, in different ways, in its book and film versions, it forefronts issues that remain unresolved in today's Cuba, issues with which Cuban artists in all genres continue to struggle. And when a Cuban work, even one based on a text written a century and a half earlier, goes out into the world, the fact that it comes from a country in revolution changes its impact and meaning: inevitably it is interrogated differently.

The novel *Cecilia Valdés* tells the story of a young, nineteenth-century mulata woman and her white lover. Race is not their only conflict; unbeknownst to them they are also brother and sister. Their ill-fated love story, a Caribbean version of the myth common to so many different cultures, is set against the beginnings of Cuba's slave rebellions. But when the novel became a film it was panned by every Cuban critic. Almost all were outraged at Solás's reinterpretation of the canonical work. The filmmaker omitted the subtext of incest but foregrounded Santería, an African religious practice that had been impossible to write about in the nineteenth century. His Cecilia is a practitioner, and he portrays that religion as the force that shapes his characters' destinies.

These are familiar themes. It isn't primarily the novel's content that claims my attention here but how Cuban artists embraced that content then and now. In the 1980s, when the film was made, Santería remained suppressed within the Revolution, and Solás's version of the story allowed him to look at something that had been driven underground but retained the power to subvert the dominant paradigms. The immediate response came from a familiar place of fear. The critic Mario Rodríguez Alemán called the film's ending repulsive and condemned it for what he termed its excessive religious charge. He claimed it overshadowed Villaverde's original political and social intentions.[14]

The *Cecilia Valdés* story continues to be the subject of symposia, lectures, and other events, on the island and beyond its borders, devoted to untangling its subtexts in twenty-first-century Cuban life. The issues of power, race, class, gender, sexuality, and ideology put forth in the novel, film, and television versions and in scholarly papers continue to kindle passions in Cuba and elsewhere. The backdrop of a socialist revolution takes these issues out of the realm of intellectual discussion and situates them within the context of social change. They evoke heated discussions and demand solutions, practical as well as emotional.

I have lingered with the *Cecilia Valdés* phenomenon because I believe that the way Cuban artists explore the social consequences of our most intimate dilemmas is one of the attributes that makes their work so powerful and augurs for a healthy freedom of expression, and also because it may be a useful backdrop when discussing the subject of this book: the Cuban Revolution's unique solidarity exemplified by its hundreds of internationalist missions to countries where most people are dark-skinned, desperately poor, and in dire need of humanitarian aid.

There is no question that Cuba follows a different moral imperative in this regard, one that has been impossible for U.S. citizens (Democrats as well as Republicans) to comprehend. Speaking about its military aid Tom Hayden put it well: "Rarely had such a small third world country intervened militarily on such faraway battlegrounds, a global reach previously monopolized by the white colonial and imperial powers. This Cuban internationalism also was contrary to the mainstream political theory that nation states follow narrow state interests and hew to their geographic spheres of interest, doctrines developed from Machiavelli to Metternich. Cuba was the exception."[15]

Cuba has also been the exception with regard to its vast outreach in the areas of disaster relief, health care, and adult education. The Revolution's extraordinary internationalism is indeed contrary to mainstream Western political theory and has become a profound aspect of the Cuban people's collective identity over the past half century. It was Fidel Castro who said "Cuba doesn't give what is left over; rather it shares what it has without asking for anything in return."[16]

I want to explore how the foreign aid offered by Cuba differs from that offered by the large imperialist nations: the United States, Russia, and China.

The refusal of the United States to peaceably coexist with the neighboring country helped push Cuba into the Soviet orb. Declaring their revolution socialist, Cuban leaders made the choice to be part of the Eastern European economic bloc. Depending on one's perspective, this move was made either freely or out of necessity; I would say both came into play. Whichever predominated, however, a country traditionally considered within the U.S. political sphere was suddenly part of an opposing axis of power.

In 1972 Cuba joined the Council of Mutual Economic Aid, the socialist bloc's internationalist collective of nations in which each was charged with producing products or services for the benefit of all, itself a form of socialist internationalism.[17] This facilitated Cuba's being able to sell its raw materials and buy what it needed under favorable conditions, but it also meant trading much farther afield, incurring greater transportation costs, and created a new dependency that in the long run proved almost as detrimental as its previous reliance upon the United States.

These and many other aspects of its particular island identity have affected Cuba's growth, development, human and trade histories, culture, and attitude toward the rest of the world—as well as the world's attitude toward it. They have made Cubans feel strongly rooted in their own cultures and history: isolated, proud, and determined, as well as capable of feeling the pain of others and ready to ameliorate that pain. (I explore Cuba's island condition more deeply in chapter 4.)

The 1959 Revolution marked a dramatic *before* and *after* for those who opposed it as well as for those who embraced its possibilities. The Revolution declared itself socialist in 1961. Ideology, history, and world events provoked an identification—sometimes easier, sometimes beset by disagreement—with the Soviet-style socialism then existent in Eastern Europe, what eventually came to be known (not without irony) as "real socialism."

This identification with the first socialist revolution is understandable. The Russian Revolution of 1917 offered a heroic history to which new generations of rebels could look for solidarity, and for clues about taking power, the ferocious counterattacks they would face, how to make a socialist society work (or avoid errors that keep it from becoming truly socialist), and how to move toward the eventual goal of communism, in which citizens contribute according to their abilities and receive according to their needs.

The exuberance and accomplishments of the Russian Revolution's first years imbued it with a glory that overshadowed the problems of subsequent decades. China provided another example, rooted in an agricultural rather than industrial model. But both the Soviet Union and China are immense countries, spanning many time zones and with a number of internal nationalities that have their own customs, belief system, and language. In both cases, as it turned out, their accomplishments and errors responded to realities too different from those of Cuba to offer much in the way of a recipe to be followed.

The Soviet Union had a strong internationalist tradition, evidenced in its interest in disseminating socialism globally as well as in the presence of its advisors and technicians in the countries it helped. A large number of Soviet internationalists fought for the Spanish Republic. Many experts from the Soviet Union and other socialist bloc countries worked in Cuba during the Revolution's first decades; I remember scientists and engineers as well as educators and specialists in the social sciences. In retrospect what is absolutely clear is that, given U.S. efforts at destabilization, Cuba could not have survived without Soviet and socialist bloc support. But as Soviet socialism became vitiated, the USSR broke apart and its aid as well as its internal political strategies acquired capitalist characteristics. This shift was experienced quite dramatically in Cuba.

It is to the Cuban Revolution's enduring credit that it eventually managed to facilitate homegrown prescriptions for change, from its particular latitude and tense proximity to its most aggressive enemy, and out of its island identity, geographical location, rebel history, cultures, racial mix, and the historic moment in which its revolution took place. It is also noteworthy that, although it has not yet been able to adequately develop its own economy, it has been so willing, indeed eager to aid those still strangled by underdevelopment.

In the Soviet Union, Josef Stalin's coercive philosophy and policies overtook less dogmatic approaches by Lenin and Trotsky, and Stalinism reigned by the time the Cuban revolutionaries came to power. The novelist, short story writer, and cultural critic Arturo Arango concisely sums up the Cuban experience with regard to its Eastern European older sibling; he asks us to understand Stalinism not simply as a dogmatic and repressive way of treating ideological processes but, above all, as a way of understanding socialism itself as a construction centralized in the state: the economy, ideology, and so forth.

In the West, Stalin is best known for the atrocities he committed against intellectuals and artists, as well as for the thousands who died of hunger during his command. For a more balanced view we should also remember that Stalin was Georgian—a hated minority—and inherited the world's first socialist revolution at a time of almost insurmountable obstacles: a backward nation of impoverished peasants and workers besieged by the entire Western world. The imperative was to industrialize as rapidly as possible while embroiled in a brutal war against fascism that took twenty million lives. There is no doubt that Stalin's measures saved an extremely complex situation, and that centralism was necessary to emerge from it. Still dogmatism (and at times a murderous brutality) led to fear, masses of dead, bureaucracy, corruption, and, ultimately, a weakening of the system itself. One of the Soviet Communist Party's debilitating legacies was its belief that one size fits all, that what worked in the motherland (or even what didn't) necessarily applied to the creation of successive experiments in social change elsewhere.

Arango looks at Stalinism with regard to the arts. It is clear, he says, that Cuba installed a Stalinist system, remnants of which remain to this day. And he focuses on one of the key features of that system: democratic central-ism.[18] We cannot know what might have happened in the Soviet Union had Lenin lived longer or Trotsky not been forced out and his more sophisticated way of looking at creativity been allowed to flourish. Arango analyzes the influence Stalinist thought had on culture in Cuba:

> Everything derives from this centralism, something that in one way or another negates the options that make possible the creation of participatory democracy. But Cuba's political and revolutionary traditions differ from Russia's and from that of the Soviet Union overall, just as Fidel and Stalin had very different personalities. Cuban culture put up the strongest resistance to Stalinism. From the nineteenth century on, Cuba possessed a cultural tradition that was revolutionary, liberating and emancipating. For this reason, after 1959 important revolutionary groups existed that were already anti-Stalinist in nature. It is important to note that Fidel's role in that period included mediating and achieving a balance between the various currents present within the revolutionary leadership, principally the July 26 Movement (in its beginnings composed of a strong bourgeois element that was later eliminated as the process radicalized), the old-time communists (all of them Stalinists), and other groups such as The Student Directorate (made up of those who came predominantly from the petit bourgeoisie).

> During those early years some strong contradictions with Soviet ideology emerged. And this is where a very important factor came into

portray as national/unique vs USSR or LatAm communist

play: Cuba's position within Latin America and its identification with the Nonaligned Nations and countries of the Third World. This is what separated us from Soviet orthodoxy. Fidel not only sympathized with this oppositional tendency, he was its leader. This generated a great many contradictions with the Soviets and also with the Latin American communist parties of the era.

In Cuba, already back then and in several different arenas, intellectual currents existed that rejected Stalinism as a cultural concept. It was too dogmatic, too programmatic for the Cuban leadership, even if those same currents supported Stalin's views with regard to the economy. One of the most important of these currents was the one that produced the magazine *Pensamiento Crítico*. Another, although with some ups and downs, can be seen in Casa de las Américas.[19]

Che saw the problems in the Soviet Union early on. He traveled to the first socialist republic as early as 1960 and questioned its cultural concepts as well as its economic model. He had read Trotsky and studied the Chinese and Vietnamese revolutions and other socialist processes. In a number of articles and speeches he made clear his disagreement with the Soviets. But Cuba had already made its alliance with the Soviet Union. As recently as 2005 Fidel Castro, the great architect of the Revolution and its most brilliant spokesperson, reminisced, "Of the many mistakes we have committed, the most important was thinking we knew about socialism, or that anyone knew how one constructs a socialist society."[20]

From its inception, and especially in terms of its aesthetic considerations, the Cuban process differed substantially from that of the Soviets. Powerful forces on the island rejected socialist realism, for example, although a core group of old Cuban Communist Party members tried to impose it, and in one notorious period their efforts gained dangerous momentum.[21] During those times when Cuba was most economically dependent upon the Soviet Union, this dependency exerted its most damaging influence. Fortunately the Revolution's history, culture, climate, temperament, originality, and Latin American—or more specifically Caribbean—identity eventually enabled it to throw off the Stalinist approach to art and letters and return to its more authentic self. I discuss this in more detail later.

By this time in my musings, however, it was clear to me that long before the 1959 Revolution Cuba had produced and nurtured cultural tendencies that made the Revolution's job easier. Central among these was its nuanced brand of nationalism. The Cuban cultural critic Julio César Guanche points out that the country's movements for independence were rooted in a strong republican or universalist ideology and were committed as well to the liberation of the other nations of the Americas.[22] In this sense Cuba's concept of *nation* was never inscribed within a narrow or chauvinist philosophy.

The nineteenth-century revolutionary intellectual José Martí had spoken clearly for a single Latin American identity and unity, and from that century on Cuban patriots conceived of *nation* in its broadest terms: as humanity.[23] This conviction powerfully underwrites Cuba's internationalism, as seen in its heroic aid to other liberation struggles and in its tens of thousands of teachers, health care personnel, and others who continue to take their solidarity to remote regions of the world.

Martí is regarded as the father of the nation, both politically and philosophically and by revolutionaries as well as by those opposed to the Revolution's socialist ideology. The cultural and literary critic Ambrosio Fornet, reviewing a study of Martí by the country's first minister of culture, Armando Hart, considers four points Hart makes as he analyzes Martí's role in shaping Cuban intellectuality.[24] Because they bear on my ideas, I enumerate them here. The first concerns the two currents present in the formation of Cuban consciousness, one intellectual in nature, the other ethical. The intellectual current is rooted in the ideas of the Enlightenment, including scientific reflection. The ethical current embraces Christianity's philosophy of morality, oriented toward human community and solidarity. The second point is that in Cuba, as in most of the colonial world, nation does not precede revolution but rather is one of its offshoots. A Cuban nationality existed before Céspedes's cry of independence in 1868,[25] but the idea of Nation, with a capital N—that is to say, a community of interests and intentions shared by the majority of the island's inhabitants—emerges organically, one might say, from that event. Third, given that a system of slavery dominated the island, coloring not only its relations of production but also its human relations into the foreseeable future, political independence alone was not enough to forge a sense of nationhood. The promise of independence had to be accompanied by a promise of social justice. Fourth, and following from the three preceding points, Martí's thought was central in shaping the political and social ideology of the Revolution that came to power in 1959.

Bear in mind that it was Hart who elucidated these four points, the person tapped as the country's first minister of culture, the man who would guide Cuban intellectuals and artists out of the repressive period that began in 1971 and could so easily have curtailed their freedom from then on. It was a complex task, requiring intellectual sophistication, intuition, brilliance, compassion, and above all confidence in the creativity of men and women with everything to give and everything to lose.[26]

This was as good a starting point as any in my effort to understand why the country's intellectuals and artists have been in the forefront of Latin American debate since the 1960s and why their poetry, prose, painting, music, and other creative production has been so outstanding when compared with that of countries with much larger populations.

Historically all the nations of the Caribbean have seen large numbers of their citizens emigrate. But up until the 1930s Cuba was more a nation of immigrants than emigrants; in other words, more people were arriving than leaving. Spaniards (from diverse provincial cultures), Africans (also of differing cultures), Jews, and Chinese all made important contributions to a multifaceted Cuban identity. Creoles from nearby Haiti arrived to work in the sugarcane and coffee fields. Mexican laborers arrived from the port of Veracruz. Cuba's proximity to the United States also made for a great deal of cultural exchange. All this produced a discourse of *mestizaje* as the essence of Cuban nationality. And this discourse, reflecting a sense of *cubanía*, also informs the Revolution's internationalism.[27] After 1959 this history, linked to a powerful antidictator stance, sparked values of solidarity toward other oppressed peoples.

The unusually powerful role Cuban poetry has played with regard to that of other Spanish-speaking countries took me by surprise. It wasn't long before I began thinking about additional artistic genres: the novel, essay, film, and visual arts, including photography and architecture, and performance arts, such as music, theater, and dance. In some of these genres Cuba also excels: its film industry has had a global impact, the *nueva trova* (new song movement) contributed powerfully to the protest song movement that swept the world in the 1960s and 1970s,[28] and the posters it produced in the 1960s, 1970s, and 1980s were enormously influential. It is clear that Cuba exerted an important influence on filmmakers, singer-songwriters, and artists in other parts of the Americas, perhaps even other parts of the world.

In other genres—architecture comes to mind—the Revolution produced renowned artists such as Emilio del Junco, Tonino Quintana, Ricardo Porro, Mario Coyula, and Roberto Segre, whose work began to speak an original, organic language only to suffer an opposition that took years to overcome.[29] Many believe architecture still suffers from that stifling. Innovative architectural design was quickly replaced by the worst elements of Soviet influence, seen in the heavy blocks of cement buildings, inappropriate to the island's heat and humidity, that still scar Cuba's tropical landscape. This may be the artistic genre in which the struggle between freedom and suppression took its greatest toll. I sought lessons from the country's intellectual and artistic successes and also from its painful setbacks (which, notably, in Cuba's revolutionary history have eventually given birth to counterattacks engendering useful analysis, reassessment, and even remedy).

From pondering the country's intellectual and artistic creativity I naturally moved on to consider Cuba's impressive outreach in the areas of adult education and health care, its twentieth-century support for the nonaligned nations movement and for liberation struggles that were taking up arms against dictatorial states, its support for other social change experiences that gained governance through electoral politics, its international primacy in sports, and its example as a tiny country resisting subordination by hegemonic powers. What struck me most forcefully was not only the fact that such a small, isolated, and besieged island nation managed to survive and develop, but that its internationalist solidarity became one of the pillars of its identity. In Cuba we have a country that has given—and continues to give—more than its share of morality, ideas, expertise, talent, heavy lifting, and concrete aid to peoples everywhere. A number of other Latin American countries—Argentina, Chile, Colombia, Bolivia, Peru, Ecuador, and Venezuela, to mention some of the largest with rich histories and cultures—have produced their share of world-class poets, novelists, painters, and public intellectuals. Yet Cuba's contributions stand out.

In the United States ignorance of all things Cuban that comes from so many years of media blackout and distortion has now been replaced by a frenzy of interest sparked by the sudden attention that began to surge when our countries reestablished diplomatic relations at the end of 2014. In a longer-range evaluation such trends tend to even out. Eventually we should be able to enjoy the more balanced perspective that will come when we are able to look at the neighboring nation and situate it realistically within its own cultural, social, and political history. Yet the current increase in attention also provides us an opportunity to examine what Cuba gives.

I lived in Cuba from mid-1969 to the end of 1980, the Revolution's exuberant second decade. I raised my four children there, worked for several cultural institutions, and wrote numerous books. Like most citizens and residents, I participated in the everyday efforts to create a different, more egalitarian society: joining a monthly street patrol to keep my neighborhood safe, doing voluntary work, and gathering with colleagues to discuss drafts of new laws. As a mother I got a close look at the educational system. I valued the safety net of universal health care and appreciated Havana's drug-free, violence-free streets. Although I wasn't yet able to plumb it deeply back then, I intuited the ways the Revolution drew on tradition as well as its particular recipe for change in attempting to shape new values.

Those were years of scarcity, rationing, and other hardships. And although we didn't know it at the time, things would get much worse in the early 1990s.[30] Yet I cannot remember ever feeling as if my family and I didn't have enough. On the contrary, I shared with others a deep sense of satisfaction at living in a place where equality was the goal. It is hard to describe this feeling to those who have never experienced it.

At the same time, as Cuba's leaders constantly reminded us, the war had been the easy part; constructing a justice-based society would be much harder. The Revolution wasn't a fairy-tale adventure; problems inevitably arose. Economic experiments didn't always turn out well, and changes in course were frequent. In the search for equilibrium bureaucracy often showed its ugly face. Repressive periods took their toll.

I can attest to this from firsthand experience. For several years, along with many others I felt the heavy hand of official marginalization. I lost my job but never stopped receiving a salary. Certain "friends" stopped coming around, yet my work continued to be published in Cuban journals. It was all very confusing. My attempts to find out what was happening and why met with a frustrating silence. At the time I had no idea that others were suffering similar dilemmas; we were all too fearful to speak openly about our situations and so were unable to see them as part of a sociopolitical phenomenon. It would take two decades for Cuba's artists and writers to grapple publicly and productively with that dark time.[31] I remained in Cuba until I received an explanation for what had happened to me.[32] Then I moved on. I did not blame the Revolution. It was always clear to me that social change is made by human beings, those who may be mediocre and cowardly as well as those who are brilliant and visionary.

So the Revolution's successes and failures were my successes and failures. When I left Cuba in December 1980, I didn't leave the country behind. My two older children stayed, and I visited often. Then, back in the United States throughout the 1990s, I periodically took groups of U.S. feminists to the island on trips sponsored by Global Exchange.[33] In 2011 I was invited to be a judge at Casa de las Américas' yearly literary contest. This was my second such invitation; I had been a member of its jury forty-one years earlier, in 1970.

In 2014 I returned to the island to undertake the fieldwork for *Haydée Santamaría, Cuban Revolutionary: She Led by Transgression*. A great deal had changed, even since my previous visit two years before. After each day's research I would meet with old friends or walk Havana's streets, noting the rehabilitation of some of the many buildings that were disintegrating from lack of upkeep. Schools and hospitals were being renovated first: Cuba still had its priorities straight.

In April 2015 my partner and I visited again, this time to participate in the thirtieth-anniversary celebration of Vigía, a publishing collective in the province of Matanzas, whose handmade books have gained worldwide recognition for their literary content and artistic beauty. Some consider Vigía an anomaly, but in my mind it is one example of the many truly revolutionary spaces that can be found throughout the island, often in surprising iterations. These spaces develop simultaneously out of a revolutionary consciousness and in response to moments of repressive error; their courage and complexity have much to teach us. Spending a week with the folks at Vigía, studying its more than five hundred titles, and observing the inclusive community-based way it commemorated its anniversary, I felt I was inhabiting a magical multidimensional venue the majority of Cuba lovers have no idea exists.

Each successive visit allowed me to witness a rapidly changing reality. The ration book, which three decades before had determined what my family and I ate, remained as a way of ensuring the basic necessities at accessible prices but had lost its centrality in Cuban life. Despite the ongoing stress of the U.S. embargo, growers' markets and moderately well-stocked grocery stores existed now. Small restaurants were everywhere, many of them independent endeavors, and their creative offerings and gracious service were proving important competition to their state-run counterparts, most of the latter faring poorly by comparison.

By 2011 a great many people had cell phones. By 2014 Wi-Fi hot spots had been established, and Internet communication with the outside world was easier than it had been, although still far from economically accessible to most Cubans. In April 2016 the Cuban government announced an average 6 percent reduction in the prices of a number of food staples and other household goods. The country's dual currency was still a problem, and when I asked people what change they would be most eager to see, without exception everyone with whom I spoke told me they needed to be able to live on their salary, lessening the temptation for petty but widespread corruption that has been a reality for several decades. To a person those with whom I spoke felt that Raul Castro, who had assumed the country's presidency in 2008, was doing an excellent job.

Although some hospitals looked rundown and I knew the country suffered from a lack of some expensive diagnostic equipment, health care continued to be exemplary. Foreigners still travel to the island for procedures that would cost them much more at home; Cuba was finally charging modest fees for health care for non-Cubans that I remember it giving freely when I lived there. Education at all levels enjoys an excellent reputation.[34]

Life for gay Cubans is markedly easier today, although prejudices remain among the older population and marriage equality has yet to be established. Raul Castro's daughter, Mariela Castro, heads a sexual outreach and education project that has achieved a good deal of progress for LGBTQ Cubans.[35] Gay Cubans appreciate her efforts, but some would like to see a movement with more effective input from the base. Hundreds of books that would not have been published even ten years earlier because their authors were considered problematic for one reason or another appear in beautiful editions and fly off bookstore shelves.[36]

The long U.S. trade embargo and the collapse of the Soviet Union have both taken their toll. Understandably in 2015 people seemed much more exhausted than when I'd lived among them. Many young people especially were leaving the country. But among the many more who were staying, that unique Cuban pride and dignity continued to be palpable.

Much has been made in the foreign anti-Castro press about the large numbers of Cubans who leave. But few speak about the many who choose to stay even now that travel restrictions have been lifted, or of the trend—involving far fewer people but steadily increasing—of those who left and are coming back as hopeful entrepreneurs.[37] Nor has there been much discussion about the tens of thousands of Cubans who immigrated to the United States in hope of a better life. Many are forced to work in jobs far below their professional level, and continue to struggle with poverty and a lack of basic human services.

Over the years, and in vastly differing moments of Cuban revolutionary history, I have written a number of books and dozens of articles about Cuba.[38] I have been engaged with the country and its revolution continually, suffering its problems, praising its achievements, critiquing the process when I felt it necessary, and delighting in its astonishing resiliency. I have close friends on the island, with whom I am in constant conversation, and close Cuban friends who have moved elsewhere, comfortable in their per-

sonal decision even as they may be grappling with that sense of displacement that transplantation inevitably brings. In spite of this long familiarity
perhaps I had internalized Cuba's solidarity to the point where I couldn't see
how unusual, even extraordinary it is.

As a poet I should not be surprised that my realization that the country's
influence is unusual came first after reading Cuban poetry. A number of
people with whom I spoke about my idea for this book urged me to limit its
scope; they feared I was taking on too much. Why don't you just write about
the arts, they said, or limit your focus to Cuba's internationalism, its outreach in the areas of adult education or public health? It's true that any one
of these subjects would make for an interesting book, but what fascinates
me is the overall phenomenon: What compels a small, poor, as yet underdeveloped country that has been forced to face more than half a century of
attack and privation to be so consistently generous with those who have
less, often in some distant part of the world? I am interested in Cuba's multifaceted interdisciplinary approach to internationalism and in the ways it
draws on its domestic experiences when it initiates programs overseas.

Cubans are not known for their inhibitions. Ambrosio Fornet writes,
"Our history is palpably marked by a lack of restraint. It might be said that to
Cubans, limited because they inhabit such a tiny floating space, the Island
has always felt small."[39] When I broached my ideas about the country's influence to another friend and cultural critic, Jorge Fornet, Ambrosio's son, he
responded with equally powerful words of caution: "What you say seems
obvious, but we need to think about it carefully. On the one hand, we Cubans
have always thought of ourselves as exceptional. On the other, we don't think
we exert much of an influence beyond our borders because in a certain sense
we do not see ourselves as being a part of the larger world. Our excellence in
all the fields you mention may give us an illusion of grandeur."[40]

As I have mentioned, Cuba's influence is not limited to the arts. The Revolution extends its outreach to humanity, in moments of natural disasters,
during wars of liberation, and in the many poor countries where health
care, education, and other requirements for human well-being are denied
to the vast majorities. Cuban teachers and health professionals have labored
in remote areas across the globe; their human and material aid to Haiti following the 2010 earthquake and their work in several African countries to
combat the Ebola epidemic overshadowed that offered by larger and wealthier
countries and has been praised by international bodies.

Another motivating factor is the Revolution's mix of ideas and praxis.
A radically changing society is ideal terrain on which to move in different

directions, assessing successes and errors. Beginning in 1959 the whole country became a laboratory, in which a vast range of talents were called upon and constant feedback demonstrated what worked and what didn't. Programs were designed to deal with specific problems or address immediate needs and were often launched before formal studies were carried out, that is to say, without the input of experts. This meant mistakes were made but also that the services were immediately made available.

These programs were particularly visible in the area of education, where the first effort was to give every Cuban child and adult the opportunity to study—even when it would be years before educational strategies could be systematized and refined. My own children's Cuban education, although wanting in some aspects, combined theory and practice, intellectual work and manual labor, in ways that produced practical benefits in their lives.[41]

Thinking of all this, I was powerfully struck, on the one hand, by Cuba's small size, scant resources, and history of resisting years of aggression and, on the other, by the quantity and quality of its output in so many different fields. Its apparent lack of self-interest and the generosity in its manner of giving are palpable. To begin to trace this solidarity it is important to look first at the initiatives taken within Cuban society. The Revolution's home-grown experiments—what has worked and what hasn't—have shaped its internationalist efforts. This is why in each chapter I look at national accomplishments before examining international outreach.

It was also important that I ask the hard questions. What is the difference, for example, between U.S. aid programs and those launched by Cuba? Does not every country involved in overseas work hope to get something in return? In terms of military involvement, how does responding to the call of a government differ from responding to the call of a liberation movement struggling against a government in power? What do the younger generations of Cubans think about their country's internationalism? And how do countries that send teachers, doctors, agricultural experts, or others to places needing their expertise hope to redeem their investment: in monetary terms? Geopolitical control? Oil? Water? Ideological currency? The simple satisfaction of having gone where they were needed?

Some nations invade and occupy, claiming they are doing so in defense of their own national security or even pretending such occupation is good for the country. They inevitably devastate infrastructures and economies, do gross collateral damage, kill tens of thousands, and turn millions into displaced persons forced into endless migration. In recent years U.S. aggression in the Middle East has created a chaos that seems irreversible and has helped spark a jihadist response that has become ever more threatening throughout the world.

Cuba continues to send its teachers and health care personnel, disaster relief teams, and experts in dozens of fields to work in countries throughout the developing world. There have been problems, and I do not claim that altruism alone is involved or that the Cuban Revolution gets nothing in return. In humanitarian terms, however, and by all possible measures, comparison favors these efforts over imperialism's bully presence.

This book is my attempt to explore a reality that has not received the attention it deserves.

2

TALENT AND INFLUENCE
BEYOND NUMBERS

My first contact with Cuban poetry was in the early 1960s. I was living in Mexico City, and the Mexican poet Sergio Mondragón and I were editing a bilingual literary journal called *El Corno Emplumado / The Plumed Horn.*[1] We were excited to receive submissions from Cuba, its revolution still fresh, exuberant, and ignored or distorted in most Western countries. We began to correspond with a number of Cuban writers and artists, published their work from time to time, and then commemorated the Revolution's eighth anniversary by devoting our entire issue 23 (July 1967) to Cuban poetry and visual art. Our U.S. readers especially were astonished. A systematic information blackout had kept poetry lovers from reading what was being produced in the mysterious Caribbean nation.

We were also surprised because, influenced by ideas prevalent at the time, we expected Cuban poetry to explicitly reflect the changes wrought by the Revolution: people being educated and able to work, a newfound equality and dignity, communal ownership of land and resources, a burgeoning sense of freedom—in other words, agitprop. In most cases these issues were reflected, if at all, by a new use of language rather than by explicit references to a more equitable ownership of production. It's not that I believe there is any subject matter that should be off-limits to a poet; good poetry depends not on its subject but on how that subject is expressed. Still this poetry, given its context, surprised me.

Cuban poets were mostly writing about things that concerned us all: the big philosophical questions of love, loss, fear, struggle, risk, courage, interpersonal or interspecies relationships, landscape, and other diverse human experiences. It was their perspective that was entirely new. And it wasn't a uniform perspective but varied, projecting unique voices, each markedly its own. The monumental effort to change society from the inside out was clearly producing work that departed in powerful ways from what we were accustomed to reading.

On the negative side of the equation, the response to our making the new Cuban work available was immediate and vehement. The Pan-American Union canceled five hundred subscriptions because we insisted on publishing work by revolutionary Cubans. We were also publishing work by Cubans who had emigrated, but this wasn't good enough for the cultural arm of the Organization of American States. It didn't want us to give space to anyone living in Cuba or who looked favorably on the Revolution. Those subscriptions had been purchased out of what seemed to be a genuine appreciation for the journal but turned out to have strings attached. For some, exhilaration was in the air. For others, fear. We learned how dangerous it could be to breach the sugarcane curtain.

So, I thought, Cuban poets are extraordinary. As a group they have influenced their contemporaries in ways that aren't true of poets everywhere, although certainly many nations have stellar poets. But why is this? Was there a particularly brilliant group of Cuban poets writing before 1959? Could it be something about the nation's size or physical qualities? Does insularity sharpen the voice, a yearning to participate in world culture strengthen it? We know that small countries often have advantages when it comes to putting complex social change initiatives in place. Manageable size can breed passion, intensity, and also a greater efficiency. Was the Cuban Revolution really able to nurture creativity in new ways? And if so, how?

In the arts as in all else the Revolution itself marked a dramatic *before* and *after*, especially for those who had already developed a mature voice. Most poets stayed, at least at first, and the extraordinary *after* took up residence in their poems—but, as I say, generally not in the ways outsiders imagined.

The Cuban Revolution provoked the intellectual struggles common to all great social upheavals. There was the promise of a breakdown in class barriers and opportunities to escape from traditional limitations. Women and Cubans of color dared to believe the biases against them would dissolve— and, although much work remains to be done in both areas, important progress has been made. People living in remote areas now had access to opportunities previously reserved for urban dwellers. Many more people gained access to education, and the most creative minds moved in exciting new directions. A sense of necessary sacrifice was added to the calls for innovation, study, and discipline.

At the same time, and in tandem with all this possibility, bureaucrats, fearful of instability, tried to rein in these new ideas. I went into some detail about this in chapter 1, particularly with regard to the danger of Stalinist influence.[2] But there were other factors. For several decades U.S. aggression made it difficult—in many cases impossible—for poets on the island to follow their own diverse creativity or connect easily with the outside world. The besieged nation struggled to survive and claimed unity (read: sameness, or common effort) as one of the necessary components needed to help keep it afloat.

The United States launched its many-pronged embargo, and Cuba fought the cultural blockade with the same tenacity it fought its diplomatic and economic counterparts. It established important cultural institutions, hosted conferences and symposiums, invited intellectuals and artists from around the world to visit the island, and supported its own creative minds.

But most poets in their prime, like most other Cubans, were unable to travel. This restriction on movement (which translated as a restriction on curiosity, experience, and contact with other literary scenes) took its toll and provoked rebellion in individual lives, causing some to emigrate. Its impact was certainly painful and negative, even in the work itself, although in retrospect it may also have had its positive side: just as it limited a close and personal knowledge of the rest of the world, the resultant tensions forged an expanded and multifaceted imagination. The painful separations when families split also imbued much of the work with a uniquely Cuban registry of loss.

Of tremendous importance was the fact that what might have reduced the island to a sad provincialism was counteracted by a push for education that from the Revolution's first days was both massive and deep. Schools were a priority, and hundreds, then thousands were built, located not only in urban areas but throughout a countryside ignored by previous governments. Today, according to UNESCO, roughly 98.4 percent of Cuban boys and 98.3 percent of girls attend primary school, with a 95 percent graduation rate. Secondary school enrollment is around 87 percent. Universities exist in every province, and their graduates are respected throughout the world. A subsidized publishing program was also very important.

The 1961 nationwide literacy campaign was key, as well as successful follow-up efforts to achieve a sixth and then ninth grade education for every adult. (I describe this campaign in detail in chapter 11.) In higher education gender disparity disappeared quite quickly in a variety of disciplines, and as many women as men, if not more, graduated in fields where they had previously had very little presence. Being from the countryside no longer meant a lack of access to higher education; systems were put in place through which Cubans, no matter where they lived, were able to achieve the education they sought. Educating a nation achieves much more than a proud place at the top of international lists of countries where learning is broad and deep: the whole pattern of social participation changes. A population's educational level is enriched by input from different cultural, regional, ethnic, and racial traditions.

Fidel Castro and other leaders constantly reiterated the emphasis on learning. Billboards proclaimed, "If you know, teach; if you don't know, learn." In March 1961, during an act of tribute paid by the International Organization of Journalists to the newspaper *Revolución*, Fidel emphasized education as he so often had before and would do innumerable times in the future: "This is the moment in which we must cultivate every intelligence, this is the moment in which we must allow intelligence to shine in every one of our citizens, in the cities and in the countryside."[3]

In a centralized system needs and the capacity for fulfilling those needs are assessed at the national level. In education this means if it was estimated that the country would require such and such a number of doctors or engineers or language teachers, roughly that many students in those fields would be accepted into the pertinent courses of study. Needless to say, personal interest and aptitude were also taken into account. You don't get a talented teacher or engineer simply by filling a quota.

Of particular importance for young people with artistic aspirations was the Escuela Nacional de Arte (National Art School, ENA). ENA appeared on Havana's horizon almost magically, a cluster of graceful arched domes seducing with their evocative architecture, lush grounds, and in-depth courses.[4] By the time several generations of Cuban poets could travel freely, they were well educated and expertly trained in the history of their art form, literarily and in terms of the requisite skills, and their experiences had produced a new perceptive edge, unimaginable to those of us who, if we have the money, enjoy the freedom to come and go but don't live in a society attempting to change itself from the inside out. ENA, now called the Higher Institute of Art, offers postgraduate as well as graduate degrees. Arts schools also exist today in the provinces: two in Camagüey, two in Holguín, and one in Santiago de Cuba.

Preparing to celebrate its fortieth anniversary, ENA's current director, Dr. Rolando González Patricio, noted, "Thirty-five graduating classes have produced more than 5,000 well-trained artists. Ours has been a selective formation, which doesn't mean exclusive, and our arts education program continues to gain in prestige internationally."[5] "Selective" as opposed to "exclusive": an important distinction, rooted in a far-reaching and tireless search for genuine talent rather than favoring certain social classes or accepting only those students able to pay an expensive tuition. In Cuba young people don't study at a school because a parent is an alumnus, or because of influence, or because they can afford the tuition. Graduates don't spend years paying education debts. Opportunity moved horizontally at first, and then enabled those with talent to get what they needed irrespective of class or other considerations.

From the beginning the Cuban Revolution defined freedom from violence, a safe place to live, decent work, education, health care, and access to culture and sports as basic human rights. For more than half a century it has had extraordinary success in being able to assure most of its citizens these rights.

The situation has been similar for those wanting to be poets and writers, respected disciplines in Cuba. Most at this point were born into the Revolution. They obtain their formal education at one of the island's universities, where they study comparative literature, philology, history, or occasionally an unrelated field. In a planned society, one that funnels its graduates into jobs in line with their interests (for poets and writers these might include working at a library, on a literary journal, in a publishing house or cultural institution of some kind), they will have on-the-job opportunities to continue deepening their knowledge and craft. Early in the revolutionary process structures were established to support aspiring writers with opportunities for peer critique, performance, and publication. Yet until travel restrictions were loosened,[6] they too saw in the possibility of journeying outside the country an experience weighted with unfulfilled longing. Poets who had never been away from Cuba wrote of their own experiences in voices that astonish and of other parts of the world in lines often filled with myth and fantasy.

For almost eleven years my own creativity was nurtured by the Revolution's commitment to the arts. I attended readings by some of the world's best poets who came to perform in the country, as well as Cuba's own. I might as well have been living in New York, Paris, London, Tokyo, or Athens instead of in the capital of a small Caribbean island. Cuba invited artists and thinkers of the caliber of Jean-Paul Sartre, Simone de Beauvoir, Ezequiel Martínez Estrada, Violeta Parra, Roque Dalton, José María Arguedas, Salvador Allende,

Rodolfo Walsh, Carlos María Gutiérrez, Arnaldo Orfila Reynal, Juan Gelman, Juan Carlos Onetti, Mario Benedetti, Julio Cortázar, Eduardo Galeano, René Depestre, Antonio Saura, Claribel Alegría, Ernesto Cardenal, Allen Ginsberg, Carlos Fuentes, Thiago de Melo, Stéfano Varese, Angela Davis, Gabriel García Márquez, Roberto Matta, Laurette Séjourné, and Betita Martínez to read, show, and perform. The educated and extraordinarily aware population they encountered made these artists eager to give of their art in remote areas as well as in the cities. Despite poverty, scarcity, and struggle on all fronts, the Revolution introduced world culture to its people, giving birth to a true sophistication that enriched the lives of visitors as well as locals.

I read my own work in many parts of the island, sometimes in formal venues and sometimes at schools, in factories, or on state farms. At first I wondered if my best poems would be appreciated by audiences I knew approached poetry from a less cerebral, more popular perspective. I needn't have worried. Invariably there were those who responded in astonishing ways. Often someone asked to read a poem of his or her own. These too could be surprising. I soon realized that I was experiencing what happens when an entire population has access to the arts and has come to believe they are important parts of life.

Despite so many years of inability to travel, this rich intellectual life made Cubans unexpectedly cosmopolitan. Cuban poets, indeed Cuban writers in various genres, have consistently won the big international literary prizes: Spain's Cervantes, Reina Sofía, Julio Tovar, Príncipe de Asturias, Renacimiento, Federico García Lorca, and Loewe; Mexico's Plural and Juan Rulfo; Chile's Pablo Neruda; Italy's Viareggio and Italo Calvino; Bulgaria's Nicola Vaptasarov; Venezuela's Pérez Bonalde; and France's Legion of Honor and National Medal for Arts and Letters, among others too numerous to list. Their recipients have been not only the older, consecrated voices but the extraordinary younger writers as well. And many of these are prizes for poetry, a genre too often ignored.

The Cuban Revolution established several institutions that made indelible names for themselves throughout Latin America and beyond. These, more than any individual, were responsible for challenging the cultural blockade, and they continue to be enormously prestigious and active. Casa de las Américas may be the most important of these. Under the brilliant tutelage of Haydée Santamaría, a revolutionary heroine and extraordinarily sensitive arts administrator, it was founded in the first months following victory and smashed the attempt at isolation, bringing the world's great artists to the island and promoting Cuban art internationally.[7]

A number of Cuban institutions began hosting massive student gatherings, congresses, symposiums, art biennales, film festivals, books fairs, and other events attended by artists and intellectuals from around the world. Organización de Solidaridad con los Pueblos de Asia, África y América Latina (Organization of Solidarity with the People of Asia, Africa and Latin America, OSPAAAL) was particularly influential as a magnet for some of the era's exceptional poster artists. Carlos Vega was a Massachusetts-based political activist whose concept of art in struggle was changed by OSPAAAL's posters. He was one of many thousands of U.S. activists who looked to Cuba for an example of what was possible and found inspiration in the way the Revolution linked the political and the artistic. In a moving tribute Vega's son Jesse Maceo Vega-Frey has written:

> The most powerful aspect of what [my father] encountered in Cuba, the thing that would direct his life and work forever after, was the value placed on culture at the center of the Revolution—a value embodied in [the] OSPAAAL posters. In his life at home, he had already delved into radical political analysis, theory, and organizing, but in Cuba he also found an unwavering commitment to music, food, art, and poetry integrated into the DNA of the Revolution and it radically transformed his ideas about the need for art and culture at the heart of work for social change.[8]

These political, cultural, and artistic practices continue to weave a fertile web in Cuba.

Several journals, most prominently *Signos, Santiago, Pensamiento Crítico, Temas, Revista Casa, Revista Unión, La Gaceta de Cuba,* and *Revolución y Cultura,* have been essential in promoting cultural thought, giving voice to a variety of progressive perspectives and space to important debate. Casa de las America's yearly literary contest awards prizes in poetry, the novel, short story, essay, theater, children's literature, writing by the indigenous peoples of the Americas, Brazilian literature, English-language literature of the Caribbean, and work by Latinos within the United States. (Casa was one of the first international institutions to recognize the porosity of arbitrary borders.) The winning books are published in beautiful editions and their authors receive $3,000—not a lot when compared with some of the more significant international literary prizes but generous in the context of Cuba's ongoing financial hardship. Casa's galleries and recital halls host hundreds of exhibits and concerts each year, free to the public as all Cuban cultural events are. A steady stream of artists from other countries visit Cuba through Casa.

Other influential institutions are Instituto Cubano del Arte e Industria Cinematográficos (Cuban Institute of Film and Film Arts, ICAIC), the Alicia Alonso Ballet, the Folklore Ballet, and the Ministry of Culture, as well as dozens of their provincial counterparts. Each city and town also has a Culture House, where local artists gather and perform, as well as theaters and recital halls. Each province has one or more publishing houses. All these entities are linked through the working chronograms a centralized system puts in place.

As I thought about Cuba's poets I realized the name *trailblazer* could be applied to those writing in several genres. I found myself thinking of novelists. Alejo Carpentier's magical realist novel *El reino de este mundo* (1949) appeared a good two decades before the boom that placed Latin America on the international literary map and brought Gabriel García Márquez, Carlos Fuentes, Julio Cortázar, Elena Poniatowska, Mario Vargas Llosa, and Isabel Allende to such prominence. José Lezama Lima's neobaroque *Paradiso* (1968) remains a highly sophisticated cult classic.

Speaking of Carpentier, there is a little-known story worth telling here because it also illustrates an attitude astonishingly before its time. *Revista Social* was a monthly magazine published in Havana from 1916 to 1933 and again from 1935 to 1938. It featured fashion as well as articles of literary and intellectual interest, poetry, and a social calendar, all illustrated in the elegant art deco style of the era. It had a female as well as male readership and, advocating for women's suffrage, provided a forum for the feminists of those years. Carpentier wrote fashion pieces for *Revista Social* and signed them "Jaqueline." Throughout history women have often written under male names; men writing under women's names could not have been common, particularly at that time and in the Caribbean. Carpentier's was an act that defied convention.[9]

Now that we think of Cuba as including its diaspora—the whole-island concept having replaced the cruel line drawn by prior political exclusion—we can also talk about poets such as José Kozer and Milena Rodríguez Gutiérrez. It is worth noting that the Cuban American Richard Blanco read at Barack Obama's second inauguration in January 2014. Blanco, born in Madrid of Cuban exile parents and raised in Miami, was not only the first with Cuban roots but the first openly gay and youngest poet to perform at a U.S. presidential inauguration.

Is this literary explosion a revolutionary phenomenon? Undoubtedly, but not exclusively. We have seen how the seeds of philosophical brilliance were planted generations earlier, long before the 1959 revolutionaries came to power, when a Cuban elite enjoyed a level of education uncommon on the continent except in certain Latin American capitals. Before the Revolution educational access was limited to the upper classes and concentrated in the cities, and many rural Cubans were unable to study at all. The Revolution made higher education available to the population at large, beginning with its extraordinary 1961 literacy campaign.[10] The Revolution fertilized the whole nation so the seeds of education could sprout more equitably. Considering culture vital to the creation of the new human being, the leaders of the Revolution also consistently supported creative endeavors, funding writers and artists even during precarious economic times. More than five decades have produced extraordinary artists and writers who would not have been able to excel without this broadening of opportunities.

The nineteenth-century patriot José Martí was a political organizer, but he was also a writer; his complete works fill more than thirty volumes and encompass political essay, cultural commentary, journalism, the novel, poetry, and literature for children. As one of the most important modernists, his literary as well as political influence has been strong throughout the Latin world.

Cuba also has fine visual artists. The artist and art historian Luis Camnitzer, who has written about Cuban art in great depth, admits that it is "tempting to judge Cuban art by international standards" but warns that doing so "one would neglect its role in national culture building, an issue not always visible but a factor in the minds of most of [the country's] artists."[11] I think the nature and predominance of the 1959 Revolution has involved all creative artists in culture building, and the effort has been largely conscious and tenacious. Because in many cases they have received the same education, even those opposed to the politics of the Revolution are engaged with the phenomenon, albeit from a stance of resistance. I will return to the issue of nation building in the context of nationalism and internationalism.

In the 1980s several schools and groups of younger artists claimed space across the island, and the *Volumen I* show gave important new impetus to experimental artistic production.[12] In response to years of relegation, religious images could be seen in much of the new work. The art remained transgressive; I would say this transgressive attitude is one of its defining features from year to year and movement to movement. Outrageous constructions and events have been staged, many of them covertly or overtly critical of bureaucratic rigidity. The installation and performance artist Tania Bruguera (b. 1968) has produced a number of controversial happenings, some coinciding with the Havana Biennale.[13] Her work is a cry for freedom of expression, no matter what official or unofficial force may be repressing it, although some Cubans living in Cuba feel her work is aimed at an audience outside the island. In early 2016 Bruguera launched an online fundraising endeavor that raised more than $100,000. With it she opened the Institute of Art Activism in Havana and announced that her first artist in residence would be the Russian feminist punk collective Pussy Riot.[14] Other performers of protest, such as the graffiti artist El Sexto, have recently appeared on the scene. Bruguera and El Sexto have produced work that goes beyond what has been acceptable in the Cuba of recent years. Both have been arrested and held for hours or days on charges ranging from disturbing the peace to misrepresenting the system. Sadly the Revolution has not yet learned to live with its most biting critics. However, I am confident that a time will come when it won't feel so threatened by these critics, when it will be able to make room for their dissident voices and coexist more comfortably with them.

A recent visit to Cuba convinced me there are plenty of talented and critical artists who show their work without problem. Alejandro González is a young photographer whose series *Re-construction* refers to the cultural repression of the 1970s (the Five Gray Years). He fashions tiny figures out of lead, arranges them in provocative ways, and photographs them. His work seems to me to follow in the footsteps of Antonia Eiríz, especially her canvas *The Baseball Game*. These artists, from two generations, in different mediums, and with very different voices, take a sophisticated and visually successful stand against any threat to freedom of expression.[15]

Culture building moved beyond Cuba's borders and into a global realm in the work of the poster artists of the 1960s to 1980s. Few of the country's writers, musicians, or visual artists were able to obtain visas to perform or show in the United States during those decades. But Cuban posters bypassed those restrictions, moving across borders through the mail or in the suitcases of the curious who defied U.S. travel bans and visited the island. In these posters political and artistic imagery (form and content) fused in innovative and powerful ways. Antonio Pérez González (Niko), Rafael Morante, Alfredo Rostgaard, and Raúl Martínez González are some of those whose images remain imprinted on my memory. Most liberation struggles throughout the world at the time were reflected in this art.

René Mederos's exquisite silkscreen images of Vietnam are still collectors' items. José Gómez Fresquet (Frémez), also working in silkscreen, drew on the opportunistic elegance of upscale U.S. advertising images when he contrasted a Vogue model's bright red lip gloss with blood of the same hue running from the corner of a Vietnamese woman's mouth. Alfredo Rostgaard's protest song poster, in which a single drop of blood hangs suspended from a rose's thorn, also references a bleeding world. The message was clear: a part of our world bled, and another part of it was causing the bleeding.

Raúl Martínez's collages of repeated portrait images might at first glance seem to have been influenced by Andy Warhol and other U.S. pop artists of that era. It is clear that there was communication and cross-pollination. But it wasn't only Martínez's subject matter that differed; the art itself was imbued with a very different attitude of what it means to live and grow in a society rooted in the search for justice at all levels. U.S. pop art took its subject matter's iconic images from a commodity-oriented society: Marilyn Monroe's seductive pout, the U.S. flag, an iconic can of Campbell's soup. In revolutionary Cuba the poster artists were dealing in praise song rather than featuring the products of a consumer society or sophisticated social commentary. These artists weren't depicting the same reality. And there was another group of artists working in the United States, social activists, expressing themselves through their art. They were profoundly moved by what was going on in the world of Cuban posters.

The dynamic posters coming out of the Revolution became familiar to those of us engaged in the struggles for social justice, against colonialism and imperialism, against the U.S. war in Vietnam, and for racial equality and women's rights. These posters were aesthetically and politically brilliant, and it was their insistence on excellence in both areas that made them so. Cubans were living an experience of social change they wanted to proclaim to the world. They also felt a deep connection to those involved in similar struggles elsewhere. A number of talented Cuban poster artists, each in his or her own way and with marked stylistic differences among them, wrote the language of the genre. This was also a two-way street: despite the rigors of the blockade, the Cuban artists influenced the U.S. artists and vice versa.

Cutting-edge urban planning and museum-like preservation have also found a home within the Cuban Revolution. A Havana city historian, Eusebio Leal, has reconstituted, refurbished, and reenergized the city's old urban center, creating a UNESCO World Heritage site that continues to expand. And this is no static museum. In its beautiful old buildings, primary school children cycle for months at a time in and out of classrooms that provide hands-on knowledge of authentic art and architecture from several cultures. No one who visits the twenty or so square blocks fails to come away impressed. In the country's interior whole small cities, such as Trinidad, also function as museums while embracing the activities of everyday life. (In chapter 13 I describe the contribution of Cuban artists to the enhancement of mental health work carried out by internationalist medical personnel in countries where natural disasters have affected large segments of the population. Painters, musicians, and circus performers often accompany doctors and nurses in order to work particularly with children. Kcho has so far taken the lead in this endeavor.[16]) As the Cuban poet Víctor Rodríguez Núñez has pointed out when speaking of his country's poets (the observation works for Cuba's visual artists as well), they "continue to be dissidents, particularly with regard to dehumanization, no matter where it comes from. Still, none of them proposes a return to capitalism, or celebrates private property, a market economy or free enterprise."[17]

Humor is another field that has produced a range of Cuban talent: cartoonists who aim their pens at contentious issues, creating characters whose job it is to keep society honest as they reflect national idiosyncrasies. One of these, Eduardo Abela (1889–1965), was also an important painter; his cross-genre work is in the Cuban artistic tradition. Cubans collectively possess a sharp sense of humor, including the ability to laugh at themselves—and at their enemies. I remember mass rallies during the years I lived on the island in which a donkey in the crowd would be saddled with a sandwich sign that protested, "Nixon is not my son!" Comic strips, cartoon contests, and caricature museums feed Cuba's tradition of humor as a respected and prolific art form.

Cuban photography has been stellar from long before the 1959 Revolution, which recognized and cultivated the genre. Images by Raúl Corrales, Alberto Díaz (Korda), Mario García Hoya (Mayito), María García Haya, Chino Lope, Ramón Martínez (Grandal), Gilda Rodríguez, Rogelio López Marín (Gory), Rigoberto Romero, Iván Cañas, Lissette Solórzano, Arien Chang Castán, and Leysis Quesada Vera are regularly exhibited in galleries throughout the world. A story that illustrates the unique challenges and socially conscious responses of Cuban photographers concerns Korda's famous portrait of Che Guevara, fortuitously taken on March 5, 1960, during the memorial for the more than eighty victims of counterrevolutionary sabotage who were killed when the Belgian ship *Coubre* exploded in Havana's harbor. Korda aimed his lens at the reviewing stand when Che suddenly stepped forward wearing his characteristic black beret with the single star and seeming to gaze into the future, and the photographer shot a couple of frames. The famous image didn't appear in the press covering the event, and Korda never tried to capitalize on it. But he kept it tacked to his darkroom wall. Years later a visitor saw it there, asked for a copy, and reproduced it on the poster that still circles the world. Without requesting permission the Smirnoff vodka company later appropriated the image in its advertising; the regulations governing copyright in Cuba at the time were, after all, vague. But when Korda discovered that his photo of Che was being used to sell vodka, he sued, winning a considerable monetary settlement, which he promptly donated to Cuba's universal health care system. There is something to be gleaned from this story, something that casts new light on a different kind of society and the artists who inhabit it.

I myself learned photography in Cuba. In 1978–79 I apprenticed to Ramón Martínez (Grandal). His wife, Gilda Rodríguez, and I decided to study with him at the same time and became co-conspirators in our search for film, chemicals, and paper. We obtained 35mm black-and-white film in long end strips from the makers of Cuban newsreel documentaries. We might get ten or twenty rolls out of each of those ends, and we hand-filled our own cassettes. Photographic paper was almost impossible to come by back then. Sometimes friends traveling to the island would bring us a box or two. We solved the problem of chemicals by making the rounds of the city's compounding pharmacies; the country had no shops where one could purchase neat yellow envelopes of developer or fixer powder that need only be mixed with water to be ready for use. We also managed to obtain the amber bottles for blending and storing those chemicals from the same pharmacies, but these were more difficult to come by. Once I inadvertently cracked a gallon jar against the corrugated side of the stone washstand where we washed our photos; Grandal curbed his usually explosive temper, no doubt realizing I felt bad enough about the accident.

I go into some detail about the difficulty obtaining the materials we needed because it was something artists in every genre suffered in a revolution whose first priority was providing its citizenry food, medicine, and other necessities. Painters needed paint and canvas, musicians were always looking for instrument strings, writers hunted down typewriter ribbons, and so forth. Along with paying a monthly stipend to artists, the government provided what materials it could to the most prominent. But the quantities were never enough.

Even when I had no film Grandal would send me out to make pictures and expect me to come back and tell him what I had shot. His response to my description of a picture taken only in my mind might be "You didn't get close enough!" Imagination played a huge role in the learning process. Yet I think back to those times with nostalgia. An integrity of intention and degree of ingenuity existed that is hard to find in today's world of ease and plenty for those able to purchase what we need. And there was a solidarity among artists in all genres that is hard to find in countries where a market economy determines who makes it and who doesn't.

If Cuban photography has achieved a level of excellence, in film Cuba has been a giant. Cuba didn't have a film industry before the Revolution. Like so many other poor countries, such an endeavor would have required an investment that didn't exist. In the months following the victory of 1959, the Revolution established ICAIC, headed by the brilliant theoretician Alfredo Guevara. The institution began producing weekly newsreels, innovative documentaries, and award-winning features. It's interesting to go back to the ten-minute *Por Primera Vez* (For the First Time, 1967). Parts of the island were still remote and inaccessible, and a *cine móvil* (movies on wheels) brought the magical genre to such areas; the Revolution was interested not only in bringing culture to places that hadn't experienced it before but in documenting such experiences. *Por Primera Vez* documents the experience of members of a small mountain community as they watch Charlie Chaplin's *Modern Times*. They had never before seen a motion picture. The short begins with brief interviews, in which the nonprofessional protagonists reveal what they imagine is about to happen. Then they watch the iconic film. Some peek behind the screen, trying to discover where the action is coming from. *Por Primera Vez* is a film within a film. Rarely has such a cinematographic event been brought to the screen with such authenticity and emotional sensitivity.

I could fill a book simply reviewing Cuban films from 1959 forward. On a randomly selected online site I found more than a thousand, most made by all-Cuban crews, some by foreign filmmakers residing in the country for a few years, and several coproductions with Spaniards or Brazilians, among others. A short list of those that continue to hold the attention of international audiences include *Memorias de Subdesarrollo* (1968), *Lucía* (1968), *La Ultima Cena* (1976), *Fresa y Chocolate* (1993), and *Buena Vista Social Club* (1999). The work of the documentary filmmaker Santiago Alvarez, including *79 Primaveras* (about the life of Ho Chi Minh), are in a class by themselves.

Artistic genres such as literature and film juggle memory in interesting ways, and I want to speak briefly about one more film, in which memory bends the viewer's consciousness through the use of innovative but inexpensive technical manipulation as well as that magic many who know Cuba associate with the country. It is *Hombres de Maltiempo*. Maltiempo was a famous battle in Cuba's second war of independence from Spain; it was waged in 1895. In a matter of fifteen minutes Cuban insurgents destroyed six companies of Spanish invaders. Seventy-three years later, in 1968, the Argentinean filmmaker Alejandro Saderman decided to feature that battle in a commemorative thirty-two-minute short. The Cuban poet Miguel Barnet wrote the script.

Because Cuba values authentic witness, the filmmakers invited a group of old men from an assisted living residence in Havana to visit the shoot, which took place at the site of the original battle. These men were veterans of Maltiempo; all were over ninety, one 109. We see them being loaded into a van, their movements slow, faces impassive. Then we see them being unloaded on location and helped into lawn chairs from which, we assume, they will enjoy watching this re-creation of the story they may remember from their distant past. The actors are ready, in period costumes and on horseback, swords drawn.

"Action," the director commands.

As the mounted actors ride into sight, something happens to the old men: they come alive. They rise from their lawn chairs, engaged now but agitated and upset. "No, no," one begins to exclaim, and goes on to critique the re-created battle scene. Another shouts, in a voice that has become unexpectedly resonant, that the horsemen are coming from the wrong direction. Yet another explains the actors aren't wielding the swords as they should. To a man the veterans begin to remember. The location, the action, all of it pulls their memory to the fore.

The film's use of solarizing emphasizes memory's nonlinear route.[18] Advisors have become actors. Before our eyes months of careful planning give way to fortuitous change. The original script is discarded for this new one, a product of having brought these old men to witness an event from their past. The interplay between veterans and actors is intense. After the remembered battle has been filmed authentically, the men return to the van that will take them back to their residence. They move slowly once more. They are no longer who they were seven decades—or an hour—earlier. *Hombres de Maltiempo* embodies so much of what I believe makes Cuban art unique: respect for history and for those who make it, an openness to ideas that may surge spontaneously along the way, innovative methods of capturing and honoring memory, artistic experimentation, and the creative freedom to play with it all.

Other artistic genres offer similar stories. Cuban dance has long been internationally acclaimed; for example, the world-renowned prima ballerina Alicia Alonso was already a virtuoso stage presence in 1959. She immediately declared her commitment to the Revolution and founded a national ballet school that attracted attention for its level of excellence and its development of new dance techniques geared to the Afro-Cuban body type.[19] I can remember seeing Alonso dancing in Havana's Lenin Park and against a backdrop of shear rock cliffs at a political event in Pinar del Río, in the spirit of making high culture accessible in popular venues. Now, a half century later, Cuba has several generations of brilliant classical dancers: her legacy. Blind most of her adult life and now at the age of ninety-five, Alonso is still attentive to Cuban dance.

Beginning in those early years folk ballet also got a boost. But here more complicated challenges existed because folk dance was often based on African religious practices. These religions are popular everywhere on the island, and there was a period in which excessive materialism was disrespectful, even unkind to these and other religious manifestations. Accusations of opportunism flared when the Revolution began nurturing Afro-Cuban culture while disparaging its adepts as believers. In time an accommodation was reached, just as happened between the Revolution and Catholics and other denominations.[20] Today Afro-Cuban dance and music enjoy ample support, and their masters travel widely as performers and teachers. A number of African musical forms are ubiquitous in Cuba; its drums can be heard in every neighborhood and on every street. Salsa has taken up residence throughout much of the world, Cuba's variety blending with its Puerto Rican and U.S. counterparts to produce ever-evolving expressions.

Cubans excel in all musical forms. After the rapprochement between Cuba and the United States that began at the end of 2014, a venue in Chicago hosted a Cuban group that had kept the spirit of jazz alive through decades of broken contact.[21] Numerous other collaborations followed, many of which had been on the drawing boards for years but had been stymied by U.S. government refusals to grant the necessary visas.

Symphonic, chamber, chorale, and early instrument ensembles flourish across the country. Classical musicians such as Leo Brower and Frank Fernández and popular figures such as Omara Portuondo, Compay Segundo, and Chucho Valdés are legends. The musical movement known as the vieja trova, with its grace and nostalgia, still fills theaters.[22] But it has been the nueva trova movement of singer-songwriters—especially Silvio Rodríguez, Pablo

Milanés, Noël Nicola, and Sara González, as well as subsequent generations of their followers—that has most palpably crossed Cuba's borders to make its mark throughout the world. These singer-songwriters compose lyrics that are both critical and poetic. They were part of the great Latin American protest song movement that exploded in the 1960s with such greats as Víctor Jara, Angel Parra, Mercedes Sosa, and Daniel Viglietti. But while the latter musicians made music in situations where repression reigned (often the individuals themselves had been forced into exile), their Cuban counterparts performed in the more complex situation of a nation in revolution. In a recent interview Silvio Rodríguez said, "The Cuban Revolution has been an immense reality, recognized in its unquestionable legacy. I have been with it the whole time. I have no doubt that another revolution exists in our future. But until that extraordinary moment comes, we must continue to evolve."[23]

When thinking about all these artistic expressions, an important question arises: How has the Cuban Revolution avoided repression and censorship permanently overtaking its cultural expression? Every revolution has had its initial moment in which creative expression has taken off, even exploding within the context of the new social paradigm. Exuberant political moments have invariably had their intellectual and artistic counterparts. The more progressive members of society were restless to break free of restrictive molds and welcomed transgressive artistic manifestations. We can trace this freedom of creative expression in the Russian, Chinese, and other revolutions. But their moments of creative possibility were generally short-lived. Consolidation and institutionalization of the political process, internal power struggles, and a tendency to revert to the safety of traditionalism took their toll. In most cases the periods of creative freedom and experimentation lasted only a few brief years and ended badly: with coercion, repression, or worse.

I'm not thinking here only about art itself but also about its encouragement and support. True artists will create in almost any circumstance; if they cannot do so freely, they will go underground, or, as in Cuba's case, during repressive periods many will emigrate. It isn't so much about making art as about nurturing it. About allowing art to flourish in an atmosphere conducive to experimentation and unafraid of currents that challenge or appear to threaten the status quo. About inviting it to help shape social reality.

These are intimately related themes. Repression introduces fear, censorship, and self-censorship. Repression can set literary and artistic movements back generations. I am talking about state sponsorship of diversity in artistic expression, a state knowledgeable, sophisticated, and self-confident enough to support a variety of artistic modes, even when some may be critical of the state itself. In Cuba this "inevitable" restriction of creative freedom reared its ugly head but didn't last. It was overcome by the writers and artists themselves as well as by a new, wiser generation of government bureaucrats. After a period some describe as having lasted five years (a *quinquenio*) and others considerably longer, a palpable (though never to be taken for granted) freedom was restored. In spite of the terrible damage wrought by El Quinquenio Gris, and in spite of the fact that its negative effects actually lasted as long as ten or fifteen years, freedom of expression rebounded with a fighting spirit and exists in today's Cuba with a deep awareness of the dangers inherent in its repression. I've been curious as to how the small country has achieved this more productive unfolding.

Like Russia's, China's, and other twentieth-century revolutions, Cuba experienced an explosion of artistic diversity in its first decade. Then this explosion came under attack. We have seen how different groups vying for power represented different trends in this respect. For a while censorship took its toll. But in Cuba creative diversity rebounded in ways that it did not in the Soviet Union and China, at least not as quickly or conclusively. One reason for this may be that during the Cuban Revolution there were always several currents competing for primacy. One might predominate for a while, but the others were never completely obliterated. During the repressive period starting at the beginning of the 1970s and not waning until the mid-1980s, fear and narrow-mindedness took over. But eventually clearer minds prevailed. Why and how did this happen?

Some point to Fidel Castro, who possessed an astonishing intellect and understood the importance of encouraging diverse expressive currents. Early in the revolutionary process he talked about its not being a question of downgrading culture for the masses but rather of bringing the entire population's cultural level up so that everyone could understand and appreciate the best art and literature. "No cree, lee" (Don't believe, read), he is remembered as saying. In 1961, at an assembly of artists and writers, he gave his famous speech, "Words to the Intellectuals." One line from that speech, "Within the Revolution every right; outside the Revolution none," has been quoted, misquoted, and taken out of context through the years. He was saying that if artists and intellectuals respected the Revolution, they would enjoy all rights; if they defied or tried to weaken it, they would have none. The Revolution itself had rights, the first of these being to protect itself. But few have remarked on how extraordinary it was that the leader of the Revolution would meet with artists and writers in an in-depth effort to explore the responsibilities the state and those creatives bore to each other.

Some point to Che Guevara, whose important 1965 article, "Socialism and Man in Cuba," defended abstract art against Soviet-inspired socialist realism. He described the latter, as it was encouraged in the Soviet Union, as

> an art that would be understood by everyone, the kind of "art" that functionaries understand. True artistic values were disregarded, and the problem of general culture was reduced to taking some things from the socialist present and some from the dead (and, hence, not dangerous) past. But the realistic art of the nineteenth century is also a class art, more purely capitalist than this decadent art of the twentieth century which reveals the anguish of an alienated people. Why, then, try to find the only valid prescription for art in the frozen forms of socialist realism? . . . Let us not attempt, from the pontifical throne of realism-at-all-costs, to condemn all the art forms that have evolved since the first half of the nineteenth century, for we would then fall into the Proudhonian mistake of returning to the past, of putting a straightjacket on the artistic expression of the person who is being born and who is in the process of making himself.[24]

Despite Guevara's warning, Cuba had to go through its own process in this respect. For a time freedom of experimentation gave way to hyperrealism, a photo-like style of painting that proposed pictorial values similar to those of its Soviet forebear, but it was short-lived and without ongoing influence.

Many speak about important figures in Cuba's intellectual milieu, people such as Alfredo Guevara (who headed the country's film industry), Haydée Santamaría (who founded and ran Casa de las Américas), Celia Sánchez (Fidel's closest confident, whose behind-the-scenes influence can be seen in several extraordinary architectural projects, including Havana's vast Lenin Park), Armando Hart (the first minister of culture), the literary critic Ambrosio Fornet, the filmmaker and cultural critic Julio García Espinosa, the poet Antón Arrufat, the cultural promoter Marcia Leseica, the playwright Senel Paz, the singer-songwriter Silvio Rodríguez, the novelist and critic Arturo Arango, and Abel Prieto (the second minister of culture). All these men and women possessed a sophisticated view of art's importance to cultural development and understood when to move energetically, when carefully. They promoted artistic excellence and a rich diversity of cultural expression.

Even as I acknowledge the enormous impact these major figures had, I want to emphasize the importance of the masses of Cuban artists and writers who invariably raised their voices against all forms of censorship. Those who have not found freedom as immediately or completely as they hoped within the Revolution have left to search for it elsewhere. Those who were able to wait and seek opportunities to help shape their milieu did so brilliantly. I believe the freedom for which the Revolution stands has influenced both groups. In this respect a reunited island speaks for a fabric that is battle-worn but strong.

The ideological struggle between the PSP, with its ties to a Stalinist vision, and the July 26 Movement, which included men and women who were much more intellectually progressive, more open to ideas, was critical through the Revolution's first two decades. This struggle involved political and economic theory and also contrasting notions regarding culture and the arts. Cuba's long dependence on the Soviet Union left its mark, but in the creative fields as well as in other areas, the Revolution eventually embraced policies more attuned to its unique particularities.

A poet myself, I see the world through poetry's eyes. I tend to explore philosophical questions and search for their answers on its terrain. But as I pondered the power of Cuban poets, writers, visual artists, musicians, dancers, photographers, and filmmakers, and their impact beyond the country's borders, I remembered that the small country has also wielded extraordinary influence in other arenas: in its internationalist solidarity and generosity, its willingness to fight against tyranny in distant lands, its embrace of the children abandoned or orphaned in so many struggles, its far-reaching educational programs, and its contribution to human health not only at home but throughout the world. The following chapters are devoted to these areas.

The questions remain: Why Cuba? And how? How much of this powerful creative reserve existed before the 1959 Revolution, and what did the Revolution do to capitalize on, institutionalize, and multiply that reserve? What did it do, from time to time, to hamper creativity? Does the Cuban Revolution's history with regard to the arts (including its darkest chapters) provide clues to its awareness of the essential oneness of the world's peoples and offer us a viable way to understand its solidarity in so many areas?

3

CUBA BY CUBA

On December 17, 2014, presidents Raul Castro of Cuba and Barack Obama of the United States simultaneously announced the renewal of diplomatic relations between our two countries, broken more than half a century earlier. For some who have followed the astonishing history it was a welcome moment we never thought we'd witness. For others it was a sign of political folly. For many it remains purely symbolic, its full potential unrealizable until the economic blockade is lifted. For still others the gesture ended their "post-Castro" dream of restoring bourgeois democracy on the island.

In Cuba itself the news was met with cautious optimism.

Within the large U.S. Cuban immigrant community, close to two million strong, opinion was split. The older generations, although dying off now, tend to hold fast to their demand that the United States alter its Cuba policy only after democracy is reinstated in their homeland. And their definition of democracy mimics this country's corrupt high-dollar brand. Among younger Cuban Americans reason has replaced rigidity, and many welcome changes that make communication, family visits, and life in their other homeland easier. They understand that half a century of failed U.S. policy toward Cuba has become a cold war anachronism.

Despite his courageous move, President Obama hasn't stopped advocating for regime change in Cuba. Nor has the United States put an end to a number of government-funded strategies aimed at unraveling the Revolution. One of these is the policy that gives special immigration status to Cubans who come to the United States illegally. Another is the systematized brain drain of professionals from Cuba. A third can be seen in a reluctance to lift the blockade and reauthorize normal trade. Even in the context of renewed relations, for example, a producer of U.S. farm machinery applied to invest in the Cuban industrial complex at Mariel on the condition that its tractors be sold only to private landowners.[1] Most important, until the U.S. Congress revokes the punishing embargo, the new relationship represents a shift in method more than in policy.[2]

What about Cuba? When will the United States move away from its condescending attitude toward other peoples and listen to what Cuba has to say about itself? The Caribbean nation has plenty to tell us and has expressed it in domestic speeches and international forums as well as in its political positions, accomplishments, and responses to continuous harassment all these many decades. When will we look without bias at the astonishing things it has done with dignity and a sense of genuine solidarity and eschewing self-promotion?

The problem is even many on the left are stuck in a kind of traditionalist mind-set that makes it difficult for them to look at Cuba without referencing previous socialist solutions. Ricardo Alarcón, a Cuban revolutionary and statesman and for thirty years his country's permanent representative to the United Nations, says:

> Marxism was represented by a set of concepts from the outside. One element that is missing in conversations about the Cuban Revolution is that a fresh and highly critical approach emerged, even among the old communist movement. We started going back to a sort of new New Left in Latin America, a new approach to socialism. The positive dimension [of the Soviet demise] was not having to have a point of reference like a Vatican or a Socialist Church. It made you go back to the socialist idea which was not represented by either the Soviets or the Chinese. We were fortunate that history continued and that Latin America evolved.[3]

The U.S. left welcomed the Cuban Revolution, albeit too often trying to fit it into one of several molds. But among the mainstream, with their sound-bite coverage of international politics, most probably would not be able to point to Cuba on a map, and those who can, wonder about the next chapter. For years I've heard people ask "What will happen after Fidel dies?"[4] Not a few now say they want to visit the island "before it changes." They envision a Hollywood-like *before* and after—not before and after the Revolution but before and after the renewal of relations, which they see as basically orchestrated by the United States.

I doubt there is a leader of any country in the world whose death has been reported more often than Fidel Castro's. For years every time the Cuban president failed to appear in public for a few days or weeks Miami gossip exploded into rumor purporting to be certainty. When he became very ill in the mid-1990s, we heard a frenzied drumbeat of such premonitions, which failed to appreciate that, as extraordinarily important as he was to the Cuban Revolution, he was a member of a party, part of a political process and system. Since Fidel's retirement in 2008 continuity has been evident to anyone willing to look.

We in the United States tend to believe we can control what happens in the rest of the world. Invade, bomb, occupy. Penetrate with the force of arms or softly through the power of propaganda, brain drain, and so-called aid programs. Speak English as loudly as possible rather than learn the languages others speak. Our presence and influence always seem to us to be the determining factor in every situation.

Because information about Cuba in our corporate media has been so skewed, most people have very little knowledge about the country that is so geographically close but ideologically distant. Such questions and comments reflect this distorted press rather than reality on the ground. There's no doubt that December 17, 2014, marked a historic shift, and a positive one. But Cuba existed in all its vibrant complexity before that date and will continue to evolve along lines of its own design despite changes in U.S. policy.

Here's a brief geographical sketch, then some necessary history.

As countries go, Cuba is tiny; it occupies less than 110,000 square kilometers. As of 2015 its population stands at slightly over eleven million. This, despite waves of emigration, is almost twice what it was when the Revolution succeeded in 1959. By comparison the United States has a territory of 9,857,306 square kilometers, with an estimated 2016 population of almost 325 million. In the Latin American context, Brazil, at 8,515,767 square kilometers, has a population of over 200 million; Mexico has 1,972,550 square kilometers with just over 218 million; even tiny Uruguay occupies more land (176,215 square kilometers), although with only about a quarter of Cuba's population.[5]

Information about Cuba's so-called prehistoric era has come down to us through conquest texts that naturally render it Eurocentric and one-sided.[6] The original inhabitants were seen through the lens of evangelizing conquerors who thought only in terms of claiming new territories and gaining a chattel labor force of salvageable souls. Columbus "discovered" the island on his first New World exploration, landing there on October 28, 1492. Our country's racist Eurocentricity causes it to date the beginnings of those civilizations on lands colonized by Europe from their presumed moment of contact, ignoring the life that existed there for centuries or even millennia. The sixteenth-century historian and chronicler Bartolomé de las Casas would identify three indigenous cultures: Guanahutubey (now written Guanajuatabey), Siboney (now Ciboney), and Taíno. Their history goes back centuries before our era. But Columbus's maiden voyage initiated the Spanish takeover and a dissemination of early descriptive texts.

In eastern Cuba the natives had heard about the atrocities committed by the Spaniards on neighboring islands. A Hispaniola-born Cuban leader named Hatuey organized his people to fight the invaders. The Spaniards captured and condemned him to be burned at the stake. Popular culture has it that just before the sentence was to be carried out a priest tried to convert him, claiming he would go to heaven if he accepted Christ's truth. Hatuey asked the priest if heaven was where the Spanish go when they die. When the priest said yes, Hatuey said he would rather go to hell. Truth or fiction, the story is referenced today as indicative of Cuban dignity and strength of character.

With a decimated native population, Spain was left with a weak labor force, and the Spanish king authorized the introduction of African slaves as early as 1512. By 1577 seven hundred were documented. But aboriginal uprisings continued. Another Taíno chief led a rebellion against Spanish rule in the 1530s, controlling a mountainous region in the eastern part of the country until 1533. These indigenous struggles would foreshadow similar attempts by African slaves in the nineteenth century to gain their freedom. Throughout the sixteenth and seventeenth centuries the isolation and ruggedness of eastern Cuba made it a haven for illegal trade with the French and English. At the beginning of the nineteenth century there was an influx of French who had fled the revolution in nearby Haiti. And cheap labor was imported from Mexico as well. The island gave birth to a strong *mestizaje*, or mix of bloods, languages, and traditions, all tempered by the social stratification that comes when some of the influx indentures others.

As slavery became entrenched, when black men and women managed to escape and hide in the mountains they were called runaway slaves or maroons. The courage of these runaways is familiar into modern times. One, Esteban Montejo, was still alive in the 1960s. He told his story to the Cuban ethnographer Miguel Barnet, and it became *The Autobiography of a Runaway Slave* (1969), a brilliant testimony that has been translated into a dozen languages.[7]

The Independent Party of Color, founded in 1908 by Afro-Cuban veterans of the War of Independence, was a nationwide organization that linked racism to colonialism and advocated against racial inequality and for the civic-mindedness of all Cubans. Its program went beyond fighting racism to include abolition of the death penalty, free and compulsory education for all children six to fourteen, equal employment, the eight-hour workday, and even a modest distribution of state lands. In 1912 the party led a rebellion in the eastern part of the country; the uprising failed, putting an end to the party.

No one writes more knowledgably about race in Cuba than Zuleica Romay.[8] Describing racism and race relations in her country in 2008, when she began an extended period of study of the phenomena, she writes, "Back then our overconfidence in the infallibility of those transformations of a structural nature had diminished, and we began to let go of the positivist enthusiasm that had led us to underestimate the weight that inherited lifestyles and culture had on the social project we were constructing. The worst years of economic crisis, following the imposition of European socialism, had demonstrated that it isn't possible to transform people's ways of thinking and acting if you don't appeal as well to philosophical and political concepts and categories, to memory, social relationships, sentiments and emotions."[9]

Spanish, British, and French colonialism competed for Cuba throughout the seventeenth and eighteenth centuries, each power alternately gaining and losing control. In 1628 even the Dutch briefly made their presence felt, plundering the Spanish fleet anchored in Havana's harbor. Britain occupied Cuba for a few months in 1762.

The country fought for its independence from Spain in three successive wars. The first (1868–78) is called the Ten Years' War. The Smallest War (1879–80) resulted from the lack of a conclusive victory in the war immediately preceding it. The final War of Independence (1895–98) won freedom from Spain, only for the country to fall into the hands of the United States, by then a world power and one that considered the Caribbean island to be within its radius of control.

Cuba's great independence leaders emerged in the last of these wars, men such as Máximo Gómez, Antonio Maceo, and José Martí, and a woman, Mariana Grajales. Today these names are familiar to every Cuban child. Less well known until the Revolution rescued her from oblivion was Carlota, a slave from the province of Matanzas who led a doomed rebellion in 1843. In 1975 Fidel Castro vindicated Carlota, bringing her name out of obscurity as he stood in an overflowing plaza and announced that Cuba's military aid to Angola would be called Operación Carlota in honor of that woman who a century and a half before had sought freedom for herself and other African slaves. (Cuba would return to Africa, then, on another kind of freedom mission I describe in detail later in this book.)

On February 15, 1898, just as the War of Independence was drawing to a close, the battleship USS *Maine* anchored at a Havana dock. It had sailed from Key West, Florida. That night an enormous explosion decimated the forward third of the ship and 274 men lost their lives. In March a U.S. Naval Court of Inquiry declared that a mine had caused the accident. Importantly the event precipitated (or justified) what in the United States is called the Spanish-American War, avoiding any mention of Cuba itself. "Remember the Maine" became a common cry.

The United States proceeded to fight Spain for dominance over the island, sending troops in June 1898. The explosion of the *Maine* would foreshadow the explosion of another ship, the *Coubre*, in 1961. It is because Cuba is an island that the devastating explosions of ships figure so prominently in its history. But I don't want to skip ahead in my story.

On December 10, 1898, Spain and the United States signed the Treaty of Paris, giving the latter control of four new territories: Cuba, Puerto Rico, the Philippines, and Guam. This was the period in which the Monroe Doctrine shaped U.S. hemispheric policy, and bourgeoisies in client countries as well as in the metropolis did not question the rightness of that policy. Each of these occupations ended differently: Guam and Puerto Rico remain U.S. territories to this day; the Philippines was a territory until 1945, when it won definitive independence. Puerto Rico continues to struggle with issues of politics, culture, the economy, and identity. As I write all these years later the island begs for debt renegotiation in its ongoing and weary fight for economic survival.

Cuba traded Spanish for U.S. domination. On March 2, 1901, the United States codified its control over the island when Congress passed the Platt Amendment, denying Cuba's right to self-determination and approving U.S. military intervention any time it might be deemed necessary to keep the territory in its domain. The Platt Amendment was also written into Cuba's 1901 Constitution, establishing servile acceptance of this arrangement. The United States installed a protectorate government, in effect through 1902, then turned the country over to a Cuban administration loyal to U.S. interests. This mock transfer of power gave rise to the oft quoted saying that Cuba was the first republic to have been "born castrated."

A succession of pseudo-independent administrations followed. Opposition to U.S. and local oligarchic domination became particularly strong in the early 1930s, and in 1933 Gerardo Machado's dictatorship was overthrown by a successful general strike, only to be followed by moderate administrations such as those of Grau San Martín and Prío Socarrás. These decades also saw a strong communist presence, with brilliant leaders such as Julio Antonio Mella and Jesús Menéndez.[10] By the 1940s and 1950s, however, opposition was centered in Eduardo Chibás's Orthodox Party, a populist configuration that gained considerable progressive support. On August 16, 1951, Chibás himself, dispirited about his party's prospects, committed suicide right after one of his weekly national radio broadcasts.

Fidel and others who would later join his movement had previously looked to orthodoxy as an answer to Cuba's aggrieved situation. In 1940 a military officer, Fulgencio Batista, had won elections judged at the time to be fair and democratic. Batista proved no better than his predecessors, though, and lost to civilians in 1944 and 1948. In 1952, rather than wait to see how he would fare in the next election, he retook power in a military coup. That coup proved to be the blow to Cuban dignity necessary to unleash the forces that would coalesce as Fidel's July 26 Movement, the organization able to bring together and lead the successful revolution. Other groups existed—including the PSP, the Student Directorate, and a fighting front in the Escambray Mountains—but eventually they would either disappear or cede prominence to July 26.

History appeared to speed up after that—of course it didn't really, but the more contemporary events are, the more they seem to follow one another in rapid succession and the more compressed the overall narrative becomes. Fidel and his followers had made their presence felt for the first time on July 26, 1953, when 165 rebels attacked Moncada Barracks in Santiago de Cuba, the country's second largest military garrison—thus the movement's name.[11] The action was a failure in the sense that it didn't end in victory or trigger the popular uprising that was its primary goal. In retrospect, however, it proved to have been a great political victory, the event that ignited the struggle. The dictatorship tortured and murdered almost every revolutionary taken alive. Those few who were captured were imprisoned and then released two years later in a general amnesty.

Trained as a lawyer, Fidel defended himself at trial. His defense speech, which came to be known as "History Will Absolve Me," was a brilliantly reasoned and detailed program for the new society he envisioned. The rebel movement gained tremendous popular support, and Cuban liberation was under way.

Perhaps even more significant, and particularly relevant to a book about Cuban solidarity, the attack on Moncada Barracks demonstrated to the people of Santiago de Cuba the existence of a group of determined and courageous young men and women willing to sacrifice their lives for a cause in which they believed. Those who took part in the action knew their chances of survival ran from minimal to nonexistent, yet they understood that although they might not live to see it, their sacrifice would help put an end to tyranny. This sort of commitment in the face of almost certain death is typical throughout Cuba's history: a domestic foretelling of the country's influence in the larger world. In the history of the 1959 Revolution a few heroic names are revered, but thousands whose names will never be known played their part in weaving the fabric that brought success and remains strong through subsequent years of struggle.

Haydée Santamaría, one of only two women who took part in the Moncada action, put it eloquently: "Moncada existed because there were dozens of young men who the people of Santiago saw tortured to death, murdered. Because the people of Santiago felt their pain, they came to understand people differently. Because they knew that not everything had gone to ruin here. They knew there were people willing to be tortured to death shouting Viva Cuba! All of that took root in Santiago de Cuba. And the help the people of Santiago gave those in the mountains was decisive, the help they gave the underground was decisive."[12]

When Herbert Matthews of the *New York Times* made his way into the Sierra Maestra to interview Fidel in February 1957, insistent rumors reported the rebel leader dead. The revolutionaries had been fighting at that point for only seventy-nine days. It was later revealed that a mere eighteen of them made up the troop Fidel convinced the journalist was much larger. But even that small a group was beginning to outfight thousands of well-trained and well-armed soldiers. In his February 24 article Matthews quoted Fidel: "I have followers all over the island. All the best elements, especially all the youth, are with us. The Cuban people will stand anything but oppression."[13] It was true: almost all of Cuba supported the uprising, and tens of thousands contributed to the victory two years later.

In the context of Latin American emancipatory efforts, Cuba's young revolutionaries defeated the dictator in record time. The victory was an inspiration to others. The United States was on guard after that, and none of the subsequent attempts by Latin American rebel forces were successful—with the ill-fated exceptions of Nicaragua's Sandinistas in 1979, Grenada's short-lived revolution (1979–80), and Guatemala and El Salvador in mediated agreements some years later. Chilean revolutionaries had taken power in democratic elections in 1970, but the United States would destroy that project too by backing Augusto Pinochet's coup in 1973. The United States would destroy the Sandinista experiment by funding the contra war and subverting Nicaragua's 1990 elections a decade and a half later. After Cuba it was careful to keep a tight hold on its client nations in the hemisphere.

The victory of the Cuban Revolution led to immediate and important changes in the country. In February 1959, just months after the rebels ousted Batista, the 1940 Constitution was reinstated. At a massive rally in March, Fidel explained that the new government would be outlawing racial discrimination and adopting worker protection laws. By April all the gambling casinos were closed and all private beaches opened to the public. In May the first Agrarian Reform Law was proclaimed. In October the formation of a people's militia was announced, putting arms in the hands of citizens who were eager to defend their revolution.

Nationalization of major industries and the bank also came quickly. On October 13, 1960, the new government took control of 376 Cuban companies, and less than two weeks later nationalized 166 U.S. properties.[14] Land reform eliminated foreign ownership of large holdings, and urban reform reduced speculative real estate and limited to two the number of homes a person could own. Education and health care were declared human rights; they were soon brought under central control and made accessible to all.

In 1960 President Eisenhower approved the CIA's Program of Covert Action against Castro, the beginning of an ongoing strategy to destroy the Revolution. The CIA began recruiting and training Cuban exiles for paramilitary attacks against the island. (It was Eisenhower who authorized the Bay of Pigs invasion, which was reluctantly and, as it turns out, half-heartedly inherited by John F. Kennedy.) When Cuba restored diplomatic relations with the Soviet Union, Eisenhower suspended Cuba's U.S. sugar quota, and Esso, Shell, and Texaco refused to refine Soviet oil in Cuba. In both cases the Soviet Union stepped in to make up the deficit. Cuba also signed a trade agreement with China around this time.

The United States authorized, funded, and trained those who participated in the April 1961 Bay of Pigs attack (called Playa Girón by Cubans). The debacle was defeated in just two days and failed miserably in its attempt to put an end to the Revolution. Each side suffered more than one hundred deaths, and Cuba captured some 1,200 mercenaries. Later these prisoners would be traded for fifty-two million dollars' worth of medicines and baby formula. If anything, Playa Girón made the revolutionary process stronger.[15]

I could go on, enumerating every Cuban revolutionary decision and every attempt by a succession of U.S. administrations to do the Revolution in. The list would take pages. Suffice it to say a small island nation declared its right to a future of its choosing, while its powerful neighbor spent billions attempting to destroy it, as it had been successful doing to so many other governments it didn't like.

Noble as Cuba's struggle for independence was, and ultimately as unthreatening to the United States, the latter went into a prolonged period of shock and petulance. In the first moments it had recognized the new government and backed Manuel Urrutia, an interim president it thought it could depend upon to defend its interests. He lasted only a few months. There followed years of subversion and outright attack, decades of blockade. Nothing worked.

After Eisenhower took the step of breaking diplomatic relations with the Caribbean country, the next nine U.S. presidents maintained the policy, some loosening their grip slightly, others doubling down. The bottom line was that little Cuba was an unacceptable communist beachhead in what the United States considered its area of control. Administration after administration supported military attack, funded covert subversion, and reauthorized the brutal trade embargo and other punishing measures against a sovereign nation that dared choose its own form of government.

The United States also made third countries pay if they defied its dictates with regard to the Cuban Revolution. After the Organization of American States (OAS) conclave that took place in Costa Rica in August 1960, the United States began enlisting the support of OAS members in its anticommunist crusade. Through its control of the organization it began barring the Cuban government from attending regional meetings. Although Cuba was one of the OAS's twenty-one founding members, the United States exerted the influence necessary to suspend its membership at the eighth general assembly, at Punta del Este, Uruguay, in January 1962. It wasn't until the thirty-ninth general assembly, held in San Pedro Sula, Honduras, in June 2009 that—due to increasing pressure from other Latin American countries—this suspension was finally lifted.

Cuba has so far refused to rejoin the OAS, although it now participates regularly in regional meetings held by organizations less dominated by the

United States (or from which the United States is absent). In April 2015 the Summit of the Americas, held in Panama City, saw the attendance of both Cuba and the United States; President Obama hoped that he would be given more of a welcome than previous U.S. presidents had received when they attended such meetings, but Cuba's Raul Castro was given far more attention. After years of bowing to U.S. interests, many of the continent's nations are taking a more independent position on all sorts of issues.[16]

Throughout the past half century, a couple of U.S. presidents proffered timid gestures of rapprochement with Cuba, briefly loosening draconian travel restrictions. Jimmy Carter made modest moves in this direction, but then Gerald Ford, Ronald Reagan, and George H. W. Bush reverted to the same old failed approach. Under Bill Clinton the Helms-Burton Act of 1996 strengthened anti-Cuba policy, making it necessary for Congress to dismantle it. Contrary to popular belief, Democrats have been almost as stubbornly antagonistic as Republicans with regard to U.S. Cuba policy. For its part Cuba consistently declared itself ready to normalize relations with the United States if that country stopped its overt and covert actions against the Revolution.

Those Cuban exiles arriving in the United States illegally, sometimes in dribbles and sometimes in waves, continued to receive special treatment from the U.S. Immigration and Naturalization Service; once on our shores they easily obtained residency or citizenship.[17] From time to time special airlifts rescued Cubans, one of them even separating children from their parents.[18] The brain drain has also been ongoing, luring everyone from well-trained doctors and other professionals to legendary baseball players. (In a later chapter I discuss how the United States praised Cuban medical support during Africa's 2014 Ebola crisis even as it was trying to lure Cuban doctors fighting that crisis to defect to the United States and attempting to block World Health Organization salaries destined for the Cuban internationalists.)

U.S. policy has forced Cuba to buy what it needs halfway around the world, thus adding immeasurably to the cost of transport. This, in addition to the embargo, has prevented the country from getting ahead economically. It has kept families separated, caused ongoing estrangement, and meant far too much in human tragedy. But none of these attempts to punish the Revolution has been able to bring it down. In Cuba, as in so many other places, a bully implacability fails to account for the power of human dignity and enduring strength of resistance. Cubans have too often had to set their jaws and tighten their belts in heroic efforts to survive as an independent state.

Meanwhile, for more than fifty years, no one in the United States in a position to undo a decision that belies every stated principle of respect for other countries and only brings continued hardship to the Cuban people had the courage to say "Enough is enough." Now the bully stance has begun to unravel. Following months of secret negotiations, Obama made good on his campaign promise to normalize relations. I hope further steps will follow.

Except to establish a context, my aim here is not to dwell on U.S.-Cuban diplomacy. I want to talk about Cuba itself, and particularly about its unique offerings, so often overlooked by those who write about the country.

Let me begin by describing Cuba in its natural Latin American milieu. It is a small island in the Caribbean ninety miles off the Florida Keys and sitting like a salt-soaked hinge between the nations of South and North America, a landmass sometimes referred to as a single continent, sometimes as two. In addition to the Latin American countries, the whole of North America is composed of Canada and Mexico as well as the United States—although Mexico is also considered part of Latin America. The United States has long usurped the name America for itself, one that rightfully belongs to twenty-six modern nationalities plus hundreds of indigenous ones. Ask anyone from Tierra de Fuego to the Arctic Circle, and they will tell you they are American.

Within this diverse spread of territories, peoples, and cultures, by all counts and measures Cuba is insignificant. Yet its power, prestige, and influence among its Latin American neighbors, especially during the past half century, have rendered it larger than life.

The Cuban Revolution of 1959 took the world by surprise. And it shaped generations. Many saw in it a beacon for humanity. Others believed it a threat to market capitalism and democracy that must be combated in every possible way. Like the roughly concurrent U.S. war in Vietnam, its political impact has been far greater than the number of people who brought it to fruition. For those paying attention, notes Ricardo Alarcón, Cuba provides us with a Latin American route to social change that is different from those of the Soviet Union or China. And this impact has not been limited to what the United States has called "exporting revolution." The moral underpinnings of its political example can be felt in its internationalism, health care outreach and biomedical research, global efforts to eliminate illiteracy, response to natural disasters, lessons from its domestic educational and health systems, and solidarity with peoples mired in poverty, hopelessness, and underdevelopment. Poor and limited in resources though it is, Cuba doesn't see social betterment in a solely national context; it consistently and disinterestedly finds ways to help improve life for people throughout the continent and world.

Why, and how, has such a small island with such a minuscule population managed to change history? I look at a variety of areas—national identity; social change; the quest for justice and equality; the eradication of disease; class, race, and gender issues; international outreach; health care; education; sports; and culture—in an effort to answer these questions. I also show how Cuban literature, music, dance, painting, photography, and film have had an impact beyond what might have been imagined. And I am interested in the shape of arcs: high points in this influence but also low, those points at which extraordinary offerings have been stretched thin by ignorance, prejudice, outside pressures, internal error, or corruption. From time to time these low points have all but consecrated the sad history of a has-been, a cold ember where the fire of hope once burned. At such times, and despite the gleeful rubbing together of naysayer hands, Cuba has invariably raised itself from the ashes of outside aggression, major international power shifts, abandonment, inadequate infrastructure, and endemic poverty—as well as from its own sad periods of repression and moral detour.

A lot of attention has been paid to the ways Cuba itself manages to resist, much less to the fact that even or perhaps particularly when it has found itself in difficult straits it has been unstintingly generous to others. Despite scarcity and rationing, when least expected the country's leaders have announced they would share what little Cuba had with those suffering attack or devastated by some terrifying natural disaster somewhere in the world. Or send well-trained soldiers to fight on unfamiliar turf. Or set up efficient clinics where free assembly-line operations restore eyesight to tens of thousands of Brazilians, Venezuelans, Uruguayans, and others suffering from cataract blindness. Or send teachers to remote areas in countries where locals are hesitant to go. Or offer a free medical education to any black or Latino U.S. American youth wishing to avail herself or himself of the opportunity.[19]

Little Cuba has long been full of surprises. These range from its inordinate number per capita of truly great thinkers, public intellectuals, artists, scientists, and sports stars to innovative ideas aimed at reducing inequality and shaping a global future of social justice. In the face of Goliath-like assaults by a succession of U.S. administrations against its territory and well-being (actions ranging from the 1961 Bay of Pigs invasion to lesser incursions, crop and swine plagues, wielding innuendo and rumor to lure a well-educated population to emigrate, attempts on Fidel's life, and a steady barrage of subversive propaganda ploys),[20] the country has invariably met the challenge, rebounded, and emerged bruised but standing.

Although it has caused great hardship, Cuba has so far survived fifty-four years of the U.S. blockade. Astonishingly it also managed to survive the 1989–90 demise of the Soviet Union and socialist bloc upon which it had come to depend for so much of its foreign exchange. The sudden loss of more than a third of its investment and overseas trade partnerships and the vast reduction in oil and other prime necessities ushered in a number of years which the Cuban leadership euphemistically called El período especial en tiempo de paz (the Special Period in Peacetime). Everything was in short supply. People went hungry but tightened their belts, and some say the effects of that period linger. But the economic and social remedies put in place proved effective in guaranteeing survival, and the country came back from the brink.

Have the Revolution's stated aims too often been forced to adjust to survival strategies? Yes. Has internal error shared the blame with outside aggression? Undoubtedly. Is Cuba changing today, as a largely hegemonic global economy demands market adjustments? Of course. But counting the Cuban Revolution out or considering it or its influence defeated would be a mistake. Despite fifty-six years of constant struggle, the country can still point to near full employment and equal pay for equal work, a highly educated population, free and universal health care, and every citizen's access to culture and sports. Many in the United States, if they could shed their fabricated fear of terms such as *socialized medicine* and *one-party state*, would be happy to have the security such well-being provides.

4

THE ISLAND

Countries that are islands are worlds unto themselves, magical spaces that imbue their inhabitants with a complex sense of identity. Isolated? Contained? Relegated? Privileged? More than others, perhaps, those who live on such small strips of land order their lives in particularly dream-based ways.

The Czechoslovakian scientist E. Kollman wrote, "The machine and the living organism seem islands in an ocean of increasing entropy of all macroprocesses on those parts of the universe inhabitable by us, islands where entropy decreases because information is accumulated."[1] Could it be that island dwellers lose that collective sense of dreaminess as they accumulate the information that comes with increased connection to the outside world?

Geographically island landmasses are defined as too small to be called continents but of sufficient size and import to escape the lesser name of islet or key. Greenland is the world's largest island, at over 2.1 million square kilometers, while Australia is the smallest continent, at 7.6 million.

Perhaps geology decides a more significant difference than size. Continents sit on the continental lithosphere, which is linked to the tectonic plates that float high on Earth's mantle. Oceanic crust is also made up of tectonic plates but is denser than the lithosphere, so it floats lower on the mantle. Geologically speaking, islands are either extensions of the oceanic crust—volcanic protrusions—or a small part of one of the continents that has broken away from the mainland. Either way they exist on tenuous terrain, more readily subject to nature's whims than larger, more stable masses of land. This origin surely determines their psychological and emotional as well as physical impact.

And islands move. Metaphorically if not in a time easily measured by humans. They are not static but can float, stray, accommodate. They may rise from the ocean floor, the result of an undersea volcanic eruption. When sea levels swell, islands seem to sink—a movement, imperceptible as it may be in real time, of undeniable importance. Think about what happens when the earth beneath our feet shifts, even metaphorically.

Travel—how easy it is to get to an island—causes islands to move closer to other landmasses, even if that movement is practical rather than geographical. A poet's imagination can pluck an island from its natural habitat and place it anywhere. Before commercial flight—rather recent in our history—islands could be reached only by boat; then those that were larger and had the necessary harbors and port infrastructures, by ship; finally by plane. Depending on their distance from the continents, access might be routine, with frequent exchange, or impossible.

Thinking of Cuba naturally leads one to ponder its condition as an island and how that all-important circumstance provides clues to its environmental, mythical, imaginative, social, agricultural, industrial, cultural, psychological, political, and even temperamental development. The containment of land surrounded by sea, often experienced as isolation, has tremendous bearing on how the people who live on it relate to the rest of the world. Emilio Comas Paret expresses this best when he says that Cuban literature does not reflect an involvement with the ocean that surrounds the country on all sides and that this points up "an equally dramatic occurrence. In spite of being an island, Cuba has lived for centuries with its back to the sea. . . . It is a country where, even at mid-twentieth century, people almost never ate fresh fish and ninety-five percent of the population didn't know how to swim."[2]

Dictionaries define the word *island* as both a noun and a verb. As a noun it is "a contiguous area of land, smaller than a continent, totally surrounded by water"; secondarily and in a more general sense it is "an entity surrounded by other entities that are very different from itself." Use of the verb "to island" is rare; the synonym "to isolate" is more common. Psychologically and emotionally "a world unto itself" may be as meaningful a definition as any. It is one that defines island inhabitants, irrespective of latitude, culture, or political system.

We may think of islands such as England and Japan that are home to once imperial powers. Relatively small and surrounded by water, yes, but because of their colonialist or imperialist history and because they have exerted such military or economic control over others, possessing a world presence whose influence has far outweighed their territorial size. Both countries are known for their elaborate rituals, evidenced in regal ceremony and class rigidity. Britain's royal lineage and changing of the guard. Japan's tea ceremony, Kabuki theater, and the way its people bow reverently in almost every circumstance. Tradition is important, and it is almost always the tradition of the owner classes and cultures. Such tradition tends to engage the world's imagination. Perhaps these powerful island nations strive to make up for in pomp what they lack in physical grandeur, although both also traffic in a great deal of grandeur despite their small size. Both have had an important influence on much larger countries: England's on India and her other ex-colonies, for example, and Japan's role in World War II.

The island that is Cuba is very different from such countries. In fact when I began asking my Cuban friends to tell me what it means to them to live on an island, a couple responded in a jocular vein: "When you asked, all we could think of was what it might be like for an English or Japanese person, and decided it must be as natural as living on a continent!"[3]

We may think of island countries that lack such impact but which for other reasons—perhaps ecological, perhaps cultural—have earned international status. Because of the menace of climate change, nine island nations in the Pacific are currently threatened with extinction due to rapidly rising sea levels. These are the Cook Islands, the Federated States of Micronesia, Kiribati, the Marshall Islands, Nauru, Niue, Palau, Tonga, and Tuvalu. Would that by pronouncing their names we might be able to save them. With greater or smaller populations (some of these countries have only a few thousand inhabitants) they have lately raised their anguished voices in world forums or at international climate change conferences. And the impact of those voices has been another sort of naming. It has endowed them with a new global importance. People listen, moved and perhaps ashamed, although it seems unlikely that those who could make a difference will heed the dire warnings.

There are other prominent islands, each unique in size, biodiversity, and culture. Madagascar lies in the Indian Ocean just off the coast of southeast Africa. Its main landmass is the fourth largest of the world's islands. It split from the Indian peninsula some eighty-eight million years ago, allowing native plants and animals to evolve in relative isolation. Because of this it is a biodiversity hotspot; over 90 percent of its wildlife is found nowhere else on earth. Its exuberant rain forests, beaches, and reefs are home to thousands of species, and it alone possesses the ingratiating lemur.

Iceland, the world's eighteenth and Europe's second largest island (after Great Britain), also draws attention for its unusual physical attributes. Geographically it is part of the Mid-Atlantic Ridge, along which the oceanic crust is still spreading and forming new mass. Iceland was created by rifting and accretion due to volcanic activity along the ridge. Its coastline of dramatic fjords holds most of its human settlement as well as attracting many visitors.

Greenland is another immense and alluring island, the world's largest. Geographically close to the North American continent, for the past millennium it has politically and culturally associated itself with Europe, especially Norway and Denmark, the colonial powers that once ruled it. As recently as 2008 the country voted overwhelmingly for autonomy and the following year gained self-rule. Today Greenland, once covered in glaciers, is being dramatically affected by global warming: we are witnessing the glacial melt and resultant web of new rivers extending across its face. This signals what we can expect in other parts of the world. We should be paying attention.

Although less dramatically than the Pacific island nations, Cuba is also threatened by the planet's warming. Experts at the Cuban Oceanography Institute believe that the most serious repercussions will take the form of morphological changes to littoral areas and river basins. Erosion will be the main force pushing back the coastline, where nearly 245 settlements currently stand. Studies show that over the past three decades sea levels rose by an average of 2.9 millimeters each year. Agriculture will suffer, as nearly 15 percent of productive farmland is already facing the effects of increased water salinity. The greatest risk of coastal flooding is faced by south-lying areas of Havana and Pinar del Río provinces.[4] A sociologist friend tells me plans are already being made to move seventy-five coastal towns and communities inland.

The Cuban Environmental Agency estimates that climate change will have a multimillion-dollar impact on a society already suffering severe hardship from the worldwide recession compounded by the additional problems of underdevelopment, long-term pressure from the United States, and oil dependency on Venezuela, a country that has lately suffered its own economic implosion. Three hurricanes in 2008 cost ten billion dollars in losses, and the droughts of 2004 and 2005 set it back another million. Additionally more than 120 million dollars in annual health expenses have been needed to combat the impact of climate change on a series of the country's conditions.[5]

In Cuba all this means dealing with the economic repercussions of lost landmass and its effects on defense, food production, and hurricane relief, rather than the potential disappearance of the entire country. At least to this point in time the country's political and cultural histories have had greater impact than how it can expect to be affected by the erosion of its coast, although global warming will bring an increase in the severity of storms. As throughout the world, climate change means a host of complex and rapidly changing problems for the Caribbean country.

Island ecosystems are extraordinary. We see this most clearly today when looking at the Galápagos group, where each island enjoys a unique system of fauna and flora. These were the laboratory for Darwin's hypothesis about the origin of the species. Separated even among themselves by vast stretches of water, none but a few migratory birds managed to travel from one to another, and a few sea turtles swim the distance. Land mass and altitude also contributed to the Galápagos's developmental differences. Over centuries each of the islands nurtured its own vegetation, mammals, birds, reptiles, and amphibians. Ships arrived from around the world, introducing rats to the environment. The same type of cactus with low hanging pads on one island developed without these on another, where large land lizards strain to reach and eat them. I have seen those hungry lizards stand upright on their short but muscular hind legs as they consume the moisture-swollen sustenance. Conversely on the small island of Rapa Nui (Easter Island) social conditions led to the disappearance of almost every tree, determining a very different history and culture. But every island environment is unique, with its particular flora and fauna, storm patterns and biological microcosms, relationship to the surrounding sea and to other human populations.

Cuba, neither tiny nor large among islands, is situated in the Caribbean, only ninety miles from the Florida Keys. Although it possesses several mountain ranges, its most salient natural feature is its coastline of pristine beaches. Water is a constant. Coral reefs are home to diverse tropical fish and other sea life. Palm trees dominate the skyline. Sports fishing, snorkeling, and deep sea diving expeditions are among its pastimes and tourist attractions. But think of Comas Paret's observation that although Cuba has an island's ready access to creatures of the sea, the Revolution of 1959 inherited a population that didn't much care for eating fish. I can remember how the government surreptitiously added fishmeal to pasta in the 1970s in order to get its stubborn citizens to consume the valuable nutrients. Today people are more appreciative of the sea's bounty, and lobster is a prized dish in Cuban restaurants.

For centuries Cuba's proximity to the North American mainland deeply influenced it in terms of politics, trade, and culture. The island was home to U.S. crime syndicate figures such as Meyer Lansky, George Raft, and Santos Trafficante Jr., who established fiefdoms not subject to mainland tax codes and similar restrictive laws. U.S. businessmen and other weekend good-timers frequently flew down in private planes to enjoy an extravagant night of drinking, gambling, prostitution, and shows featuring women clad in feathers and fake fruit. Stereotypes such as Carmen Miranda and Our Man in Havana summed up Cuban culture for its neighbor to the north.

The Revolution of 1959 broke with those denigrating images and the reality behind them. Almost from one day to the next, U.S. crime syndication was out, reform in. High-class call girls fled with their mainland pimps, while the Revolution established a school where local prostitutes could acquire new skills leading to a choice of more dignified work. A night out at a lavish club, ironically still featuring women as sex symbols, would now be offered as a reward to the most productive Cuban workers. Unfortunately, with the recent revival of tourism as a source of much needed revenue, images of voluptuous bikini-clad mulata women have reappeared in advertising. The truth is, those images were never entirely eradicated.

From 1959 forward the Revolution's more socially conscious measures and what they stood for were less palatable to a succession of U.S. administrations. Still only ninety miles away, the island had become a "dangerous communist beachhead" in the discourse of its northern neighbor. Cuba lost its closest trade partner, and U.S. Americans suddenly had to travel south by way of Montreal or Prague. This "sugarcane wall" has stood for more than half a century. Yet baseball continues to be the national pastime in both countries, and jazz, blues, Afro-Cuban music, salsa, rap, and hip-hop have gone their separate but related ways. A cultural identification exists that political enmity has been unable to erase.

Another important element in Cuba's identity was the predominance of its forced African immigration during the years of the Middle Passage. The island was a temporary way station for slaves eventually sold to U.S. plantation owners and also a destination in its own right. Slave labor, fortitude, tribal belief systems, melancholy, dignity, resistance and resilience, and multiple cultures from several west African countries contributed to Cuba's nationhood. Its island identity also affected runaway slaves: in Cuba they had nowhere to go but into the mountains to live constantly threatened as maroons. In the United States slaves escaping the South had a well-organized underground railroad system that took them north and even across the

Canadian border, where a jurisdiction more favorable to their freedom existed.

The U.S. naval base at Guantánamo is like an island within an island, a point of contention within a larger political complexity. It is located on 120 square kilometers of land and water at Guantánamo Bay in the eastern part of the country. The United States originally leased this piece of Cuba in 1903 for $2,000 a year until 1934, and $4,085 a year from 1938 to the present, but since the 1959 Revolution Cubans have cashed only one rent check; they claim the occupation is illegal. The United States points to that single cashed check as its justification for staying.[6]

As outrageous as the colonialist land grab, or more so, is the fact that George W. Bush turned Guantánamo into an illegal detention camp, much like those operated by the Third Reich. Its existence and what is perpetrated there negate those basic rights embodied in the Magna Carta (1215), the Habeas Corpus Act (1679), the U.S. Constitution (1789), the Geneva Convention (1949), the Universal Declaration of Human Rights (1948), and the Convention against Torture (1987), among other hard-won agreements. Michael Ratner, a human rights lawyer who defended Guantánamo inmates ranging from Haitian refugees suffering from AIDS to an illegally imprisoned Australian and civilians picked up in Afghanistan who had nothing to do with fighting U.S. forces, wrote:

> Guantánamo has become a symbol of much that is wrong with our society. It is a complex of brutal prisons where hundreds of men and boys from all over the world, many of whom we believe are neither guilty of any crime nor pose any danger to the security of the United States, are being held by the U.S. government under incredibly inhuman conditions and incessant interrogation. They have not been charged with anything, they have no access to counsel or the courts, no right to a hearing of any kind, and no idea when, if ever, they will see an end to their plight.[7]

Before the Revolution several thousand Cubans had civilian jobs at Guantánamo. After the Revolution the base became a problem, with frequent epithets exchanged between each country's guards who faced off across a no-man's land. In 1991 a coup overthrew Haiti's first democratically elected president, Jean-Bertrand Aristide, triggering a flood of refugees fleeing that island. Within six months the United States had interned more than thirty thousand of those refugees suffering from HIV or AIDS in a camp at Guantánamo Bay Naval Station. The conditions were deplorable.[8] Over the years

Cubans who had been picked up by the U.S. Coast Guard trying to reach the United States also ended up at Guantánamo. The island within an island has seen tremendous human misery.

September 11, 2001, only ushered in a worse chapter at the prison camp. Soon afterward the United States began housing at Guantánamo Bay Detention Camp combatants who had been captured in Afghanistan, Iraq, and other countries during its unending war on terror. Many prisoners have been held for years without formal charges or trials. Cases of torture have been condemned internationally.

By then Cuba had prohibited new recruitment of its civilian citizens, and in 2006 only two elderly men, Luis Delarosa and Harry Henry, still crossed the base's North East Gate each day to work. They retired in 2012. Cuba has reiterated its right to its territory and demands that the base be returned. In 2009 President Obama signed an executive order directing the CIA to close what remained of all secret overseas prisons, including Guantánamo, within the year. In 2011, however, he issued another executive order, this one permitting ongoing indefinite detention of Guantánamo detainees. He has continued to move prisoners not considered dangerous off the island, but it is unlikely he will be able to close the prison camp before he leaves office. The island within an island seems to possess a half-life similar to that of radiation.

Even Puerto Rico, considered a sister nation by its inhabitants as well as by Cubans, exerts far less world influence than its sibling. This is because Cuba achieved independence, albeit a mediated one, in 1902, and definitive independence in 1959. Puerto Rico remains a U.S. territory, with all that means in terms of dependence, confused identity, and off-balance cultural syncretism. The two countries' flags are identical in design except for the placement of their colors: Cuba's displays a single white star on a red triangle with blue and white stripes, while Puerto Rico's white star rests on a blue triangle and its stripes are red and white.

The islands of the Caribbean used to be referred to as the West Indies. There are seven thousand of them, of which thirteen are now independent states. Haiti was the first Caribbean country to win its independence from Europe, in 1804, but it has yet to achieve liberation; a succession of dictators and one democracy that was too short-lived to bring real change have spawned ever-increasing poverty, violence, and despair. In recent years horrendous natural disasters have combined to keep the country bleeding. Its misery and oppression have made Haiti an object of world concern rather than influence. And Haiti presents a particularly interesting geopolitical picture because it is really only half an island. Joined by a common border, Haiti and the Dominican Republic are at opposite ends of the economic and racial spectrums. Both countries are poor, but the differences between them are dramatic. The Dominican Republic, wealthier and lighter skinned, fears and denigrates its poorer, darker neighbor. One can see this dichotomy even from a plane, looking down on lush fields on one side of the border and barren wasteland on the other. This sad history plays itself out today in immigration struggles: the Dominican Republic's government expels Haitians it is glad to use as cheap labor but refuses to support. (I have already mentioned early Haitian immigration to Cuba; in chapter 12 I argue that Cuban generosity has been particularly important in today's Haiti.)

A few other Caribbean islands have made their international mark: Jamaica and Trinidad-Tobago in the realm of music; Nassau, Bermuda, the Bahamas, and a few others as tourist destinations. Tiny Grenada (less than 350 square kilometers, with a population of 110,000) had its moment of glory from 1979 to 1983, when Maurice Bishop and his New Jewel Movement staged a coup and established a revolutionary state. Bishop wanted to move slowly toward socialism while continuing to encourage a mixed economy and developing the island for tourism. The experiment was short-lived. A hard-line faction led by Deputy Prime Minister Bernard Coard wanted to move faster and staged a countercoup. With the country under martial law, the United States was able to invade, destroying the revolution. Cuba had supported Grenada's short-lived exercise in freedom, and a number of Cuban internationalists working in the construction of an airport in the capital city of St. George died in the counterrevolutionary attack.

Perhaps beyond any of the aforementioned qualities or indicators, however, islands have a sort of magical aura that comes from their being enclosed within themselves. An island identity always affects import-export, and Cuba is no exception. Before the Revolution, Cuba got about a third of its imports from the United States.[9] In fact the United States traditionally tested products in Cuba; those that sold well there were exported to the rest of Latin America. The implementation of the U.S. blockade against Cuba, most damaging in its economic embargo, not only ended trade between the two countries; it also impeded trade between Cuba and most other nations of the region.[10] And the United States embarked on a policy of punishing countries that traded with Cuba by refusing their ships entrance to U.S. ports for six months following each such infringement.

Cuba's island condition is essential to its sense of self. Cubans experience who they have been, are, and may become very much as islanders: a people proud in their separateness and with a deep need to make themselves known beyond their sea-lapped coastline. A people both established and floating, rooted in place and in perpetual movement.

As I've said, poets are a nation's social conscience, and they also create and project its imaginary. So I have asked some of my Cuban poet and writer friends what inhabiting an island means to them and have received a range of responses.

Nancy Morejón responded to my request for her thoughts with the following:

> The word *island* is an entire experience that goes beyond any geographical category. Cuba is an Island, and so its natural neighborhood is made up of the Greater Antilles, and the Lesser as well. Cuba is part of that archipelago. From remote times, at the end of the fifteenth century, when a number of cultures from three continents (Europe, Asia, Africa) came together on this Island, we began to be called the Key to the Gulf. This Island, the largest of them all, experienced the passage of navigators, chroniclers, and conquerors. And this is why we've earned the right to such an integrated culture, one of archipellic implications, as the Martinique poet Edouard Glissant liked to say.[11]

Roberto Fernández Retamar pondered my question for a few weeks before answering with the following:

> Obviously, in my earlier years, I felt my condition of islander strongly. Proof of this is the fact that the last section of my second book, *Patrias*, written between the ages of nineteen and twenty-one, is called "Dulce y compacta tierra, Isla" [Sweet and Compact Land, Island]. Two romances in that section bear the same name. There are also three poems in the *décima* form called "Sobre la Isla, el sol" [Over the Island, the Sun], and another poem in which I wrote, "Te acercas a mí Isla, la copias y propagas" [You approach me Island, multiplying and extending yourself]. Curiously, I don't think I refer to my Island in any of my later verse. And yet my essay, "Caliban," which has been reproduced so often, is about an island. When I traveled outside the country I always missed the sun and sea, which undoubtedly has to do with being an islander. But after the victory of the Cuban Revolution, in 1959, I would learn to feel more like the resident of an archipelago, made up of the islands of the Caribbean.[12]

Mirta Yáñez wrote:

> The first thing that comes to my mind is what we learned from the moment we went to kindergarten: land completely surrounded by sea. The sea is important in my life. Although it may seem paradoxical, I feel claustrophobic when I'm not close to it. On the other hand, as I said in my novel, no one leaves an island simply by walking away. I feel like an islander in every way.[13]

Kelly Martínez, who left Cuba with her parents at the age of thirteen, also references the sea, but more dramatically:

> As a child I probably didn't think consciously that much about it, but I did have the sensation that it didn't matter how far you went or in what direction, you'd always come to the sea. And beyond the sea was the rest of the world. The sea was a barrier one had to cross. I was only thirteen when I left, but I had seen a great deal. To live on an island meant being separated from others, as if you were a rare and exotic creature. I also knew that the sea surrounding us was filled with dead bodies, with those who had tried to cross it on makeshift rafts. The Island was a dot suspended in nothingness.[14]

A thirteen-year-old who imagines the sea filled with dead bodies undoubtedly sees the world in a particular way. In Cuba's case the waves of illegal emigration have affected everyone—those who stayed as well as those who left. Some have family members or close friends who died attempting to get to the United States on flimsy or overburdened rafts. The horror stories are legion. Others who remained on the island and had relatives who made it safely to Florida spent years receiving snapshots of carefully staged refrigerators, their doors ajar and showing an exuberance of food. They heard stories of opulence that often had more to do with justifying departure than with the reality of life on the other side. Today, when travel assumes a more ordinary face, the stories are more credible. Still almost every Cuban family has a narrative of separation.

Alfredo Zaldívar responded to my question thus:

> Isolation? Perhaps. But that idea of water everywhere seems exaggerated to me (Virgil was excessive). I accept the circumstance, because water really does mark us. Water is endemic to an island. Loynaz said we are

"island creatures."[15] We are also defined by the risks we run having to fly or travel over water in order to reach solid land. That's why so many fish and so many birds. Although sometimes, in the case of this particular island I feel as if I am inside another island and sometimes on a great continent. It all has to do with mood and circumstance.[16]

Laura Ruíz Montes wrote:

Every coin has two faces, and what I like about living on an island is also what I don't like, as is so often the case. I like being surrounded by water, to walk along Matanzas's streets and look down toward the sea. When I've been traveling and approach home, I like suddenly catching sight of the bay. As the plane circles above my coastal city, I love seeing all the different shades of blue. I like Cuba's shores. I like to believe that salt air heals my wounds. I love that sensation of pure air and freedom that comes from so much ocean. I love going to the beach, swimming, submerging myself beneath the surface of the water. . . .

The other side of the coin is not being able to cross easily from one country to another. I find it oppressive that all exits and entrances are by air, that everything ends "there," at that edge. I find the idea of living on an island oppressive. It reduces everything to a smaller scale. It is asphyxiating to always see myself in a landscape that sometimes seems monotonous: green land, green sea. . . . But these dislikes have to do with something besides living on an island, and I'm aware of that. Maybe if I lived on an island where I could come and go as I pleased or was able, according to personal needs and possibilities, I would be telling a different story. It frightens me—with something like a childhood fear—to live on an island, as if it might sink one day. And it fascinates me—with an infantile delight—as if it were one of the most unachievable of the world's "torments."[17]

When I posed the question to Laidi Fernández de Juan, a doctor of internal medicine, short story writer, and internationalist who spent two years in the African Republic of Zambia, she responded with this:

A curious question. I don't believe one possesses a consciousness of being an islander until one has experienced another type of life, one with borders and neighbors on the other side of those borders. In general, I don't believe that living on a strip of land surrounded by sea entirely explains the contagious joy or sensuality attributed to us Cubans. Rather, those heightened sensory qualities—smelling, tasting and hearing the sea from the moment one opens one's eyes each morning—are as natural to me as the twenty times per minute I breathe or the eighty beats of my heart. Nothing soothes my spirit like contemplating ocean water. Havana is prodigious in this respect, which is why it would be impossible for me to live anywhere else. In Zambia, aside from missing my family and my sense of displacement far from home, I suffered the horror of a place without sea, an inland country. When I was able to visit a river for the first time, although it wasn't enough—almost an insult to my intense need for saltwater—I spent hours crying on its bank. I think that was the first time I assumed my condition of islander and recognized the curse of my need for the sea, something I don't imagine will ever leave me. Like the song, I can say: "El mar, espejo de mi corazón" [The sea, mirror of my heart].[18]

Like all to whom I asked how living on an island has shaped them, these writers speak of duality, grandeur and smallness, insignificance and uniqueness, a sense of containment and also of freedom. Perhaps the country's island identity endows Cubans with a perpetual sense of enigma, in and of itself a defining quality.

Milena Rodríguez Gutiérrez, a Cuban poet who lives in Spain, has a poem called "Innocence among the Waves" in which she speaks of islands as toys. Within the space of a few brief lines the reader falls into the sea and it becomes unclear who is the toy and who is playing with it:

Islands are children's toys,
balls someone tosses
upon the waves.
Sometimes, in the middle of the game,
the islands deflate
and you must blow, blow
until you fall into the water.
Then, who knows
if the island or you are the toy,
if we float exhausted
or it's the island that's bored
with the game of blowing,
with having to pump us up again.[19]

5

CUBAN SOLIDARITY
AFRICA

As individuals the leaders of Cuba's insurrection had previously joined other struggles, and it is now known that members of several liberation organizations were training on the island as early as a few months after victory. But the first time the new Cuban state came to the aid of another fighting for independence was in December 1961. The Revolution wasn't yet two years old. Algiers was locked in its ferocious war of liberation from France. Cuba sent a shipload of arms to the struggling African nation. That ship, the *Bahía de Nipe*, tied up at a dock in Casablanca and unloaded weaponry destined for the Front de Libération Nationale (National Liberation Front). The gift, a well-guarded secret, was not exempt from irony: the weapons had been manufactured in the United States.

The *Bahía de Nipe* returned to Cuba with seventy-six wounded Algerian fighters and twenty refugee children. Some of those children had been orphaned by the war; others had been scarred by the fighting or otherwise injured. Cuba took them all in. Most of these Algerians needed physical and emotional healing, and a number required prostheses. After recovering, most of the children remained in Cuba to study and some went on to complete their university education.[1] The episode set a standard for the human dimension of the involvement for which Cuba would eventually be known.

Two years later, in 1963, Algerian independence was still being threatened. This time Cuba came to its aid with 686 armed ground troops, accompanied by Cuban doctors.[2] This was the first occasion on which Cuban doctors went overseas to save lives. Today they work in more than seventy countries.

Portugal's 1974 Revolution of the Carnations had put an end to one of Europe's most ferocious dictatorships.[3] In turn it had allowed progressive forces in Portugal's African colonies to contemplate independence. The African countries under European rule had been divided according to the brutal whims of the colonialist mentality, rarely taking tribal territories, languages, and customs into account. In Angola the vision of independence might have died before it was born had President Agostinho Neto not asked for Cuba's help and had the small blockaded island thousands of kilometers away not responded as it did.

The African countries were rich in natural resources, exploited by huge transnational companies as well as by the powerful nations where those countries were headquartered. The European governments that had colonized Africa and were now losing those colonies had strong allies in apartheid South Africa and the United States. Cuba came to the aid of the African revolutionaries, and it wasn't the first time. In 1961 it had supported the Algerian rebels. In 1964–65 Che Guevara and some one hundred Afro-Cubans went to assist the Congo in its struggle to liberate itself from Portuguese rule; in the face of untenable conditions there the Cubans pulled out in less than a year. From 1966 to 1974 it made a decisive contribution to Guinea-Bissau's war of independence from Portugal. Thus began Cuba's tradition of fighting with and for others involved in national liberation—sometimes discreetly, sometimes openly—and attending to such internationalist endeavors in a socially responsible way: not staying on after their job was done, not sacking natural resources as the bounty of war, and always including health personnel or teachers along with military advisors and fighters.

In an effort to reclaim the specious accusation, I call this book *Exporting Revolution: Cuba's Global Solidarity.* Yet I do not mean to imply that Cuba fomented liberation movements; to be authentic these must originate in a nation's own history, culture, and particular repressive situation. Cuba could offer its aid only where such a homegrown movement existed and wanted its help.

The forebears of the Russian Revolution understood that they needed to expand the promise of socialism internationally, but that process became distorted. The Soviet Comintern adopted the practice of shaping other communist parties to its image, a policy with dire consequences.[4] More lucid minds better understood the complicated conflicts between capitalist and socialist hegemonies.

As children, Cuban internationalists had chanted "Serémos como el Che" (We will be like Che). Now they would go to Africa, as Che went to

Congo in 1965, and emulate the greatest of all internationalists as they generously gave themselves to several struggles for justice. Che's time in Congo ended badly, but most of the Cubans who accompanied him on that mission felt they were making an effort on behalf of a fraternal movement.

In April 1973 some two hundred Cuban military advisors went to the People's Democratic Republic of Yemen, then the Arab world's only Marxist state, where they trained local revolutionaries as well as those in the neighboring Dhofar region of feudal Oman. Until the massive 1975 intervention in Angola, more Cuban troops went to Syria than anywhere else. (This was not today's Syria, but that of Bashar al-Assad's father, Hafaz al-Assad.) Between November 1973 and May 1974 Cubans using Soviet tanks directly engaged Israeli forces in the Golan Heights. Cuba's humanitarian aid to China and Pakistan has involved extraordinary efforts. Revolutionary Cuba has had an intense internationalist involvement in Africa, Asia, and the Far and Middle East, arguably a much more positive one than the United States has had.[5]

The United States has always been ready to accuse the Cuban Revolution of exporting revolution, even as it has waged its imperialist wars with impunity. As a world power the United States assumes the right to engage in actions it criticizes (and punishes) when committed by others and to develop propaganda strategies (read: lies) to obscure its actions. Sometimes the cover-ups have been exposed years later, long after the damage was done and the statute of limitations ran out. Some cover-ups remain in place even today. As I hope I have made clear by now, Cuba's internationalist missions bear no relationship to these U.S. attacks and occupations.

Cuba aided revolutionary forces in a number of nations in Africa recently freed from European colonialism that were fighting to consolidate their freedom. Following official independence these nations were vulnerable to a mammoth effort by apartheid South Africa to step in where the European governments had lost control. South Africa was protecting apartheid rule throughout the southern part of the continent and had been waging a long war of economic destabilization against its neighbors Angola, Botswana, Lesotho, Malawi, Mozambique, Swaziland, Tanzania, Zambia, and Zimbabwe. South Africa supported a coup in Lesotho in 1986 and backed an unsuccessful mercenary intervention in the Seychelles in 1981. It was behind a coup attempt in Tanzania in 1983 and provided continuous military support for armed elements in Zimbabwe after that country's independence. South Africans carried out raids in Mozambique, Zimbabwe, and Botswana and attacked refugees in Swaziland.[6]

The United States, always denying its covert role, aided South Africa in each of these conflicts. As much of the rest of the world protested apartheid, the U.S. military effectively supported and empowered the apartheid regime. While the U.S. government accused Cuba of exporting revolution, it was secretly putting its own military advisors, advanced weaponry, and considerable financial power at the service of those intent on preserving their power and control. The CIA was behind the murder of the Democratic Republic of Congo's first prime minister, Patrice Lumumba, in 1961. There was grave concern for the losses African independence would mean for U.S. companies dealing in diamonds, copper, and iron, among other natural resources. But I believe that the greatest fear of the United States was geopolitical: losing influence with and control over Africa's more than fifty as yet nonaligned nations.

Years later, when the warring factions in Angola finally came to the negotiating table, Angola and Cuba sat on one side of that table and South Africa and the United States on the other. The Western media of the time portrayed the United States as a peacemaker at those meetings; the truth is, it had been a supporting and advisory force.[7]

When Cuban soldiers traveled to distant lands at the request of governments or movements that needed their expertise and support in battle, the force of arms may have been their decisive contribution, but it wasn't the only one. In Angola, for example, Cubans found backwardness, poverty, and desperation that shocked them. They held regular literacy classes for native soldiers, built schools, fashioned toys for children who had never before held a toy in their hands, and set up field clinics where they treated illnesses previously considered incurable due to lack of medical attention. There is even a story of the Cubans giving a name to a young boy who didn't possess even that elemental identity.

As with its early aid to Algeria, the Cuban Revolution quietly supported liberation struggles by bringing their members to train on the island. From Africa alone, fighters from Congo, Zaire, Tanzania, Sierra Leone, Equatorial Guinea, Cape Verde, and Guinea-Bissau trained in Cuba, and Cubans took part in some of those struggles as advisors as well as with troops on the ground.

Cuba's legendary aid to Angola's war of liberation probably had its antecedents in a meeting that took place between Che and Neto during Che's travels to Africa in 1964–65. That meeting would lead to Cuba's full-fledged involvement a decade later and to its soldiers remaining in that country for two decades more.[8] Whereas some of its other efforts were covert, Cuban participation in Angola was public and large scale. In November 1975, on the eve of Angola's independence from Portugal, apartheid South Africa, backed by the United States, threatened the new state before it had a chance to consolidate itself. Neto asked for help, and Cuba launched an important military intervention in support of the Movimento Popular de Libertação de Angola (People's Movement for the Liberation of Angola, MPLA), which was spread much too thin to defend its homeland from the aggressions being waged by South Africa and Zaire. The operation was named Carlota, in honor of the female slave who led an 1843 uprising at the Triunvirato sugar mill in the Cuban province of Matanzas. Carlota's rebellion had been short-lived. More than a century and a quarter later Cuba's expedition to Angola brought her name from obscurity and honored her attempt.

Cuba had a historic reason for its massive involvement in Angola: its recognition of the role played by African slaves in the foundation of its society. Going to fight in Africa was also part of a worldwide movement to achieve social justice. And there was a third reason. As already discussed, the very early 1970s were fraught with political and cultural struggles, and a repressive period in the arts had taken its toll. The Soviet Union was supporting Cuba economically to a considerable extent, and that aid had brought with it the threat of Stalinization. While maintaining genuine gratitude to the Soviets for their necessary aid, the Revolution needed to express discrepancies with the Soviet line, a certain independence. No one explains this better than Jorge Fornet in his brilliant book *El 71*, a blow-by-blow account of what went on during that complex year. Fornet extends his cultural analysis to Cuba's role in Angola:

Cuban intervention in Africa, beginning in the mid-1970s, was a way of actively participating in global politics and clearly delineating its geopolitical role. The Revolution also wanted to promote its line among the young African republics, since that wasn't possible in a Latin America submerged in its long night of dictatorships. It was also a way of establishing a line that differed from that of the Soviet Union. For Cuba, at least, the period of peaceful coexistence was over. The Revolution was determined to take up arms in support of the consolidation of African socialism. Naturally, because of shared interests, its public disagreement with the USSR had its limits. But the truth is, if you look at the headlines starting in 1976, the speeches of that era, the songs, testimonies, films and even anecdotes, and the discourse running through Cuban society, you can see the change the country's presence in Africa (mainly Angola) was provoking in the country.[9]

At first Cuba sent advisors to train MPLA's revolutionary soldiers. On December 2, 1975, in the area of Caporolo, a group of Cubans and their trainees found themselves in unexpected conflict with the enemy. This was only the beginning of what would be a protracted war of liberation, in which Cuba would contribute definitively to Angola's freedom, help bring about the liberation of Namibia, and join in dealing a death blow to South African apartheid.[10]

In the 1980s Cuban troops intervened in Angola once more, to help avert military disaster when the Soviet-led Forças Armadas Populares de Libertação de Angola (People's Armed Forces for the Liberation of Angola, FAPLA) launched an offensive against those still trying to maintain counterrevolutionary power on the continent. The battle at Cuito Cuanavale is considered the turning point in that war. In August 1987 the South African Defense Force (SADF) sent a heavy contingent of troops to aid the União Nacional para a Independência Total de Angola (National Union for the Total Independence of Angola, UNITA) in the south. Neto sent an urgent message to Fidel Castro, asking for help. Cuba complied and from November 1987 into February 1988 was decisive in routing South Africa from Angolan soil. The siege of Cuito Cuanavale ended after the SADF agreed to withdraw from Namibia. Cuba lost thirty-nine soldiers in the battle, FAPLA several thousand. Horace Campbell, a noted international peace and justice scholar, writes, "There was some dithering at the diplomatic level as the prime minister of South Africa tried to get Zaire to continue the war, the Americans tried through third parties to pressure Angola to form a government of national unity with UNITA, and the Western press tried to link the South African retreat to the withdrawal of the Cuban troops from Angola."[11]

According to sources on both sides, after Cuito Cuanavale Cuba could have marched into Namibia. It did not. The decisive battle not only defeated South Africa and its supporters in Angola; it paved the way for a political conclusion to the war and for Namibia's independence. At the peace talks Cuba and Angola asked that the United Nations verify Cuba's troop withdrawal, a request that demonstrated the seriousness with which Cuba concluded its military mission. Alicia Céspedes Carillo, whose presence throughout much of Cuba's campaign in Angola, along with exhaustive research, was the basis of her book *Angola: Tortuoso camino hacia la independencia* (Angola: Torturous Road to Independence), was the interpreter for Cuba's delegation at the negotiations. She writes about the reaction by South Africa and the United States to Cuba's demand that the UN verify its troop withdrawal,

"[The demand] took the United States by surprise. The South Africans looked interested, while those from the United States were taken off guard. They didn't expect that. The head of the mediating delegation, Under Secretary of State for Africa Chester Crocker, never really believed in Cuba's decision to retire its troops. To the last minute he thought it was a scheme on Cuba's part to cover who knows what unholy plan. Maybe that's why he fiddled with his earphones and asked, again and again, that Cuba repeat what we were saying. His preconceptions didn't allow for our position."[12] Peace talks finally led to the New York Accords, the agreement by which Cuban and South African forces left Angola, and South West Africa gained its independence.[13] The Cubans retained a lesser peacetime presence in Angola until 1992, when the civil war finally ended.

In 2005, celebrating the thirtieth anniversary of Cuba's heroic Angolan intervention, Fidel said, "For the first time, on a far-off bit of African soil, Cuban and Angolan blood flowed together to fertilize the freedom of that suffering land." Later in that same speech he added, "War is humanity's most terrible, heart-wrenching and difficult endeavor. Rarely has it been waged with such a high level of humanism and modesty on the part of the winners, despite the almost total lack of these virtues in the ranks of those who were defeated. A solidity of principles and purity of goals explain the absolute transparency of every action undertaken by our combatants and internationalists."[14]

Thirty thousand soldiers and almost fifty thousand civilian workers went to Angola in the first phase of Cuban involvement, many on more than one tour of duty.[15] At one point in the second phase fifty-five thousand Cuban soldiers were fighting there. During the lengthy deployment 2,070 Cubans died; Ethiopia claimed the lives of another 160, and 113 fell in other African wars. Cubans continued to go on military missions to Angola throughout the 1980s, and many noncombatants remain there today. The anticolonialist leader Amílcar Cabral said of the Cubans who fought in Africa, "We also want to lay special emphasis on the untiring efforts—sacrifices that we deeply appreciate—that the people of Cuba . . . are making to give effective aid to our struggle. For us, this is a constant source of encouragement, and it also contributes to cementing more and more the solidarity between . . . our people and the Cuban people, a people that we consider African."[16]

Nelson Mandela, the great South African leader who spent twenty-seven years in apartheid prisons, was finally released on February 11, 1990. In July of the following year he traveled to Cuba to personally thank the people and their leaders for their decisive aid in freeing his homeland. Among the many moving things he said in his speech was the following:

I was still in prison when I first heard of the massive help the Cuban international forces were giving to the people of Angola. The help was of such a scale that it was difficult for us to believe. . . . In Africa we are used to being victims of countries that want to take from us our territory or overthrow our sovereignty. In African history there is not another instance where another people has stood up for one of ours. . . . I should mention that when we wanted to take up arms, we approached numerous Western governments in search of help and we could only talk with the lowest level officials. When we visited Cuba we were received by the highest authorities who immediately offered anything we wanted and needed. That was our first experience with Cuban internationalism.[17]

The foregoing is all from speeches, news reports, and history books: the facts, dates, and numbers regarding Cuba's military involvement in Africa, and statements by the political leaders involved. Moving as they are, however, they do not touch on the more profound aspects of the reason for Cuba's internationalism, or the more intimate sentiments of those who served. Cuba responded to Neto's plea for military aid because the country had a fraternal relationship with the African nation and Cuba's leadership accepted the fight against apartheid as a matter of principle. These would have been reasons enough, putting its participation on a par with the efforts of those who took up arms to defend the Spanish Republic or the antifascist resistance during World War II, both worthy endeavors in necessary struggles by standards freedom-loving peoples continue to revere. But Cuba's relationship to black Africa had an additional component.

In 1974, when Fidel explained the decision to send Cuban troops to Angola the following year, he spoke to more than a million people gathered at the Plaza of the Revolution. I was one of them. It was a typically sweltering summer day, and we stood close together beneath the Caribbean sun. Hour followed hour, yet no one moved or spoke. I remember an impressive silence as Fidel explained that Cuba had been populated by Africans, brought over as slaves. African blood runs in our veins, he memorably said, and we have an obligation to help Africa emerge from colonialism. Those of us hearing his words felt them in every fiber of our being. This represented a unique decision in the annals of modern military history, a profound solidarity with those whose ancestors had been kidnapped and harnessed into slave labor to help build the country those listening had inherited.

This sentiment was experienced deeply by many of the Cubans who volunteered to fight in Angola. Pedro Núñez Mosquera took part in the first phase of the war. The following anecdote expresses southern African reality at the time and Núñez Mosquera's visceral reaction to it:

> Mine was a modest contribution to our people's effort during the actions that eventually guaranteed Angola's freedom, the independence of Namibia, and the eradication of apartheid in South Africa. I arrived in 1975 aboard the SS *Vietnam Heróico*, to command one of the antiaircraft artillery guns. We landed in Luanda and immediately began our offensive to the south. . . . Our main mission was that of contributing to expelling South African troops from Angola. . . . We left Angola in June, 1976, also by ship. But we were different then. We had been through an unfamiliar experience, one that heightened our ability to feel and to love. Our time in Angola increased our sensibility enormously. We also left with the sense that we'd paid a debt we had with a fundamental part of our roots, the part that had been most exploited, had suffered most.
>
> So you can better understand what I'm talking about, I'll tell you about something that happened in Calueque, a spot on the southern border of Angola with what was called South West Africa back then. This was territory occupied by South Africa that is now the Republic of Namibia. Since I knew some English, I was ordered to be part of the group of comrades leading our advance on the heels of South Africa's retreat. We got to the border, began organizing the first posts and—young guys after all—started socializing with the South African soldiers who were also young. We took pictures of ourselves with their FALs and they took some with our AKMs.
>
> In one of our conversations, a young South African soldier asked me when we Cubans would be leaving Angola. I told him we'd be leaving as soon as the Angolan people were able to defend the independence and sovereignty to which they had a right. And I asked if he didn't agree that they had a right to that. Totally convinced, he said: *No, because they're blacks* [in English in the original]. . . . I knew about apartheid . . . but this incident helped me understand that apartheid was a perverse ideology, and very deeply engrained in South Africa's white population. Maybe this is why President Mandela's presidency gave me such joy.[18]

Although official statistics put Cuba's black population at around 12 percent, roughly the same as that in the United States, which has been calculated at 12.5 percent, this figure has always seemed low to me. Many Cubans speak of themselves as being part of a black nation and so many are of mixed origins that I think a true percentage has been difficult to assess. Almost everyone possesses some quota of African blood.[19] At the time Cubans understood that by fighting apartheid in Africa they were paying an old debt, which no doubt accounts for the fact that so many volunteered and why those not accepted were upset, even resentful at not being allowed to enlist.

In Angola and in other African countries Cuba went to war fully conscious of the fact that great numbers of Africans had been kidnapped and brought to the island as slaves, that their country had been built upon that tragedy. Darker- and lighter-skinned Cubans fought harmoniously beside their black African counterparts. An emotional as well as political rightness accompanied the gesture. Fornet notes that Cuba's participation in Angola "included the vindication, in political discourse, of a genealogy that was now *latino-africano*, and that could be traced to slave ships having come to the Island."[20]

In light of this it is interesting—complex but disappointing—that in more than half a century the Cuban Revolution has not been able to go further in dealing with racial prejudice. It put antiracist laws in place, and periodic efforts at reeducation have been made. Still, just as with gender equality, many Cubans are troubled by a certain stagnation in both areas. Traditional values and attitudes have proven resistant to change. Zuleica Romay has an interesting analysis:

> Racial prejudice and discrimination in Cuba are reinforced today . . . by the classism that is beginning to reemerge, along with cultural practices that would seem to recycle the behaviors of our republican bourgeoisie. . . . Such tendencies come up against the unprejudiced attitudes of a sector of mature adults who have been educated in twentieth-century socialist experiences. . . . What this means is that Cuban racism functions like a complex system of forces in equilibrium, the dynamics of which, influenced as they are by economic and cultural but also social and political factors, aren't easy to analyze and also are not predictable in the medium term.[21]

There is another very serious issue I feel obliged to mention with regard to Cuba's participation in Angola. It doesn't detract from the great sacrifices so many Cubans made to help free the African country, but the meaning of freedom would not be served by remaining silent about it. Commonly referred to as the Ochoa affair, it involved the 1989 arrest, conviction, and execution of General Arnaldo Ochoa, head of Cuba's troops in Angola; Colonel Tony de la Guardia, an official of the Ministry of the Interior charged with breaking through the U.S. economic blockade; and their aides, Captain Jorge Martínez Valdés and Major Amado Padrón Trujillo. A number of others were also arrested and tried but received less drastic sentences. The accused had been advised not to hire lawyers and at the last minute were assigned public defenders who expressed distaste for the jobs they had been given. What I can only describe as a show trial was followed in detail in the country's press, and people were still in shock when it ended.

These men, all of whom had accrued decades of brilliant service to the Cuban Revolution, most of whom had also done important tours of duty in other countries and were beloved comrades up to and beyond the moment of their arrest, were convicted of illegal drug trafficking, the sale of black market ivory, and keeping relatively small amounts of dollars in offshore accounts. The last charge was preposterous when one considers that their revolutionary tasks called for acquiring international currency.

By the late 1980s the Angolan war had become complicated and, due to the breakdown of the Soviet Union, Cuba's economic situation had as well. Books have been written about the Ochoa affair, and I am not going to go into a lot of detail here, among other reasons because I do not believe we yet know the truth about this sad chapter in Cuban history. What I will say is that I think there is more to the story than what is publicly known. Perhaps serious ideological differences among the Revolution's upper echelons, for the accused spoke approvingly about Gorbachev's perestroika. Perhaps suspicion of an attempt to grab power. Perhaps one or more of the charges were true, in which case I cannot imagine that the highest ranks of revolutionary leadership were not aware of and had not tacitly agreed to what the accused had been doing. The drug trafficking charges seem to have some truth to them; the United States apparently got wind of that activity and finally had something it could pin on the Cuban Revolution, and the Cubans may have felt they had to make scapegoats of some high officials in order to save face. If so they could have done so without taking the lives of men who had only been trying to do what they believed was expected.

Ochoa maintained to the end that his involvement in illicit activities, although wrong, was in order to feed and pay his troops. There was never any evidence of personal greed. He did not live luxuriously; on the contrary, his lifestyle was far simpler than that of most Cuban leaders. No matter which charges were true and which false, I believe the trial was a sham and the executions a horrendous miscarriage of justice. Perhaps one day we will know the truth.

Particularly moving to me is the book *El furor y el delirio* by Jorge Masetti, a longtime colleague of Tony de la Guardia and his daughter Ileana's husband. Masetti writes, "The dynamics of the Angola expedition were clear. Cuba launched [the last phase of] that war during the Brezhnev era. In the division of labor, Cuba provided the troops and the Soviets the logistics. Later Andropov came on the scene, and the 50,000 Cuban soldiers remaining in Angola found themselves in extremely precarious conditions. A general such as Ochoa had to feed his troops and resolve infrastructural problems, knowing full well that he could not count on funding from any quarter."[22]

As I say, the Ochoa affair is a black mark on the Cuban Revolution. Every country, sadly including those we may admire most, has such horrendous moments in their history. In my mind this one, grievous as it was, does not detract from the extraordinary generosity of Cuba's internationalism nor from the heroism of the hundreds of thousands of Cuban men and women who fought and the more than two thousand who died for Angola's freedom. Neither, however, should it be erased from history.

Moving as speeches and news reports are, they cannot fully capture the experience for those who survived an internationalist mission. Ventura Carballido Pupo, who fought in Angola, remembers what it was like. The following are excerpts from an interview conducted in 2015:

On the flight home from Luanda . . . I meditated on the ethical issues that may be unfamiliar to those who do not think as we do, . . . those who don't understand how we were educated or what we did, who don't understand the grandeur of what we fought for when we risked our lives without any promise of material reward. In the belly of that plane we had no suitcases filled with souvenirs we were bringing back to family and friends. As hand luggage I had only the small bag provided by the Angolan airline. Its most valuable contents included two women's handkerchiefs that a member of Angola's Civil Defense in Cabinda had given to me, a pack of Cuban export cigarettes my anguished father sent on one of the cargo ships traveling to the Congo, underclothes and the clean shirt I would change into once I got to Havana, documents that reflected the stimulus given out by the political section of one of the units in which I had been deployed, and my tag number 54295, that I still have and cherish. I had no money in my pockets, because we weren't mercenaries who had gone to war to risk our lives for riches. We descended from that huge

Il 62-M Soviet airliner carrying nothing material. We didn't have any luggage to pick up. Our greatest reward was moral.[23]

This is but one of hundreds of such testimonies.

Many of Cuba's fighting contingents have been accompanied by specialists in a variety of fields, whose generosity wasn't felt on the front lines but was equally valuable to the country struggling to emerge from colonialism. A dear Cuban friend who is a sociologist served two tours of duty in Angola, neither as a soldier. On the first he was an advisor to that country's secretary of state for social affairs. On the second he headed a Cuban-Angolan research team that studied the many ethnicities in the People's Republic of Angola, with an eye to helping it develop a viable policy of nationalities. When I asked if that policy had been implemented, he said it was, and added (after some prodding) that President José Eduardo Dos Santos of Angola had referred to the investigation and to the importance of its findings in his speech at the opening of the MPLA's first congress.

Since Cuba's military aid to Angola it has continued to help the country in a variety of ways. In 2015, on the fortieth anniversary of the joint fighting venture, Angola's minister of national defense, Cándido Pereira Dos Santos Van Dumen, reminisced about the war and spoke about Cuba's collaboration:

> Without Cuban military aid, and considering the state Angola was in at the time, the recently constituted government would not have been able to withstand foreign invasion. . . . As those Cubans and Angolans who participated directly have reflected, we understand how dynamic the political and social processes have been. . . . Beginning in the 1970s, Cuba has played an important role in our health care, education and civil construction. . . . At the moment more than 3,000 Cubans lend their services in those areas as well as in agriculture. And in Cuba more than 1,000 young Angolans are studying a range of specialties, that will also help our country to develop and move forward.
>
> Angola's economy is going through a very energetic moment. In the past thirteen years, with a gross national product of $131 billion, and according to International Monetary Fund statistics, we can expect three and a half percent growth in 2015–2016. This makes ours one of the most prosperous countries on the African continent. In sub-Saharan Africa, it is one of the countries that has had the highest increase in its gross

national product. . . . From having a single university in 1974, we now have fourteen university cities. We have been able to construct more than 5,000 new homes, and are projecting seventy to eighty percent growth in this construction by 2025. Today, although we have many challenges ahead, we are a positive example for the region.[24]

6

CUBAN SOLIDARITY
LATIN AMERICA

Latin America is twenty-one mestizo nations, several of them with official languages other than Spanish, five territories whose inhabitants possess a strong sense of nationhood, and hundreds of (recognized and unrecognized) indigenous nations with their own cultures and languages. It is a landmass that once included an important part of the southwestern United States. The Caribbean is home to twenty-eight island nations, fourteen of which are still ruled by foreign capitals, including the Netherlands, France, the United Kingdom, and the United States. A Caribbean character has increasingly emerged as separate from Latin America, although on the islands where Spanish is spoken there is also a sense of identification with mainland identity.

It doesn't help the image of relations with Latin America that the United States appropriated almost half of Mexico in the 1846–47 Mexican-American War, continues to claim Puerto Rico as an unincorporated territory whose citizens pay taxes but are not protected by the U.S. Constitution and do not have full congressional representation, or that over the past half century a succession of U.S. governments has destabilized or destroyed democratically elected governments in Guatemala, the Dominican Republic, Chile, Nicaragua, Honduras, and Venezuela, among others. Its record of assaults against the Cuban Revolution has been particularly tenacious and brutal.

Despite their discrete nationalities, Latin Americans also think of themselves as a single entity: residents of the continent Simón Bolívar and José San Martín hoped to liberate from European colonialism, the land José Martí knew would have to make a collective stand against U.S. domination. Which is to say, there is a strong Latin American identity, born long before northern designs on the region. Latin Americanists still argue about whether the continent is one or many, but even as they recognize and pride themselves on national differences, in important ways Latin Americans identify as a unified bloc.[1]

The story of Latin America's liberation contains many pages, recording devious as well as brilliant actions, going back to the fierce regional battles waged by a number of highly advanced indigenous peoples. In what today is Mexico, Moctezuma II (ca. 1466–1520) ruled the Aztec kingdom of Tenochtitlan from 1502 to 1520. The first European contact with the indigenous civilizations of Mesoamerica took place during his reign. He welcomed but soon was forced to defend his kingdom against Hernán Cortés and his troops, who finally betrayed and murdered him and tens of thousands of his people.

In what we now call Peru, José Gabriel Túpac Amaru (1738–81), known as Túpac Amaru II, was a model of indigenous resistance. He was actually a mestizo who received a Jesuit education but claimed to be a direct descendant of the last Inca emperor, Túpac Amaru I. For organizing and leading a campaign against Spanish rule in the area of his hometown, Cuzco, Túpac II was quartered and beheaded by the colonial authorities in 1781. His wife and most valued military strategist, Micaela Bastidas (1744–81), also fell to the wrath of the Spaniards.

The Mapuche people have a long history of resisting domination. Between 1861 and 1883 the Republic of Chile conducted a series of campaigns that ended Mapuche independence, causing the death of thousands through combat, pillage, starvation, and the introduction of smallpox. Argentina conducted similar raids on the eastern side of the Andes in the 1870s.

These are but three examples, among hundreds, of indigenous uprisings throughout the Americas. Some lasted decades, but superior weaponry eventually won out. It would take a more even playing field—both sides in possession of the same type of arms—for Latin America to defeat European colonialism.

Creole liberators had even broader visions. In the eighteenth century Simón Bolívar (1783–1830) freed a vast region of the northern part of Latin America, encompassing what is today Venezuela, Colombia, Bolivia, Ecuador, Panama, and Peru. José de San Martín (1778–1850) routed the Spaniards from Latin America's southern cone: Argentina, Chile, and Peru, where he eventually met up with Bolívar. These two men are the most prominent among those responsible for Latin America's freedom from European domination, although others, such as José Artígas (1764–1850), freed Uruguay and adjoining territories (*las tierras orientales*). I won't dwell on this early history except to say that the stories of liberation of the nations of Latin America—from the earliest indigenous uprisings to the creole wars against European powers and those later waged against the United States—are intertwined and in important ways a single story.

The legacy of struggle, only touched on here, continues to fan the flames of hope for peoples throughout the continent, who long to live on their country's natural riches without becoming indebted to neoliberal demands, enslaved to impossible debt, or exploited by local oligarchies. When Cuba made its successful revolution in 1959, it gave Latin America's peasants, working people, students, and intellectuals a powerful jolt. They saw a vision of change. The rebels of the Sierra Maestra quickly became a symbol, a force to be revered, emulated, and supported, a modern-day reference for people throughout the region.

There is continuity on both sides of this history. Every U.S. administration in recent memory has supported repressive regimes throughout Latin America and the Caribbean, providing economic support and military aid and training to keep them in power. There is ample propaganda for the American Way of Life, dazzling everyone who has access to the media, Hollywood films, or even imported comic books in which the U.S. is idealized. Among working people in the countryside and cities, however, there is frustration and collective resentment as deep as cellular memory. The love-hate relationship many in Latin America feel for the United States is deceptive and complex.

Throughout the twentieth century, across the mainland and islands of the Caribbean, rebellion grew against the voracious North. And U.S. administrations have treated the Latin America and Caribbean peoples as ignorant underlings, incapable of shaping their own destiny, basically theirs to control and plunder. Domination, greed, and corruption produced dictators as cruel as any in history: the Dominican Republic's Leoncio Trujillo, Cuba's Fulgencio Batista, Nicaragua's Anastasio Somoza, Paraguay's Alfredo Stroessner, Argentina's Jorge Rafael Videla, Uruguay's Juan María Bordaberry, and Chile's Augusto Pinochet. Several of these strongmen represented dynasties of horror. They and their cronies were responsible for torturing, murdering, and disappearing whole generations.[2]

The Mexican Revolution preceded Russia's by almost a decade. Mexico's Lázaro Cárdenas (1895–1970), president from 1934 to 1940, was a communist who tried to give continuity to the social and economic aims of the 1910 Revolution, protecting workers' rights, distributing land, and nationalizing the country's oil reserves. After leaving office he continued to support progressive causes, including Castro's July 26 Movement; when the Cuban rebels regrouped in Mexico he gave them valuable aid.

More recent struggles grew out of and reflect those that took place centuries earlier and influenced those to come. In 1954, before he joined up with Fidel and his men in Mexico, Che traveled through Guatemala in the immediate aftermath of the CIA's ouster of Jacobo Arbenz. There he met Hilda Gadea, the Peruvian revolutionary who would be his first wife and would introduce him to the Cubans.

Cuba's victory against Batista in 1959, Chile's three years of socialist government (1970–73), the ten years of Sandinista rule in Nicaragua (1979–90), and several less successful liberation struggles are all part of this tradition. Near the end of the century Hugo Chávez in Venezuela would call his revolution Bolivarian, claiming Bolívar as his forebear. The Frente Amplio (Broad Front) would take electoral power in Uruguay, and Evo Morales, Latin America's first indigenous president, would install a socialist government in Bolivia.

The stance of the United States—every administration from Monroe to the present—toward the countries of Latin America has historically been one of superiority, paternalism, and condescension. Even today ignorance and provincialism keep many U.S. theorists from understanding the profound cultures and vast erudition of those "other Americas." Endemic racism also plays its part, in that such biased analysts see all darker people as primitive.

The declassified CIA and FBI reports on the Latin American liberation struggles of the 1960s to the 1980s and commentary on the ideological development of the Cuban Revolution itself contain erroneous analyses in stunningly bigoted terms. For example, in 1958 a CIA document described Che as "fairly intellectual for a 'Latino,'" and as late as 1964 an agency informant rendered the opinion that Cuba would not end up communist because Cubans are "a mercurial people, capable of sudden, swift bursts of emotional enthusiasm, but without the staying power which the creation of a communist state demands."[3]

The United States claims its neoliberal recipe offers democracy to the countries in its sphere of influence. In reality this recipe has only increased dependency, deepened poverty, and provoked years of suffering—at its most extreme during the years of the dirty wars waged by dictatorships on the continent's southern cone. In concert with local oligarchies a succession of U.S. administrations has exploited and oppressed the peoples of these countries, pushing them to rebellion. I agree with John Beverley's assessment: "There can be no question that the main enemy of democracy in Latin America has been U.S. hegemony over the region—time and again democratically elected regimes have been overthrown with U.S. support or connivance . . . but the obstacles to democracy and social equality are also *internal* to Latin American nation states; indeed . . . it is often those internal barriers— invariably tied to forms of racial and class privilege—that U.S. policy has used historically to destabilize the Left and democratic regimes."[4] This situation has begged redress throughout the region.

Just as the Cuban rebels of the 1950s looked to previous revolutions, it was logical that after 1959 groups of mostly young people all over the continent looked to Cuba for a model of struggle they might fashion to their desperate needs. On the small Caribbean island they found a solid welcome and unwavering solidarity. Many of these young people traveled to Cuba in search of advice and training. Fidel, and especially Che, had dreams of broader liberation. The former's job was to build the socialist society he had envisioned long before the 1953 defense speech that described the July 26 Movement's program for change. After a number of years in which he too worked hard to shape Cuba's future, Che declared, "I return to the trail with my shield on my arm."[5]

"To create two, three, many Vietnams" was the rallying cry of 1960s revolutionaries, implying that if people throughout the developing world could organize and resist as the Vietnamese patriots were doing, imperialist forces would be spread thin and it would be impossible for them to defeat every such aspiration.

From the 1960s to the 1980s uprisings were happening across the Third World, and liberation movements were active throughout Africa, Asia, and Latin America. Barely two years after the Cuban victory, on February 4, 1962, the Second Declaration of Havana was issued. More than a million Cubans subscribed to the manifesto, which proclaimed support for the liberation of the Americas, declaring simply that "the duty of a revolutionary is to make the revolution." In 1966 OSPAAAL was established to coordinate support for these efforts.[6] In the Cuban Revolution's first decade a special government agency was set up to organize the training and often also the logistical support for dozens of movements intent upon liberating their countries. Manuel Piñeiro, called Barba Roja (Red Beard) because of the color of his hair, became its general coordinator.[7]

And it wasn't only the fighters themselves but also their offspring who received Cuban help. Over the past half century Cuba has taken in tens of thousands of children who had no other place to go. Until recently the Isle of Youth was the site of dozens of schools for children from Nicaragua, Chile, Uruguay, Namibia, Angola, Ethiopia, and other nations where the turmoil of war had eradicated the possibility of a decent education. These were not attempts to colonize those young people; the schools employed teachers from their countries of origin who taught classes in their native languages, served food familiar to them, and maintained cultural traditions aimed at preserving their national identity. Every student received a free education, and attention to physical and mental health was part of the package. Cuba provided the welcome, the warmth, and the opportunity to learn a discipline that would be helpful to the healthy development of the students' country when they returned home.

My own family was a recipient of Cuba's generosity in this respect. After the defeat of Mexico's 1968 student rebellion I suffered a crippling repression, was forced into hiding, and sent my four small children to the island. Too many sons and daughters of those involved in our decimated movement were being discovered dead on the volcanic fields (known as the *pedregal*) outside Mexico City. I wanted to keep my children safe until I could find a way to join them. It was wrenching to have to send off my eight-, five-, and four-year-old and three-month-old. Elsewhere I have written about having to wean my baby in one day. But I had confidence in Cuba's sensibility and ability to care for my son and daughters, and that confidence was more than justified. It was July when they boarded a plane in the Mexican capital. In Havana, after thorough physical and psychological checkups, the three oldest were taken to a summer camp at Santa María Beach; there they adapted to the sudden upheaval in their lives in the company of children from a number of African and Latin American countries then at war. My son later told me about a new friend who had lost a leg to a land mine, and another whose body bore the terrible scars of napalm.

My three-month-old stayed in Havana, at a clinic for well children that had previously been home to the Bacardi rum family. On weekends a government official would bring the older kids into the city to spend time with their baby sister; it was a way of helping them preserve a sense of togetherness. When my partner and I arrived in October, we were all reunited. The children's trauma had been minimized as much as possible. Thus began my eleven years in Cuba.

It is worth mentioning that the Cuban Revolution has been generous to architects of and refugees from other social experiments, whether or not they followed Cuba's prescription for change. During my years on the island I knew Brazilians, Bolivians, Nicaraguans, Guatemalans, Mexicans, Colombians, Venezuelans, Haitians, Argentineans, Uruguayans, and revolutionaries from El Salvador and the Dominican Republic. Some were from parties that had adopted the Cuban model; some favored other lines. These men and women had come for training, a safe place to meet with members of their own or fraternal organizations, medical aid, or rest and renewal. We knew they would eventually make their way back to their respective battlefields. When they disappeared no one was surprised. We silently wished them well.

In 1970 Chile's Salvador Allende and his Unidad Popular demonstrated that socialism could also be brought about through democratic means. The Cuban Revolution fully supported the Chilean experiment by sending material aid, knowhow, and advisors and specialists in diverse fields. And when a CIA-backed coup put an end to Chile's democratically elected government, Cuba offered refuge to tens of thousands who survived that terrible defeat. The Chileans flooded Havana beginning in the last months of 1973, scarred by their burden of loss but trying to figure out how to adapt to the brutal takeover and continue their struggle. In a country suffering from its own scarcities and privations, housing and jobs were made available. The support that had been so evident during the three years of Chile's socialist government was transformed into a new type of solidarity, one the survivors needed in order to move ahead. It was hoped that freedom without bloodshed would succeed in Chile, but it lasted only three brief years, and the U.S.-backed coup that ushered in seventeen years of dictatorship was born in a bloodbath of disappearance, torture, imprisonment, and exile. Those who rail against the violence implicit in armed struggle rarely speak of the routine horror of state violence, in which human degradation is honed to a science, systematic, widespread, and protected by bourgeois money and manipulation. Poverty, hunger, illness, and hopelessness kill as surely as weapons. They just take longer.

Elsewhere in Latin America rebel groups chose to follow the Cuban example more closely; they believed that nothing short of armed struggle would make it possible for them to throw off foreign and oligarchic control. In retrospect it is clear that this recipe, although necessary in many cases, was applied too uniformly. In the Dominican Republic, Colombia, Bolivia, Peru, Venezuela long before Chávez, Uruguay, Argentina, southern Mexico before the Zapatistas, Guatemala, El Salvador, and Nicaragua, guerrilla movements trained and partially funded by Cuba attempted to rout dictatorial regimes. They adopted Che's *foco* (small group) theory, the idea that a small group of armed guerrillas could take an area, set up a base of operations, and gradually recruit workers and farmers to their cause.[8] Most failed miserably, but all planted seeds and contributed to an ongoing history of resistance.

Nicaragua's Sandinistas took power in 1979 with a great deal of help from Cuba. Their experiment lasted ten years, until it too was ravaged by U.S. machinations and its own internal problems. Nicaragua's current president is a Sandinista in name only; his policies belie everything the Sandinistas of the 1960s and 1970s fought and died for. Sadly we learned that revolutionaries can become power-hungry and corrupt, just as bourgeois political figures can.

For years the U.S. government and corporate press accused Cuba of fomenting revolution throughout the continent. This accusation was meant to justify U.S. Cuba policy and every covert and overt act of aggression against the smaller nation. All the while the United States was supporting dictatorial governments favorable to its interests and was behind every attempt to effect a change that might strengthen its control. As mentioned before, the School of the Americas at Fort Benning, Georgia, trained generations of Latin Americans in counterinsurgency, destabilization, and torture. U.S. administrations, in coordination with the CIA, have been behind numerous military coups, many of them against democratically elected governments. U.S. accusations that Cuba exported revolution while engaging in its own continuous attempts at regime change have been disingenuous to say the least. It is time we recognize Cuba's aid to other revolutionary efforts as a proud page in Latin American history.

Over more than half a century the United States has invested billions in its attempts to defeat the Cuban Revolution. The 1961 Bay of Pigs invasion and subsequent coastal incursions, Radio and Television Martí, a series of animal and crop plagues, and attempts on Fidel's life are just a few documented examples. Another is the Travelers Project. According to USAID documents, a program calling itself by that name was presented as a program for HIV/AIDS outreach. It was described as the perfect vehicle to recruit political activists from Peru, Venezuela, and Costa Rica from 2009 through 2012 to run and participate in civic programs in Cuba while secretly stirring up antigovernment activism. Behind this façade USAID directed agents to act as tourists, socialize on college campuses, and hold gatherings that allowed them to profile and organize potential dissident youth leaders. Such subversion has been denounced by, among others, U.S. democratic Senator Patrick Leahy.[9]

From the end of the nineteenth into the early twentieth century the United States, through its control of institutions such as the International Monetary Fund and World Bank, has imposed neoliberal economic policies on all the developing nations. This imposition, in Latin America as elsewhere, has devastated local strategies and initiatives that might have put national economies on a sounder footing. Under the guise of aid the United States has kept much of Latin America subservient to its own interests. Only those countries that have managed to escape this domination through revolution or successful electoral processes have been able to find remedies more appropriate to their needs.

Time-lapse scrutiny has so far protected U.S. covert operations: by the time the details of its interference in Guatemala, the Dominican Republic, Chile, Panama, and other Latin American nations was revealed, the damage had been done. And over the past three or four decades covert action has almost seamlessly become overt. I remember the official denials that the U.S. government had anything to do with ousting Guatemala's Jacobo Arbenz, or with backing the failed Bay of Pigs attack, or with invading the Dominican Republic, or with overthrowing Chile's Allende, or with underwriting the Nicaraguan Contras. In time irrefutable proof of U.S. involvement in all these crimes would sound loud and clear. But by then the damage had been done; there was no turning back. Cuba has been the single exception in the United States' near-perfect record of keeping countries in its orbit. It was an exception that a succession of U.S. administrations found impossible to forgive.

Claiming it is leading "coalitions of the willing," the United States believes it has the right to go where it wishes, killing hundreds of thousands, destroying cultures and economies, and wreaking a devastation that may never be reversed. Over the past two decades U.S. administrations have concentrated on the Middle East. Free from such intense scrutiny, the countries of Latin America have gained in regional power. But now, embroiled in chaos in the Middle East, the United States is once again paying more attention to its neighbors to the south. Under the cover of a war against drugs or beneath the banner of a fanatical patriotism, sparked by the terrible attacks of September 11, 2001, any new adventure may be deemed "keeping America safe." National security, waged unilaterally, has become a cover for illegal rendition, secret offshore detention centers, holding prisoners for years without trial, and brutal torture disguised as "enhanced interrogation methods." Among nations, as among individuals, might makes right.

In contrast little Cuba represents the dreams of peoples struggling for independence from the world's major powers. It represents choosing another route and a people's right to make that choice. Exhausted by decades or centuries of colonialism and imperialist voracity, a group somewhere decides it has had enough. It is logical that its leaders, especially in Latin America, have looked to Cuba for guidance, training, a certain amount of material aid, and a geographical rearguard where its foot soldiers may find medical help, rest, and renewal before returning to the front lines.

To pretend that these efforts are equal in weight or impact is absurd in the extreme. The first is orchestrated by a world power intent on domination and accustomed to getting its way. It is the stance of American exceptionalism, so popular among our most ignorant politicians. The second involves indigenous rebels with nowhere else to turn. The first seeks to benefit its interests. While the second certainly has its own ideological interests, its main goal is to more fairly distribute natural resources and the profits of labor. The first hides state violence beneath a rhetoric of "spreading democracy," while accusing the second of illegitimate guerrilla warfare. The second almost always attempts to reach its goals first through legal means, resorting to the force of arms only when it has exhausted all alternatives.

United States corporate media, with its myth of impartiality, has gotten generation after generation to believe its lies about the small Caribbean country to our south, and the U.S. education system's failure to teach critical thinking keeps people from asking the logical questions. We have been fed lies that range from painting socialism as a dictatorial system to describing universal health care as dangerous to a population's well-being. Choice is held up as the most important of all options, without acknowledging that in order to exercise choice one must have access to real information, health, work, safety, education, and equality of opportunities. All this has produced a situation in which large numbers of U.S. citizens accept the official story, believe that anything called communist or socialist must be bad (though they often cannot explain why), eschew universal health care and free education as unachievable or lacking in options, and defend a version of democracy that for many election cycles now has produced leaders according to how much money they spend, the false promises they make, how deftly they can twist the facts, and how convincingly they lie. To pretend that this is democratic is a farce, but sophisticated propaganda keeps the myth alive.

There is simply no comparison between U.S. global domination—military, economic, trade, and ideological—and what the United States has called Cuba's exportation of revolution.

It is also a mistake to assume that Cuba's influence on and support for liberation movements throughout Latin America was devoid of successes. In this respect we need to consider more closely what constitutes success and failure. We look to Chile, Nicaragua, and Venezuela, but we should also consider experiences of social change that have drawn on Cuba's example less directly. Today's progressive governments in a number of Latin American countries evolved out of a history in which Cuba or its influence played an important part. In El Salvador the fighting forces of the Farabundo Martí para la Liberación Nacional (Farabundo Martí National Liberation Front) morphed into a government with some progressive members and a number of projects aimed at alleviating poverty and inequality. In Guatemala decades of armed struggle eventually ended in negotiated peace accords. Although a series of quasi-democratic or repressive administrations followed, an undefeated spirit of rebellion can be seen in the 2015 ouster of a corrupt president and ongoing mobilizations aimed at holding him accountable for his role in the genocide of the 1970s and 1980s. Cuba supported the Colombian peace accords.

Throughout Mexico and Central America people are caught between the big drug cartels and vicious gangs. Violence threatens to consume whole nations. As it has in other parts of the world, the United States often supports one of these criminal groups in an attempt to defeat the other. As a result U.S. money and weaponry too often find their way into the hands of those fighting its soldiers, who in turn have been tricked into believing they are sacrificing themselves to keep their country safe.

From 1968 to 1975 Juan Velasco Alvarado governed Peru with a populist hand and ideas that favored society's abandoned members; important mobilizations took place, antipoverty programs were put in place, and the nation's Quechua-speaking majority was recognized in ways it had not been before. This positive moment evaporated with Velasco Alvarado's early death, but its spirit remains and has fostered subsequent initiatives. Hugo Chávez modeled his Bolivarian revolution in Venezuela on elements of Cuba's as well as on Bolívar's much earlier campaign. For a while Venezuela and Cuba were unified in their resistance to U.S. control of Latin America. Since Chávez's untimely death, the ineptitude of the country's current leadership, and continued destabilization efforts on the part of the United States, its future is uncertain. But tremendous improvements for the poor, especially in the areas of education, housing, and health care, cannot be denied.

In the southern cone, where repressive forces had crossed borders and worked together during the ugliest years of dictatorship, progressive politics have also had some successes. After its twenty years of progressive coalition-building Uruguay's Frente Amplio is the most solid of these. The country is well on its way to total energy sustainability, poverty has been reduced, and social legislation is the most progressive on the continent. The Frente Amplio has benefited spiritually and in terms of material solidarity from Cuba. Argentina, alone in the southern cone, has tried and convicted some of the worst criminals from its Dirty War. As I write this a progressive administration has been replaced by one that is conservative, and the consequences for the population have already been palpable. The pendulum may swing back and forth in these countries, but once the grip of dictatorship has been broken governments more responsive to human need are bound to have their day. Since the fall of Pinochet in Chile, that country has had both progressive and conservative administrations.

Mexico and Cuba have had a complex relationship. When the United States forced other nations to cut ties with the island, Mexico refused. It thus enjoyed a defiant status while surreptitiously serving as a way for Interpol to keep tabs on those who traveled to Cuba. In the 1960s and 1970s southern Mexico was the scene of several attempts at armed struggle initiatives, most notably those headed by Lucio Cabañas and Genaro Vázquez. I remember the noble, mild-mannered country schoolteachers from Vázquez's group who came to Cuba after kidnapping a local authority in the early 1970s. They had fought a modern army on horseback and with what seemed like nineteenth-century methods. Cuba managed a generous reception for these brave men while maintaining the special status of its relationship with their homeland.

It wouldn't be until 1994 that the Zapatistas emerged out of Mexico's Lacandón jungle, with their ancient ideas about power and life. They are the first armed movement that does not seek state power but rather, as set out in an early declaration, demands that the government address eleven points: work, land, shelter, food, health, education, independence, freedom, democracy, justice, and peace. They want dignified jobs, literacy, respect for their culture, the creation of more hospitals in Chiapas and other poor regions, an independent press, reduction of hunger and malnutrition, municipal self-government, economic and cultural autonomy, equality for women, and an end to the brutal exploitation of Mexico's indigenous peoples. They believe they can achieve these rights without taking state power. The

Mexican government, however, has not attended to any of them, and the two sides remain at a standoff.

Brazil's armed struggle organizations of the 1970s fed Luiz Inácio Lula da Silva's Workers Party, followed by Dilma Rousseff's continuation presidency. Both administrations have had progressive initiatives, resulting in notable improvements in the quality of life for the majority. Both have faced U.S.-backed opposition. A conservative opposition has gained the upper hand and as of this writing Rousseff is facing an impeachment trial. More exciting have been that country's massive grassroots movements for land and sustainability. And despite Che's devastating 1967 defeat in Bolivia, a direct line can be drawn from that failed history to the socialist state: one of its survivors years later becoming a member of Evo Morales's government.[10]

Cause and effect have a way of unfolding in mysterious ways and often take circuitous routes. Governments throughout Latin America today run the gamut from democracies in name only, those still beholden to neoliberal policies but that refrain from the extreme repressive measures responsible for so many deaths and disappearances in the 1970s and 1980s, to several that resist neoliberalism in a solid attempt to prioritize human need. If we look beneath the surface of these disparate histories, Cuba is there: by example, in dignity, and in many cases via a narrative that includes years of solidarity at a variety of levels.

Cuba—with Che's notions of justice for the most disenfranchised and Fidel's and his comrades' vision of a new social organization—played a role in every one of these experiences. Cuba encouraged, trained, funded, and provided refuge and rearguard bases for them all. I believe history will vindicate its role. Its peacetime contributions have been even more impressive. (In later chapters I document the tens of thousands of Cuban internationalists who have brought disaster relief, health care initiatives, and educational programs to peoples throughout Latin America.)

There is one more issue I must address while on the subject of the Revolution's military involvement on foreign battlefields, and that is the distinction between those collaborations sponsored by the Cuban government and those launched by Che after he renounced his Cuban citizenship and public offices and left the country. For the United States, as for the rest of the world, Che's guerrilla effort in Bolivia was emblematic of Cuban policy and symbolic of its internationalist strategy from the 1960s through the early 1980s. The Cuban Revolution certainly claims Che as one of its major heroic figures. Yet it was the same United States, and the counterrevolutionaries it supported, who spread the wildest rumors about a supposed falling-out between Fidel and Che, some positing the idea that Che's failure in Bolivia may have been due to a lack of logistical support from Fidel, and a few even trying to promote the ludicrous idea that Fidel murdered Che as a result of a ferocious argument. Such rumors run from the troubling to the outlandish.

As those who have read my book about Che know, I do not subscribe to these hypotheses.[11] It should be noted that in his farewell letter to Fidel, Che explicitly renounced his Cuban citizenship and the positions he'd held within the revolutionary hierarchy. He took special care to praise Fidel's leadership qualities, saying that he only regretted not having recognized them earlier. He made it clear that he owed some of his moments of greatest pride to Cuba and its revolution, but that the time had come for him to continue on his very personal—although deeply political—journey to liberate other peoples from oppression. And he stipulated that he was leaving nothing material to his wife and children because he knew the Revolution would care for them.

There is ample evidence that, even when he may have disagreed with Che's chosen destination, Fidel made every effort to provide support. The two men had very different historic responsibilities, and I believe each respected the other's while assuming his own. I also believe that, although burdened by some degree of irresponsibility toward the men he took with him into battle, and in other ways toward the peoples he hoped to free, Che's motives were genuine. In retrospect it is easy to point to errors of judgment regarding chosen combat locations and even certain methodologies of struggle. My great interest in Che resides in his intellectual contributions, ethical stance, and willingness to put his life on the line for his beliefs. But the question here is this: Should we interpret his ultimate adventure in Bolivia as exporting his own revolution or Cuba's?

My conclusion is that, as much as Che's operation in Bolivia reflected Cuba's line, it cannot be laid at that country's feet. Herein are all the unresolved issues regarding Cuba's support or lack of support. In his role of statesman Fidel was forced to tread a delicate line. I have always felt that the two men's last conversation, which was witnessed but not overheard at the training camp in Pinar del Río from which Che departed on his final journey, held clues regarding their differences of opinion about which we can only guess.[12]

As we know, however, perception frequently speaks louder than fact, especially when passions run high or such important questions hang in the balance. Although by the time of Che's final offensive the Cuban Revolution itself was moving away from active military involvement in other liberation struggles and even beginning to wind down its training camps for foreign revolutionaries, it is clear that the United States equated Che's presence in Bolivia with Cuba. When the CIA ordered Che's murder, it believed it had won its long ideological struggle against people's power on the continent. It would soon discover it was the one that had been defeated.

7

INTERNATIONALISM, CUBAN STYLE

There are several definitions of international aid. Some claim to be initiatives, such as the U.S. Alliance for Progress and President Kennedy's Peace Corps, through which legions of altruistic young people travel to remote parts of the world to teach hygiene or build latrines. But these have had their problems. It wasn't long before contingents of the Peace Corps' "returned volunteers" were getting together to denounce the strategy in which they had participated without being fully aware of what they had been asked to do. The U.S. Agency for International Development (USAID) and other programs have also been problematic, failing to address systemic problems while exhausting the economies of debtor nations.

Nor are a number of ostensibly private institutions exempt from critique. Fulbright has been denounced for collecting confidential data on peoples the United States proposes to help and using that data to support U.S. policy aimed at controlling population groups receiving its aid. The Oklahoma-based Summer Institute of Linguistics, a Christian organization that freely admits its goal is to translate the New Testament into every language on earth, is not transparent about the ways it attempts to subvert other peoples' cultures and beliefs. Many other charities have been accused of hidden motives and inflated overhead.

In terms of the impact each nation's idea of internationalism has on its own population, this has been palpably stronger in Cuba than in the United States. Most Americans are oblivious to U.S. foreign policy initiatives, and faith-based programs generally attract only members of a particular congregation. By the end of the twentieth century a single aid worker for every 35,760 U.S. citizens had been in the Peace Corps or worked for USAID. In Cuba, on the other hand, by January 1990 one out of every 228 citizens had served on overseas missions. More recently the ratio has been estimated at one in ten.

The United States has promoted some famously bipartisan initiatives, such as the Clinton-Bush Fund, which President Obama suggested and former presidents Clinton and George W. Bush launched following Haiti's 2010 earthquake. Because of its name recognition, this particular response received an enormous amount of press and popular support. U.S. citizens were urged to follow the example of the major figures from opposing political parties who seemingly cared enough to work together. The Clinton-Bush Fund was established within weeks of the quake. Like so many other charities, it promised that 100 percent of donations would go directly to relief efforts, yet it soon became apparent this wasn't happening. As months passed and 1.3 million people were still living in makeshift tent cities, much of the money remained unspent and the victims were still struggling, threatened by a serious cholera epidemic as well as the approaching hurricane season. The backstory was even more insidious, and it wasn't publicized in the corporate media. Those willing to do the research discovered that the Bush administration had blocked millions of dollars in loans from the Inter-American Development Bank for public water infrastructure in Haiti's central region and that Clinton, while in office, had pressured the Haitian government into slashing tariffs on imported U.S. rice, thereby devastating the country's rice farming economy.[1] That is, the very men charged with solving the extreme poverty that made earthquake recovery impossible were those whose policies had helped create that poverty. Some media attention was eventually directed at Clinton's and Bush's failed strategies in Haiti and to the fact that much of the money collected was not distributed. But except for a few courageous bloggers, the story faded quickly from the news.

It is only fair to note that there are some private initiatives based in the United States that do make valuable contributions to solving global problems of poverty, illness, and lack of education. The Bill and Melinda Gates Foundation has spent its considerable riches to wipe out epidemic diseases and provide clean water to millions. In December 2015 Facebook's CEO Mark Zuckerberg and his wife, Priscilla Chan, announced the arrival of their baby daughter, Max, and pledged in her name to donate 99 percent of their Facebook shares over the course of their lives to the Chan Zuckerberg Initiative.[2] Although this sort of giving provides tax relief to the givers, it clearly is important as well for the recipients. In the context of major giving, it is ironic—and sometimes embarrassing—that in the United States the private sector often plays a more positive role than government.

Despite the good intentions of many contributing individuals, when a U.S. administration has engaged in aid programs its main objective has been influence or domination: military, political, and cultural. Its aim has been to spread an idealized version of the American Way of Life while increasing its own control and coffers. When it has been faced with disasters in different parts of the world, it has invariably come up short in its immediate response. Smaller, poorer nations that give more have sometimes shamed the United States into increasing the amount of its aid.

Upon close inspection it can also be seen that the United States almost always offers such aid in the form of high-interest loans, difficult or impossible to repay. Faced with periodic efforts by nations strangled by debt to achieve some degree of debt forgiveness, the United States has invariably rejected a workable alternative. This country has very rarely given truly disinterested support, the only kind that can help mitigate the terrible human drama that accompanies underdevelopment, war, and natural disaster. Even the term *natural disaster* bears closer scrutiny. Those whom injustice keeps in systemic poverty are invariably the people hit hardest by earthquakes, typhoons, fires, or mudslides; it is overwhelmingly their flimsy hovels that go up in flames or are swept away.

By comparison Cuba's variety of internationalism is disinterested and involves immense sacrifice by both the government and the people. As a socialist country Cuba can look to the great internationalist actions of the Soviet Union for precedent and example. It can also look to the fight for the Spanish Republic, an effort joined by some forty thousand internationalists from all over the world. More than one thousand volunteers from Cuba went to fight in Spain, an extremely high number for such a small country. In the much larger United States, the Abraham Lincoln Brigade had 2,800 members. And the Cubans made their sacrifice despite the generally anti-Spanish sentiment at home at the time. Their contribution to Spain's civil war went beyond national interests to a yearning to defeat European fascism.[3] There were also some direct links between those who fought in Spain's civil war and the Cuban revolutionaries who ousted Batista in 1959.[4]

Today's Cuban internationalists address the immediate problems caused by dictatorship, foreign attack, or natural disaster, and then begin laying the groundwork for ongoing collaboration in which leadership shifts to the local people. Their strategy is to help the host country strengthen its own social programs, so that when future problems arise it will be better able to deal with them. Many Cuban specialists remain in these countries for years, setting up rehabilitation and mental health centers and training local personnel. Tens of thousands of victims of disaster have been brought to Cuba, where they receive ongoing medical help. Thousands of students from throughout the developing world also study for free at Cuba's international medical school, Escuela Latinoamericana de Medicina, and return home with an education that makes them better prepared to face future disasters.

There is no question that in certain quarters Cuban internationalism has meant good press for the Revolution. But this has not been its motivation. To begin with, Cuba has never sent advisors or aid without an explicit invitation from the receiver nation—represented by a government or well-established opposition force. Cuba's internationalism is one of the most prominent faces of its vision of global justice and a primary ingredient in the Revolution's reimagining of values, both collective and individual. Undoubtedly, especially in difficult economic times, there have also been a few who have gone on overseas missions to gain status or extra perks, but these have been exceptions. I would have thought Cuban internationalism might have received more positive attention than it has, even in the Western press.

Many have asked how Cuba has developed this policy of internationalist aid in the face of its own ongoing economic stress. The first answer is that, from the beginning, the Revolution's internationalism has been a part of its political identity. As early as February 1959, a mere month after taking power, the revolutionary leadership was making contact with liberation movements involved in their own burgeoning struggles. For example, Che Guevara took time from the multiple tasks of those first days to meet with Haitians intent upon unseating the dictator Papa Doc Duvalier.[5]

The U.S. revolutionary and public intellectual Tom Hayden emphasizes that "the Cuban revolutionaries were conscious of belonging to [what C. Wright Mills and the U.S. student movement of the 1960s and 1970s called] 'the hungry bloc,' the third world instead of the first or second."[6] Hayden goes on to explain that after the Revolution attempted to establish a "live and let live" relationship with the United States in 1961, 1963, and 1964 and had been rebuffed at each attempt, Fidel concluded that the best defense was offense.[7] Hayden's book *Listen, Yankee! Why Cuba Matters* is based in part on conversations with Ricardo Alarcón, a high-ranking Cuban official who played an important role in the diplomacy that followed a number of his country's military efforts abroad.[8] Alarcón tells stories that illustrate how the Cubans were regarded by ex-enemies as well as friends. Here he is in Windhoek, the capital of Namibia, after the Angolan peace accords:

Suddenly we crossed near a low wall and saw painted there a Namibian slogan, "Long live MPLA! Long live Cuba! Long live SWAPO [South West Africa People's Organization]!" We asked [our hosts], "Can you stop for us to take a photo?" When we got out of the van, a very old man was coming, walking with difficulty, and he saw us taking photos of this completely illegal graffiti. He asked us who we were, and when we said Cubans, he said, "You are Cubans from Cuba? I have a grandson on the Isle of Youth!"[9]

Another time when we were in Cape Town I needed something for my stomach, an antacid, and was accompanied by a Namibian security officer to a store. Very close to me was a black South African. When I was going to pay, the security guy said, "Don't charge him taxes, he's a diplomat." "Where is he from?" the black man asked. "Cuba," they said. "That's not true. Cuba doesn't support the apartheid regime!" It was very confusing for him, but it shows how much the local people knew.[10]

Through every phase of its development the Cuban Revolution has given to those less fortunate, even when doing so has meant its own people have gone without. This solidarity remains emblematic. From time to time it has even raised complaints. On October 5, 1973, weeks after Chile's Popular Unity government had been overthrown by Pinochet's coup, the Cuban ship *Imías* was forced to suspend its delivery of a large donation of Cuban sugar in the Chilean port of Valparaiso.[11] U.S. authorities tried to stop the operation, and the ship departed with some of its cargo still on board. By the time it reached Panama the event had become an international scandal. Some Cubans grumbled that it was wrong to give Chile sugar when their own sugar was rationed, but the revolutionary leadership argued that the Chilean people were worse off than they were. Such internationalist examples have become an everyday part of Cuban practice. In fact most people agreed: "That memorable day when Fidel asked us to donate one pound of our sugar ration to Allende's Chile, the decision of those present—a million people raising their hands in symbolic vote—was not collective but personal."[12]

I've already spoken about the dozens of schools on Isle of Youth. Each of these hosted from five hundred to eight hundred students, and they operated for more than forty years. In addition thousands of students from North Vietnam, Cambodia, and Laos, and in lesser numbers from other countries, studied free of charge at Cuban universities. Many attended summer camps situated on the beaches east of Havana.

From the beginning of the Revolution Cuba made provisions to care for victims of political repression, especially the youngest. This effort emerged naturally from its attitude toward its own children, summed up in the motto *Los niños son los mimados de la Revolución* (Children are the Revolution's favored ones). Even in periods of greatest scarcity, Cuban children always came first. And the Revolution extends the same sensibility and care to children from other countries. It brings them to the island, houses and schools them, and attends to their health and emotional needs. During the last decades of the twentieth century it might have been a string of brothers and sisters whose parents died in the struggle or were in prison or underground somewhere. I remember Minou, whose mother and two aunts had been murdered by Trujillo, the Dominican dictator; four small Panamanian brothers; and of course hundreds of Chileans. It might have been a single frightened boy or girl for whom only a loving family would be able to help remake his or her life. These children would arrive alone and disconcerted but soon feel the warmth of a system that cared about and for them. It might have been a widow with children, or an adult participant who had been released in one of the dramatic prisoner exchanges of the 1960s and 1970s.[13] Cuba's leadership set the example: Haydée Santamaría and Armando Hart made room in their family for a dozen or so Latin American children who needed a home. In the building where for many years Fidel Castro and Celia Sánchez lived in different apartments but shared certain aspects of family life, they too took in a number of Latin American orphans.

During the years of revolutionary struggle, housing was always in short supply. Despite several massive building programs, the number of new units never managed to keep up with the growing demand. The famous *microbrigadas* were constructing four-story twenty-apartment units in Alamar, an immense new community along the coastline east of the capital. The state would supply the materials, and workplaces would delegate a couple of workers to the project; these would continue to earn their salary while the rest of the workforce pitched in to keep production up. When the apartments were ready, those awarded the new housing would be chosen by their colleagues exclusively on the basis of need. In other words, an office employee turned construction worker hadn't necessarily labored most of the year for his or her own place. Instead someone with five kids and dramatically inadequate housing was likely to be awarded the new and completely furnished home.

Here too Cuban internationalism was evident. The Cuban Revolution has consistently tried to share its national solutions with others, modifying them as circumstance, need, and local custom require. I remember the Alamar apartment block they called the Chilean Building. Refugees from the Chilean Movimiento de Izquierda Revolucionaria (Movement of the Revolutionary Left) took part in its construction. It was to house groups of orphaned Chilean children or children whose parents were returning home to continue the struggle after the fall of Allende. In each apartment a couple would function as foster parents to a group of four or five young people. The project was a moving example of internationalist solidarity for many years. Decades later one of those children, now an adult, made a film about the Chilean Building. Viewing it, one feels the anguish of those children left behind and the anguish of the parents going off without them. One also feels the extraordinary, creative solidarity Cuba provided in such dramatic situations.[14]

Cuba has also practiced its particular brand of solidarity by inviting large contingents of U.S. young people to spend three or four weeks cutting cane, harvesting vegetables, or working in construction. These contingents pay their way to the island, but Cuba covers all in-country expenses. Thousands have been touched in this way by the reality of the Revolution. Fair Play for Cuba sponsored early trips.[15] During the 1970s and 1980s the Venceremos Brigade was pivotal for generations of young Americans.[16] And toward the end of the 1980s the Antonio Maceo Brigade invited the sons and daughters of Cubans who had left the country to experience for themselves the Revolution their parents had fled.[17]

Subsequently U.S.-Cuba solidarity organizations such as the Center for Cuban Studies in New York City and Global Exchange in San Francisco have sponsored group trips throughout the long decades in which U.S. travel restrictions made it difficult for individuals to visit. Visitors on each of these people-to-people journeys invariably meet with a warm reception from the Cubans, who have been educated to understand that aggressive counterrevolutionary policy comes from the U.S. government, not its people. This ability to separate a people's good faith and openness from their government's politics has been relatively unique on the Caribbean island. Only in Vietnam, when I visited toward the end of the war, and in Nicaragua, when I lived there during the Sandinista administration of the early 1980s, have I observed a similar attitude.

In the United States, especially during the 1970s and 1980s, when a solidarity movement was most active, hundreds of Sister City initiatives paired a city in the developing world—many of them Cuban—with one in the

United States. These projects allowed Americans to come in people-to-people contact with a Cuba they couldn't read about in the news.

Then there have been the hundreds of conferences, large and small, that Cuba has hosted in education, health policy, the social sciences, energy, political ideas, and the arts. One deserving of special mention was the huge Cultural Congress of Havana, which took place in January 1968. Six hundred delegates—philosophers, indigenous leaders, religious figures, writers, artists, and others—came together in five commissions. More than a thousand journalists attended. I was at the gathering, and it was a turning point in my life. The opportunity to meet and listen to so many thoughtful representatives of so many countries gave me my first in-depth perspective on what people in struggle were thinking, feeling, and doing. That conference had originally been planned to garner support for continental liberation, symbolized by Che's guerrilla movement in Bolivia. But Che's force had been defeated and its leader murdered just a few months earlier, in October 1967. The Congress then shifted its focus to a vibrant many-voices discussion of the strategies and tactics for social change, as well as a collective commitment to resist policies aimed at neutralizing and subverting peoples' struggles.

Over the years hundreds of thousands of Cubans have given generously of their expertise throughout the world. Wherever a government invited them, they have gone, in the early years even bringing with them their own money, foodstuffs, and cigarettes so as not to have to deplete the already diminished larders of the people they served. This disinterested aid is still offered freely to impoverished nations, while those that can afford to pay, and want the Cubans because of their skills and experience, establish reciprocity with the Cuban government. These are doctors and other health care workers, teachers, and specialists in everything from fishing and agriculture to sustainable energy.

And yes, there have been military advisors as well, and companies of foot soldiers (described in more detail in chapter 5). The United States dubbed such wartime aid "interference" and pointed to it as proof that Cuba was exporting revolution, helping governments unfriendly to U.S. interests. Of course they were. Just as U.S. advisors, bombing raids, and fighting men and women have shown up in every theater of operations where homegrown revolutionary projects have attempted to lay the groundwork for social change, and many where they are simply defending U.S. interests overseas.

It is astonishing, in light of Iraq, Afghanistan, and the dozens of other nations decimated by U.S. invasion and occupation, that a succession of

U.S. administrations can continue to claim we are "keeping the world safe." Some would say it is beyond astonishing that a president who during his two administrations has presided over unending war was awarded the Nobel Prize for Peace. There is no doubt that Obama inherited untenable overseas dilemmas from his predecessors and that his ability to bring about change was severely hampered by strong Pentagon influence, not to mention a Republican-controlled Congress that would do anything to keep the first Afro-American U.S. president from succeeding. It is also true that Obama has continued to engage U.S. war policy, economic support, weaponry, and troops in too many parts of the world, often inadvertently aiding factions that turn out to be humanity's worst enemies.

When I lived in Nicaragua in the early 1980s I traveled to the threadbare Atlantic Coast. The helicopter I arrived in was carrying a bag of mail for the small hospital at Puerto Cabezas; I offered to deliver it. When I arrived at the simple wooden structure a couple of Cuban doctors were performing a cesarean delivery accompanied by a Uruguayan nurse and a Bolivian anesthetist: evidence of the multifaceted Latin American solidarity of those years. When they finished they removed their white masks, and the Cubans began opening letters from home. I still remember their delighted grins. I have witnessed many such scenes over the years, examples of a shared solidarity that reflects a different way of positioning oneself in the world.

The year before, while I was still living in Cuba, my youngest daughter's fifth grade teacher volunteered to work in a remote region of Nicaragua. Another fifth grade teacher assumed the double burden her absence created: a class of sixty students. Parents pitched in to help. We all knew we would make it through, and we as well as our children were immensely proud that this teacher had answered the call to labor for a couple of years in a place where she was so desperately needed. This was the spirit of internationalism that permeated Cuba throughout that era and can still be felt. No matter the conditions, most people want to serve. Bringing Cuba's notions of justice to a place where people are less fortunate is considered a revolutionary virtue and a genuine desire shared by the vast majority of Cubans.

Hundreds of thousands of Cubans fought in Angola, Congo, Mozambique, Ethiopia, and other African countries. Countless others took part in follow-up programs. Their actions helped put an end to apartheid in South Africa and brought about the liberation of Namibia. Many Cubans died in battles such as the one that took place at Cuito Cuanavale and was so definitive in winning that war. Others returned to life on the island. A customary quiet surrounded those departures and returns. People didn't generally ask where a friend or relative had gone; they knew, and also knew that discretion was in order. I was aware of more than one volunteer who felt deeply affected by not being chosen for one of those overseas missions.

It is also worth noting the differences returning U.S. and Cuban troops experience upon coming home. Compare, for example, the instances of posttraumatic stress disorder (PTSD). Many U.S. veterans feel confused, hopeless, even betrayed. They realize the premises upon which they went to war are not what they believed them to be, that too many civilians are killed in such conflicts, and that their sacrifice had nothing to do with keeping America safe. They return to the pain of people who cannot know what they have endured and a system unable to care for them. They lack adequate physical and psychological attention. Many of these veterans end up on the streets. Although today there is an increased consciousness of the seriousness of issues provoked by war, a stigma persists for individual soldiers seeking psychotherapy; the military culture continues to consider them weak. Trouble getting or keeping a job, divorce and other family problems, and a high rate of suicide are being recorded. Cubans coming home from fighting overseas suffer from the horrors of war as soldiers have in all cultures and eras. But while in the United States the problem of PTSD is at epidemic proportions, in Cuba the psychological trauma of war has been destigmatized and aid is freely accessible; those needing it receive adequate community and therapeutic help. Cuba's veterans of foreign wars believe in what they have done and are proud of their service.

I asked a Cuban sociologist friend how the country handled the PTSD I assumed must have overtaken many of its veterans returning from Africa. He surprised me by saying it hadn't been a problem. I couldn't believe that and asked another friend, a U.S. psychiatrist who has worked in Cuba for decades. "What PTSD?" she responded. I explained that mental turmoil, uncontrollable flashbacks, extreme depression, and suicide among veterans of Afghanistan and Iraq had reached epidemic proportions in the United States. She kept insisting this wasn't the case in Cuba.

In Paysandú, Uruguay, I caught up with Dr. Francisco Morales, an eminent Cuban psychologist currently working at the University of the Republic and himself an internationalist. He supported the conclusions of my two previous respondents but went further: "It has something to do with how one defines PTSD, and clearly individual cases do exist. But we have not seen anything near an epidemic. Cuban internationalists believe deeply in the work they do, whether as soldiers in wars of liberation or in other areas.

They are well trained and cared for upon their return. Socialization and motivation play key roles in their ability to readjust to civilian life. Those with problems receive the appropriate psychological help."[18]

As each of these conversations unfolded, it became clear to me that when soldiers return from foreign wars in which they can believe and to a home country that provides free and adequate health care, such ills affect far fewer people. Elements of PTSD may be inevitable, but I am speaking of a social phenomenon of despair. The Revolution, with its vastly different priorities, is able to lessen the burden. When people have a meaningful personal narrative they are more easily able to enjoy a sense of well-being.[19]

Profound internationalism is definitely a Cuban characteristic that originated with the 1959 Revolution. But as with its influence in other areas, its roots may precede that historic event (as was evident in the Cuban contingent that fought in Spain). Like people everywhere, Cubans have a generosity of spirit that shows itself in numerous small acts of kindness. This generosity of spirit is frequently offered as a matter of course among neighbors and in the community at large. When natural disasters strike, these people open their homes. Those who know hunger are quick to feed the hungry. Those whose coffee is rationed offer strangers a rich dark demitasse of the drink. The Revolution institutionalized this generosity and shaped it as solidarity, naming it a collective value and national characteristic capable of bringing aid and hope to peoples in places too numerous to list.

We might ask if the Cuban Revolution constructed this quality out of sheer ideological momentum, or if Cubans arrived at the year 1959 possessed of an unusual propensity for helping those needier than themselves. I've long been struck by Santamaría's pondering the question of whether Ho Chi Minh was who he was because he was Vietnamese or if the Vietnamese people were so selfless and purposeful because they had Ho as a model. It is one of those chicken-or-egg questions that don't really have an answer.

Cuba and Vietnam have an interesting internationalist history. During the U.S. war in Vietnam Cuba's aid to that country was a priority and it supported the war-torn nation in every way possible. Thousands of Vietnamese students attended Cuban universities; young men and women in white shirts and dark pants thronged Havana's streets. The women wore their hair in long braids, vowing not to cut it until they had routed the invaders from their beloved homeland. Cuban shortwave radio donated repeated twenty-minute segments each day to the Voice of Vietnam, programming in English aimed at a U.S. listening audience. Cuba sent shipments of sugar and coffee to the Southeast Asian nation. Toward the end of the war Cuban construction workers were battling Vietnam's extreme summer heat as they labored on building projects in the devastated northern half of the country.

Among its trading partners in Asia since 1960 Cuba's trade with Vietnam is second in volume only to that which it sustains with China. Years ago Cuba helped Vietnam develop its coffee crop. Then, due to internal problems and international market fluctuations, Cuba's production declined. Vietnam has since sent coffee to Cuba and helped the Caribbean country improve its crop. More important, as Cuba has adopted some free-market measures to ease its reintroduction into the world economy, it has learned from Vietnam's experience. Today Vietnam is repaying Cuba's years of solidarity by sending experts on rice, soy, and maize to advise on crop yield. Vietnam, now the world's second largest exporter of rice and the largest exporter of coffee, has much to offer. At the end of 2015, in celebration of the fifty-fifth anniversary of relations between the two countries, a large delegation of top-level Vietnamese traveled to Cuba to explore increasing bilateral agreements in grains, production of petroleum, and sale of such Cuban products as detergent and pharmaceuticals.

Cubans have long been known for their determination in the face of seemingly impossible obstacles and challenges. Fidel and his core group were themselves heavily imbued with these characteristics and drew on the solidarity of their contemporaries. With victory, and as they set about to construct a new society, they nurtured this attitude. "Serémos como el Che" (We will be like Che) is the uniform pledge of the country's youngest schoolchildren as they gather each morning to begin another day of school. The children too take their internationalist responsibility seriously. La Colmenita (Little Beehive) is a world-renowned children's theater group based in Havana that has taken its magic to twenty-five countries, including the United States. The company offers a high-energy mix of dance and music with a message. Productions draw on rock and roll and fairy tales to promote ideas of justice and peace. One of the plays, written by the children themselves, is *Abracadabra*; its name derives from the ancient Aramaic language and in this production becomes an incantation for staged magic tricks. La Colmenita's director, Carlos Alberto Cremata, hopes to develop an understanding between Cuban children and children in the rest of the world. Cremata comes from a family of famous Cuban artists and is also a noted film director. His father was an airline worker who was killed in the

1976 terrorist bombing of Cuban Airlines Flight 455.[20] He created the group to perpetuate his father's legacy.

"We may be poor, but we are proud" was a phrase one heard repeated by many through the Revolution's first years. This pride, especially as demonstrated in internationalism, carries the beauty and power of Cuban culture to places far from the Caribbean island.

8

EMILIO IN ANGOLA

Emilio Comas Paret fought in Angola. He wasn't a professional soldier but a member of the people's militia accustomed to weekend training exercises and an occasional slightly longer maneuver. He was married, with two children, and two others from an earlier marriage. When he deployed, Emilio was working as a history teacher and studying his third year of pedagogy at night. His tour in Angola, from February to September 1976, interrupted all that. Upon his return he went to work for the Ministry of Education in the province of Sancti Spiritus, heading its Department of Science, Culture and Educational Outreach. He eventually earned his pedagogical degree from the University of Las Villas. Later he moved to Havana, where, until retiring, he worked in the Cultural Section at the Central Committee of the Cuban Communist Party. Today he is dedicated to his own writing.

On New Year's Eve 1975 Emilio had no idea why he had been called to his military committee. When we spoke in Havana in February 2016, he told me that accepting the mission to Angola was completely voluntary, although it is clear from his novel *Desconfiemos de los amaneceres apacibles* (We're Suspicious of Tranquil Dawns) that certain social pressures as well as a deep solidarity propelled people to sign up and that some of those who fought lacked in-depth knowledge of the African movements they were enlisted to support or fight against. Although most were proud of their involvement, some ended up disillusioned with proclamations of noble missions and proletarian internationalism. Emilio says his novels are not autobiographical and that their characters are composites. What draws me to them is their complexity. In his own life twenty-five days of intense training prepared him for combat, and he was off—one of the tens of thousands of Cubans who took up arms against apartheid on the other side of the world.

Emilio had written and published prior to his tour of duty in Angola. He'd finished a book of stories and another of poems, both of which saw the light after his return. His work won a couple of prizes for beginning authors. After Angola, like so many Cubans who'd participated, he felt compelled to write about the war. But it took a while. His first book on that theme, *De Cabinda a Cunene* (From Cabinda to Cunene), was published in 1983, six years after his experiencing, witnessing, or imagining the events it describes. A second, *Desconfiemos de los amaneceres apacibles*, appeared in 2012, thirty-five years after his return. It is from this second volume that the following fragments are taken. In 2016 he finished a third book, which he says has turned out to be "something of a memoir."

During Emilio's time in Angola he worked as the military historian of Cuba's high command in Cabinda, giving him access to information about a number of events in which he did not personally participate. He describes his books as testimonial literature but says he's never been that interested in genres. "I consider *Desconfiemos* to be fiction, a re-created history," he says, "in other words another version of history, which is what literature always is."

Although not all the events in *Desconfiemos* happened to Emilio or to someone close to him, the text leaves no doubt that the powerful perceptions and analysis are his. Angola represents a heroic page in Cuban internationalist history. Most of the books that have been written about the campaign are official texts, told with the pomp and circumstance the amazing feat deserves but lacking in nuance and contradiction: the problems, doubts, and horrors all wars entail and that humanize the experience. Not so for either of Emilio's books. I asked him if he had suffered reprisals of any kind, or if anyone had objected to his way of writing about the mission. He said no. *Desconfiemos*, in fact, won an important literary prize from a unanimous jury. The book also received excellent reviews. No official voice was ever raised against its publication, although silence reigned in some quarters. And he adds, "I confess that at the end of every year, when the clock strikes twelve I always cry for my friends who died; my memory doesn't forget them."

DESCONFIEMOS DE LOS AMANECERES APACIBLES (FRAGMENTS)

One

If someone at that moment had told me I'd never see you again, I would have told them to go to hell.

But throughout my life, reality—my realities—have always overcome my fantasies.

They'd been talking about Angola, its war and Cuba's participation, and it all seemed like something far off, military issues I should be enthusiastic about but nothing more.

I was supposed to have been on my way to Caibarién to wait for the new year as they celebrate it only there, with monkfish and potatoes in broth and lots of rum and beer. But I got a call that complicated things. It was December 31, 1975. If I hurry, I thought, I can be home on the morning of the first, after another visit with you, of course.

When I arrived at the Military Committee it felt strange, officers I'd never seen before and an atmosphere unlike those I was used to on weekend maneuvers or those stupid early morning mobilizations they were always thinking up for no reason other than to test the disposition of the troops. We were a small group that had been called up, militiamen from different companies standing around in the patio, and right off the bat these officers we'd never seen before began to interview each of us. My turn came and I stood before the trio. One of them, without any sort of preamble, asked if I was willing to fight to free the Angolan people from the apartheid that had taken hold of their country, and what I thought of all that.

Right then and there all hell broke loose.

Throughout their lives, men confront extreme situations that tend to modify any plans they may have, change them completely, make them into something they never wanted to be. This was one of those situations.

The first thing out of my mouth was no, I'm not a soldier, I've never been a soldier, and, well, fighting someone who is threatening my homeland is one thing, but going off to another country to fight, that's a horse of a different color. As I began to voice these doubts, I heard another officer talking about internationalism, about Máximo Gómez who was Dominican and that guy Reeves they called the Little Englishman. That officer gave a whole class on Cuba's War of Independence. I understood it was going to be impossible to say no and maintain any sense of valor, keep anyone's respect, and I figured the word *coward* was going to be used pretty freely by friends and family. So I said yes, I was willing.

The only guy who said no right off the bat was Miguelito.

He had his reasons. His wife was about to give birth, she was just days away, and there was no one but him to deal with that. His parents were old, and his wife's family lived far away in Oriente. He'd have to take charge, with the help of some of his good friends. When he told the officers, one of them said, "Look, I'll leave a blank after your name. I won't put down that you got cold feet. Go on out there and talk to your buddies, tell them you aren't going, then come back in and let me know. Okay?"

What the officer imagined would happen, happened. When Miguelito told us he couldn't go, the laughter and taunts began. Someone even said he was afraid. No one took the birth story seriously.

Miguel was livid at first, indignant. Then he turned red as an apple. Without a word, he turned away from us, went back into the recruiting station and, interrupting one of the interviews, told the guards, "Put down there that I'll go, and let God answer for the consequences."

Miguelito died. He was the first among us they killed. The morning we got to Cabinda they selected him to join a caravan to Punta Negra, in Congo. His first caravan and his last. He was on the truck bed when they hit the ambush. A blast from an antitank rocket took him out from behind. Its effect was such that they found only fragments, little pieces that they quickly put in the wooden box that was much too big for him then. His sudden death shocked us all. His was the first corpse we saw of someone we knew. Unfortunately, it wouldn't be the last. . . .

Two

"The sea is everything, its breath is pure and exhilarating. It's a desert grandiosity in which man is never alone because he feels life's palpitation all around him. The sea is the vehicle for a supernatural and marvelous life, movement and love, the living infinite." That's what Captain Nemo said in *Twenty Thousand Leagues under the Sea*, a novel someone gave me to pass the time as I headed to war on a cargo ship.

At last I was at sea, something I'd always dreamed of, to travel the ocean and spend hours gazing at it, the sky's monotony in symphony with the water, without a single bird to break the calm. Only water and sky.

But I was on a cargo ship, an old tub built for a crew of twenty or thirty that now carried fifteen hundred soldiers and several tanks and tanker trucks filled with gasoline on its deck.

My dream of traveling on a cargo ship had come true, but I had to pay a price, a high price in fact, and of course the conditions weren't what I would have wanted on this trip, but life can be capricious. Sometimes it gives you what you want but on its own terms, according to its whim, without taking you into account, without asking your opinion. That floating tub began its route at night along Cuba's coast. When I woke up the following morning, all I could see was sky and water: my landscape for many days to come. Midmorning they passed out the dog tags. I thought of that story by Che, the one about when he was taking off on the *Granma* and someone asked who they should notify in case of death. I felt the same sort of tremor. The dog tag was our identification in case of death. They would stuff it in the cadaver's mouth so it wouldn't get lost in decomposition or disappear into earth and rot.

My dog tag was number 28810. Two eights in a row. The Chinese say eight is a lucky number. I'd never before had an eight among the numbers that identified me. Papá did. Papá was born in 1918 on August 8, in other words the eighth month. He was born in Villa Clara, which is the eighth of Cuba's provinces counting from west to east or east to west. He was born in Remedios, also known as the eighth town founded by the Spanish colonizers. He was the last of eight children and was born at 88 Justa Street. I hope these two recent eights in my life will bring me luck and delay my death if it approaches. . . .

Around eight in the morning, after ingesting a couple of stale crackers and coffee with milk that I didn't finish, we got ready to disembark. The boat was tied up at the pier, but a distance of more or less three feet separated it from the dock, and you had to make a small leap to get across. For those of us who were used to moving around on boats it was easy, but for those frightened farmers it was yet another test of their courage to jump across that space with the sea moving beneath them and make it safely to land—all this after seventeen days in perpetual motion. I was one of the last to leave the ship; I was in the farthest compartment and watched the whole process. As our soldiers disembarked, fear took hold of them. The morning breeze also picked up and the ship moved more, complicating the scene. But the leader of the regiment took no pains to stop a panic that was quickly becoming collective. Maybe it was his false sense of manhood, or maybe it was his own fear he was trying to hide. Whatever, it obviated logical decisions, decisions that might have made our landing easier. Just then it was a young boy's turn. He stumbled toward the edge of the ship, which moved just as he jumped, and it was as if he were suspended for a moment in midair. He fell so hard that part of his body landed against the dock with his legs dangling above the water. They were able to grab him and avoid his going into the sea. But he lost his rifle in the dark and fetid water. After that the officials took measures and found some planks we could walk across with all we had to carry on our backs (backpack, rifle, canteen, infantry shovel, bayonet, and whatever else we could hang from our belts). . . .

Our troops were picked up in trucks and we quickly left the port. Someone told us we were going to Cuando Cubango, further to the south, to fight against UNITA. We ended up on other trucks, though, and they took us to Banga, a neighborhood in Lobito that had been inhabited by white Portuguese who'd left in a hurry. When the enemy occupied the city they gave them twenty-four hours to get out or they'd die. Banga had been the barracks of the two groups we were fighting against. You could see crudely written slogans on the walls, one of which really surprised us. It said "Savimbi is Africa's Che." We thought Savimbi and his troops were the enemy, so what were we to think of an African Che? Could it be that Savimbi was a revolutionary who was trying to free his people from residual colonialism? And if that was true, why were we fighting against him? Someone said that Savimbi had gotten guerrilla training in Cuba. No one had an explanation, and all of us who thought for ourselves had grave doubts. Our more ignorant comrades, no. Someone said, "That Savimbi must be one son of a bitch!," and everyone laughed.

This was a modern residential neighborhood, its large homes painted in pastel colors and with gardens of dying roses. Everything abandoned, dirty. Across from this neighborhood, against a hill, you could see the homes of the poor constructed of reddish clay. The sun's reflection made them seem as if they were on fire. Later we were able to see how they built those houses. It was curious, because first they made blocks of clay, like bricks but heavier and wider, and placed them so they could raise four walls. They left holes for doors in front and back, and then they gathered pieces of wood and trash, filled the houses with them and lit fires. The heat from those fires cooked the clay and made it hard. They fashioned roofs of coconut fronds or palm leaves, a door of the same material braided, and that was it. . . .

Three

"To remember is to submerge oneself in nostalgia, and it's a lie, because the years blur what happened and then we have to invent, re-create. We make it up all over again in order to go on remembering. Think about it: our memories never get old. When we remember a woman we never remember her old and ugly, but always young, and if possible naked, her flesh strong and shiny, in perfect condition."

That's Cecilio, another of my acquaintances from the old neighborhood who accompanied me on my explorations. He always finished a conversation with a solemn phrase, profoundly philosophical, and since he's a mulato of Chinese origin, the guys called him Confucius. The name stuck. Cecilio, or Confucius, or Cecilio the Confucian to those who knew him best.

Our second night ashore, finally free of the sea's continuous movement, brought a collective reflection on life, always a continual apprenticeship, or on the evidence at hand that ours might be short, especially now that we were in the midst of a war. And because we didn't know how short it might be, it was simply for each of us to figure out what we wanted from it and pursue that. The thing was to live as well as you could and try to go out without pain, without a lot of wailing, without sadness. "If you get a lemon, make lemonade. I don't know if you get what I'm saying," said El Niño with some wisdom, trying to put an end to a conversation where he found himself on foreign ground. Cecilio, without being an intellectual, had read a great deal, different sorts of things. He knew Socrates, Plato, Aristotle, all of whom he'd read in the Jackson Classics Collection at the municipal library, he said, as well as more contemporary authors such as Nietzsche, Schopenhauer, and Sartre. And with all that conceptual material, much of it upside down, he prepared his own arguments and pronouncements, making it all understandable to an inexperienced public. That was his finest quality. He never gave himself airs but tried to help with his reflections so that things would seem clear. "Let's see if he can conjure us a woman's breast," Chubasco said, and everyone laughed. . . .

We found a very modern print shop. Everything was scattered about, but the presses looked like they were in working condition. None of us knew anything about running them, nor did we care if they worked or not. The place looked like someone had messed it up on purpose, for the pure joy of breaking things. We found some papers with the initials of the FNLA [Frente Nacional de Libertação de Angola, National Front for the Liberation of Angola]. We used them to write home. I found an identity card. On one side it had three colored stripes: one white, one red with a white star in the center, and one mustard yellow. There was an inscription that read F:N:L:A.— LIBERDADE E TERRA. On the back it said FNLA/ELNA and underneath Exército de Libertacao Nacional de Angola [Army of National Liberation of Angola], COMANDO DO ESTADO MAIOR, ANGOLA, and there was a space for a name and address.

That was the enemy. It was fighting for freedom and land. It called itself Angola's Army of Liberation. So, why were we fighting each other? Why were we killing each other like beasts? Because we too were fighting for freedom and land for the Angolans. Who was right? Both of us? It was war, like always, incomprehensible war. . . .

We lacked information. If you send a man off to kill or die, at least he should know why he is doing what he is doing, what he is getting in return. It might be the satisfaction of doing something well or it might be a lot of money. It all depends on the man and his circumstances. But in war there is always a lack of information, and the soldier becomes a machine. He defends himself out of fear, kills out of fear, and can become a bloody monster out of the fear of becoming a bloody monster. . . .

We spoke with some Angolans, the first we'd seen, and we understood each other pretty well. As always gestures substitute for language when needed. The men wear European clothing, trousers with wide cuffs, Hawaiian-style shirts, and platform shoes. Women dress more traditionally, with long dresses of course, a cloth on their head, and their child tied to their back with a shawl fastened beneath their breasts. They go barefoot; a few wear cheap plastic shoes. The men always walk ahead, carrying a tiny bag, and the women walk behind, burdened like mules. (I saw one with a portable stove on her head. It was lit and she was cooking something as she walked!) But they are always smiling, as if they're happy, although they greet us with a respect that looks like fear. It's natural: they're at war, we're soldiers, white soldiers and foreigners. Later we would understand how strong that combination was for them: soldier, foreigner, white man. . . .

Eleven

. . . The earth is something basic for the soldier, your only friend, your brother, your mother. You get your energy from her, and hold onto the earth when danger approaches. When you're on the verge of panic, earth helps you control it. She helps you steady yourself until you begin to shoot. Shooting is like opening a pressure valve, and fear, shock, cowardice, terror, panic itself begin to flow. And you feel strong and powerful, the bestial instinct fully awakened. All this happens unconsciously but also very fast. You move forward without thinking. Sometimes you shoot from a distance without anyone ordering you to, like something automatic. Then you feel the explosion and the hot shrapnel rains on your back. No one told you, no one gave an order, it's only your instinct fleeing from death. . . .

Twelve

Today I woke up thinking about the other. . . .

And the question I asked myself was: Why does the enemy fight us? What motivates him? The word *enemy* can have a broad meaning. He might be a class enemy, an ideological enemy, a political enemy. He might defend racist or fascist positions, ideas that belong to the past. Or not. He might think like most of us think and aspire to a life free from wars, where technology works for the human species and not the other way around, as it does now. He might be a progressive individual, a leftist obliged to fight us by circumstances, obliged to confront us, to be our enemy. Because war is filled with absurdities and the military system itself turns you into a robot. From one moment to the next you find yourself in combat without even knowing who you are fighting, or if you even care. The main thing is not to lose your life, not to give up your skull, as El Niño says. The enemy might also be the South Africans, who defend apartheid, racial segregation. It might be black people, who own these lands on one side of this war, or the whites who own it on the other but of course are better off. Or it might be those we are fighting now. It would be logical to imagine they're on our side, because we are defending justice for them. They are poor, almost miserable, have no education, many speak a language that isn't yet written, they've been exploited for centuries, their ancestors were slaves in our land, their natural resources have been taken by the great monopolies. Apparently the MPLA, who are our allies, want the best for them, for all of them, because you can count on the fingers of your hands the inhabitants of Cabinda who own something besides misery. . . .

Twenty-One

My people welcomed me home more or less as I expected them to.

When I got to the house the door was open. I went in and found Papá seated in an armchair reading the paper. He looked at me incredulously, got a strange expression on his face and shouted, "Woman, goddammit, bring me a handkerchief!"

Mamá wasn't as pathetic. She hugged me to her, her tears soaking my olive green shirt with its stench of a thousand pestilences.

"A bath!" I shouted. "Draw me a bath!" . . .

I'm home, but it's as if I haven't arrived. Darkness descends upon the trees in the yard and envelops me. Night comes on like fog, and I feel like a single step separates me from over there.

One of our own, who got home before I did, has been talking shit in the neighborhood. What can I say now? Will I speak about the times I was saved from dying like Chubasco? Will I tell about how they surrounded us at Alto Maiombe, about Buco Zau, about the fear and thirst and hunger? . . .

The war in Angola will go on for a long long time, because all wars are motivated by ambition, and unfortunately Angola has many natural resources, riches to be exploited by men who have never even seen Africa in the movies . . .

Many, the majority, talk about our noble mission, about the inhumanity of apartheid, about proletarian internationalism and the construction of socialism in Africa. Others, very few, ask if all that death and all that sacrifice were worth it.

What will happen with the passage of time? . . .

Twenty-Two

But it was all a dream.

Once more the soldier's imagination played tricks on him, this time definitively.

He couldn't get to Punta Negra, or return to Cuba. . . .

He didn't really suffer as he died. Submerged in a deep sleep he just went off and he left us his serene countenance, as if he was satisfied that it had all ended.

No one knew his name.

His dog tag was 28810.[1]

NANCY IN ETHIOPIA

More than half a million Cubans, out of a nation of eleven million, have gone on internationalist missions at some point in their lives. Men and women. Young people and retirees. They are carefully chosen in accordance with their will, expertise, psychological makeup, professionalism, other talents, stamina, and aptitudes for such missions. They go as teachers, doctors and other health professionals, military advisors and soldiers, and technicians in dozens of fields. They go not to earn the higher pay dangerous work may offer in many countries, but often without earning anything besides their meager home salaries. These days they are sometimes paid by the World Health Organization or another international body. Always their going involves sacrifices: leaving home and family, working in areas where poverty and disease may be rampant, taking on challenges that try the strongest and best prepared.

Leaders such as Fidel and Che, Celia Sánchez and Haydée Santamaría often spoke of internationalism, touting it as the highest revolutionary value. At home, work was never seen as drudgery, but always as privilege: the privilege of helping to create a new society. And this new society was not for the island alone, but something Cuba might help give the world.

It is enormously interesting—and a contribution to contemporary thought—that the Cuban Revolution made such a strong connection between the manual and the intellectual, the arts and the sciences, liberation and culture. In Cuban schools hands-on and theoretical work are combined to teach the student the value of both and what they mean to one another, how they interact. The Revolution's multidisciplinary approach to education, health care, and internationalist missions increasingly stresses the importance of the arts in conjunction with the social and hard sciences. And when Fidel spoke at Che's public wake, the "rank" he conferred upon his fallen comrade was artist.[1]

Nancy Alonso spent almost two years in Ethiopia, fourteen thousand kilometers from home, teaching physiology to students with whom she had to engage in a language foreign to them all. She is a physically small woman, endowed with an enormous spirit. Her tour of duty began in 1989, when Cuba had yet to feel the full effects of the Soviet Union's abandonment. She came home in 1991, to a country experiencing extreme scarcity and hardship difficult even for those who had previously endured three decades of privation.

In February 2016 in Havana Nancy told me how her internationalist mission to Ethiopia came about and some specifics of the experience:

I was a professor of physiology at the University of Havana's Medical School, and my dean asked if I would be interested in a stint at the Jimma Institute of Health Sciences, a teaching hospital in Ethiopia. Four years earlier Cuban collaboration had been involved with opening that institute. I said I would like to go. We continued to draw the same salary we were making in Cuba at that moment—they paid it to our families—and Ethiopia gave us a stipend of four hundred *bir* to cover our basic needs of food and clothing. We didn't pay for our lodging, electricity, or water, or for our yearly vacation in Cuba. Ethiopia gave the European professionals working there ten times what they gave us, that is four thousand *bir* a month, although the Europeans had to cover the costs of their yearly trips home.

We lived in a compound composed of ten houses, five on either side of a paved pathway. It was three hundred meters from the teaching hospital. There were thirty of us in the Cuban brigade at Jimma, and we had six of those houses. The Ethiopian administrators lived in another three (the director and assistant director of the institute and the chief of nursing), and a Canadian couple lived in the tenth. We called them *Water Supply*, because the man's job had something to do with the town's aqueduct. Each of those houses had three bedrooms, with two people in each. They also had common areas, such as a living and dining room, kitchen and bath. And in each house there was a local woman who helped with the domestic chores; we called them *mamitas*. The woman who lived in my house was Sahai, which means "sun" in Amharic. When we met she was eighteen, a single mother with an infant.

I wanted to know what a typical workday was like for Nancy.

I would get to my office before eight a.m. Two or three times a week I would meet with my students in the mornings, and once a week we had a seminar or practice session in the afternoon. When I wasn't teaching, I would spend my time at the office or at the institute's library, studying or preparing my classes. Midday I'd go back to the compound for lunch, and then I'd return to the hospital to spend time with the two Ethiopian professors who were my counterparts there. My job was to make sure they were current in subjects having to do with physiology and pedagogy. They gave lectures too, and I would attend those to get a sense of what they knew. They were the ones who would take our places after we returned to Cuba. The idea was always that the Ethiopians themselves would be able to take over when we left. I also spent some time designing teaching materials. It was hard work, made harder by the fact that we had to teach all our classes in English, and the materials we prepared had to be in that language as well.

I asked Nancy if she had been able to visit other parts of Ethiopia while she was there.

Only the capital, Addis Ababa, and the road between it and Jimma. For security reasons we Cubans weren't allowed to leave town. With Cuba's help the conflict with Somalia had just ended. But the country continued to be at war, on several fronts, with a number of guerrilla groups: the Eritreans, the Oromos, the Tigers, etcetera, all of them fighting President Mengistu Haile Mariam's army. And there were border problems with Sudan. The Sudanese government was fighting those who opposed the Ethiopians, and the Ethiopian government was fighting the Sudanese. Jimma was less than one hundred kilometers from the Sudanese border, and in a village just a bit closer to that border a small group of our people had been kidnapped. There were five of them, doctors and nurses. They took them into Sudan and demanded the liberation of Ethiopian political prisoners. The exchange never took place, but the Cuban group had a hard time of it. Coincidentally the head of that group, Humbertico, had been a student of mine in Cuba.

I asked, "What were some of the cultural differences you noticed between Ethiopians and Cubans?"

Ethiopians are very introverted, reserved. It's hard to know what they may be thinking, whether about a local situation or world affairs. But when you get to know them, they are very loyal and friendly. Compared to us, the difference is obvious: we are extroverted and talkative; when we've known someone for five minutes we already say we're friends. They speak in whispers. We shout. Although it took me a while, I got used to the spicy food, and came to like it.

"Anything else you can add?"

At the end of March 1991 all the country's universities closed in order for the students to join the army. Some of us—those who only taught classes—had no work then, while those who were doctors continued treating the population. At that time the Oromo front was advancing toward Jimma. When they were less than forty kilometers away, we received the order to evacuate to the capital. Our mission ended abruptly, and we'd all be returning to Cuba.

We knew the Ethiopians didn't want to see us go, so we planned to leave in the early morning hours. That day, when we emerged from our houses at three a.m., the compound was filled with dozens and dozens of people grieving our departure, bidding us farewell with tremendous love and gratitude. I'll always remember that scene.

You know, none of those internal wars had anything to do with us. Whenever a group of guerrilla fighters was going to occupy a village they always wanted the Cuban doctors to stay. It wasn't possible, because when the fighting began you couldn't know where the bullets would land or who might die. Before I got to Ethiopia, Cuban soldiers helped the Ethiopians contain the invasion from Somalia, and our caravans, which sometimes had to go through Eritrean territory, were never attacked. They always let them pass because the Eritreans didn't want the Somalia occupation either.[2]

Nancy's Ethiopian service would also have an artistic component, although this wouldn't become clear to her for a number of years. She went to Africa as a physiologist and came back as a physiologist and writer. She says she hoped to write a book of African stories, but after finishing three in-spired by her Ethiopian experience, the situation at home pushed her to write about Cuba instead. Still I sense that more of her African stories are waiting in the wings. Here is one that captures some of the dramatic issues that assaulted a Cuban woman in remote Ethiopia.

MAY ALLAH PROTECT YOU

The sound made me uneasy. I couldn't tell where it was coming from or what it meant. As it intensified I was able to make out that it was something like a song, or a man chanting a litany, and I felt a mixture of fear and intrigue. The unknown can seem threatening and attractive at the same time. As the voice filled the space around me, I could feel my ears tingle and my skin prickle. Curiosity gave way to fright. The sounds became more and more mysterious, in a language I couldn't understand. In spite of the darkness of the surroundings, I tried to get away and quickened my pace while trying not to give in to panic. I kept thinking to myself, "If I can't see *him*, he can't see *me*." And that conclusion sent me running toward a site where, to my surprise, the chanting was even louder.

I woke up with a start, all sweaty and not recognizing the room in the semi-darkness. Utterly strange moments like this one seemed to confirm my premonition that any day without warning we could be catapulted into another reality. And that reality would shatter our connection with routines that, whether happy or miserable, were at least familiar. In front of me and a little to the right, instead of the door to my room, was a chest of drawers with a mirror on the upper part. The hollow in the middle of the bed wasn't the right shape, and when I stretched out my arm I found only sheets and no evidence of my customary companion. As I was getting up and looking for my shoes, my feet touched the plush of an unknown rug. I searched in vain for the switch to turn on the lamp, and at that moment a light came on in my head. I was spending my first night in Ethiopia, in room 509 of the Africa's Hotel, more than fourteen-thousand kilometers from Cuba. I looked at the clock. It was five o'clock in the morning.

After I calmed down, I again could hear the plaintive voice of the dream. I went to the window but found no indication of the source of the strange song that surely was waking up the entire city. I had completely forgotten the presence of Rafaela, my roommate, who was sleeping on the other bed in the room, until she said: "It's nothing to be afraid of. What you're hearing is the Muslim call to prayer, calling the faithful to the first prayer of the day."

"What, they pray here in the hotel?"

"Of course not. They pray in a nearby mosque that has loud speakers."

Rafaela was a veteran and knew everything there was to be known about Ethiopia. After finishing her vacation time in Cuba, she was back to complete her last year of mission work. In Addis Ababa, we were waiting to depart for our work locales. She would go to Harare, toward the east, to continue her work as a pediatrician, while I would teach physiology in Jimma, in the southwest of the country.

That morning a group of us, the rookies, went out with Rafaela to walk toward the market near the hotel. As we entered a spacious avenue crowded with vendors, we came face to face with the mosque, an enormous temple with yellow painted walls that extended over an entire block. At the top were two blue domes with the Islamic symbol of a half moon above each one. The smaller dome topped the larger one because it was situated on a tower. I imagined a man high up in that spot at five in the morning calling the believers to unite in prayer to Allah.

The large door at the entry way allowed us to catch a glimpse of the interior courtyard that was as full of people as the market. At that point I determinedly invited my companions to go in and take a look, but Rafaela warned us: "Don't even think about it! Infidels are not permitted to enter the mosques."

"You mean I can't enter the mosque?"

"Not unless you can pass for Muslim . . ."

I remembered the movie *Yentl*, where Barbra Streisand disguises herself as a man so that she can attend a study center that's closed to women. I could see myself passing not as a man but as a Muslim woman covered with black veils. The problem would arise, however, when I was inside the mosque and would find myself obliged to participate in rituals completely unfamiliar to me.

Later on I found out that one could visit mosques by getting permission. The exception, I was told, was the Great Mosque of Mecca. No one would give a dime for the life of a nonbeliever who was found inside that mosque looking at the sacred stone. And even though I had never thought of going to Saudi Arabia, I was enraged by the exclusionary discrimination. It was another example of prejudice, and I had seen many in my lifetime, not to mention what I had suffered in the flesh. Right then I resolved to go to battle and see that mosque in Jimma, even if it meant I had to convert to Islam.

It didn't take long for me to realize that the challenges of my work in Africa went far beyond the goal of entering a mosque. In the classrooms of Jimma's Institute of Health Sciences, forty-eight demanding and stern judges were waiting for me. To establish effective communication with the Ethiopian students, I would need to overcome obstacles I had never faced before. My being a foreigner made for a certain distance between us and, what was worse, a lack of trust. For my students who were accustomed to pursuing cultural studies in English, my difficulties in expressing myself in that language might be taken as ignorance. For a woman in an African country with a strong Muslim influence, doors were not going to be opened, much less those of mosques, so that one might pray for a little tolerance. Besides, my diminutive stature ended up confirming my disadvantaged position for the majority of the students, with the possible exception of the three girls in the class.

I confess that my zeal to become as Ethiopian as possible began with purely professional motives. It was the best way to reach my students. But then the whole country began to fascinate me. A culture so different from mine challenged me with its secrets. Perhaps for this reason, I made a special effort to understand, from my stance as an inveterate atheist, the religiosity of the Ethiopian people. My efforts at assimilation were rewarded, and I saw more of Ethiopia as little by little the veils that covered its face were lifted.

I found out that half the population was Christian, belonging to the Coptic or Catholic churches, and that the other half adhered to Islam. Nonetheless in Jimma there were few Muslims, and in my class there were only four, one of whom was Jemal, head of the classroom and liaison with the professors. I was struck by the fact that such a leadership role was held by someone in the minority until I realized that Jemal was the most intelligent, most generous and most polite of the students. He simply was the best at everything.

One day at the end of class, I ventured to ask for Jemal's assistance to visit the town's mosque. And that young man, who was half as old as I and almost twice as tall, seemed genuinely pleased by my interest in his religion and promised to help.

From that moment on, Jemal became my teacher about Muslim customs. Thanks to him I learned how to recognize an Ethiopian Christian from a Muslim by their form of greeting. Christians shook hands or kissed on the cheeks, like the French do. Muslims embraced, lightly bumping shoulders—first the right one and then the left—or clasped right hands, palm to palm, allowing each hand to be kissed on the back. Whether for Christians or Muslims, the greetings were repeated as many times as the degree of acquaintance warranted.

From Jemal I learned that one of the Muslim obligations was to pray several times each day facing Mecca, which was located north-northeast of Jimma. With this piece of information, wherever I was in the town, I could orient myself geographically without a compass or an astral chart and know in which direction Cuba lay. All I had to do was to observe a Muslim praying and if I made a ninety-degree turn in relation to his position, I would be facing the Caribbean.

I ascertained that Jemal was not a very orthodox Muslim. He didn't pray five times a day, because that would have taken too much time away from his studies, not just the time it would take to say the prayers but also the time required for ablutions: he would have to wash his face, hands and feet before each session of prayers from the Qur'an.

For Ramadan, the month of fasting practiced by followers of Mohammed, there was no eating, smoking or even drinking water from daybreak until nightfall, as long as the sun shone, and I became worried observing the physical effects on *my* Muslims. By that time they were my students, *my* girls, *my* boys, *my* Christians and *my* Muslims. On the fifteenth day of the fasting, I happened to see them in a cafeteria at noon on a day when the sun was crackling hot and bearing down hard even on the sacred stone of Mecca. There they were eating vegetables and drinking cold soft drinks. To my surprise, Jemal just laughed and told me that surely Mohammed had never been in Jimma, nor had he had a professor like me who obliged her students to expend so much energy studying.

Every so often I would ask Jemal when we'd be able to visit the mosque, and he always responded with a smile and "Don't be in such a hurry, Professor, I'm working on getting permission."

In the mean-time I would gaze at the mosque from the outside. It was smaller than the one in Addis Ababa but equally enticing, and I had to control my impulse to simply cross the threshold of the main door and walk right in.

On the few occasions that I led Jemal to the thorny topic of the role of women in his religion, I sensed that he was not very orthodox in this regard either, although perhaps that was wishful thinking. I inquired about the same topic with my female students and they recounted tales of suffering in a country of brutal *machismo*. There was no difference between Christians and Muslims: all male Ethiopians looked down on women. Next to Jemal, nonetheless, they felt comfortable and not like fifth-class citizens.

From time to time, from my privileged position, I was a voice of retaliation, taking up the cause of my female students, and not missing an opportunity to highlight Rahel's intelligence, Alem's tenacity and Aida's beauty. After all, they were *my* young women. I could always feel Jemal's approval and solidarity in my little reprisals.

Toward the end of the course I'd begun to lose all hope of entering the mosque and had stopped asking Jemal how the request for a visit was going. On the day of the final exam, I took a Bible and read from Ecclesiastes the verse that says, "To everything there is a season, and a time to every purpose . . ." (3:1). I apologized to my Muslim students that I had not found a copy of the Qur'an in English, but in wishing everyone "God Bless you, both Christians and Muslims," I knew that Jemal understood, and I guessed that in his eyes there was a "May Allah bless you, Professor."

After the exam was over, Jemal told me very contentedly that they had authorized him to take me to the mosque. The appointed time was for the following day.

I could hardly sleep that night with the imminence of the long awaited visit before me. I could imagine it all: the solemn atmosphere of the temple and the satisfaction of the young man in being able to satisfy my request. I envisioned myself discovering one of the hidden faces of Ethiopia, one that I had made such an effort to see.

At the appointed time, Jemal arrived elegantly dressed. He was wearing a beautiful Muslim cap, and underneath his arm was a small rug for him to use while he prayed. At the break of dawn we were in front of the mosque, and I was astonished by the throngs of believers who were already filling the place. Jemal asked me to wait outside so that he could announce my presence. After a few minutes he returned, looking a little pale and nervous with the news that it would be impossible to enter the mosque that day. Seeing him so perturbed by the setback, I felt sorrier for him than for myself. I decided to go home and put behind me what had turned out to be an embarrassing moment for both of us.

As I had done so many times before, I held out my hand to say goodbye, but Jemal responded to the gesture by taking a step backward, as if he were afraid of me. At that moment fourteen centuries of Islam came crashing down upon me: the weight of traditions, the black garments, the veils and the humiliations endured by Muslim women everywhere. It made no difference that I was Jemal's beloved professor, the Cuban who wanted to be Ethiopian, and the one who had been at his side to teach and to learn. He hid his hands in the prayer rug and begged my pardon because he had already carried out his ablutions. If he touched a woman he would be sullied and have to repeat the cleansing. Thus I saw another side of the enigma that had stayed with me since the long-ago morning in Addis Ababa, the day when I first heard the mysterious sounds of the Muslim call to prayer and had wanted to enter a mosque.

Jemal made another gesture. With his foot he swept aside some pebbles on the ground, avoiding my look and perhaps feeling ashamed. I wanted to keep believing in him and I called out: "May Allah bless you, Jemal!" Although I was really thinking: "May Allah protect you, Jemal, from your own traditions."[3]

Much later, by then a consummate writer and in an interview for a Cuban book, Nancy spoke about her time in Ethiopia and its role in promoting a talent she hadn't previously explored. Here is a fragment of that interview.[4]

Interviewer: As a biologist, what made you begin to write stories, or to publish what perhaps had seemed like something more private?

Nancy: It's true, I graduated in the biological sciences, and until 1998 taught physiology at the School of Medicine. And for two years I was a professor at a medical school in Ethiopia. The time I spent in Africa was a powerful experience for me. I began writing letters to my friends and family, with my vision of that culture that was so different from ours. When I came home in 1991 several people, and above all Mirta Yáñez, told me my letters showed a talent for describing something beyond the purely circumstantial, and they encouraged me to try to write about my life in Africa. I resisted. The idea seemed absurd to me. How could I think of writing fiction when all I'd ever written were letters and professional articles?

Interviewer: It's true, then, you never wrote fiction before?

Nancy: Never. But Mirta kept insisting, and in 1994 I began to reread what I had sent back to Cuba. I began to revisit my own words, and to reawaken the details of my life in Ethiopia. Around that time Mirta showed me a book by Laidi Fernández de Juan, *Dolly y otros cuentos africanos* [Dolly and Other African Tales]. That book narrates her experience as a doctor in Africa. I told myself: these are many of the things I want to say. What could I possibly add? "Your point of view," Mirta told me.

That summer was the great exodus of the rafters.[5] I lived in Alamar at the time, right across from one of the piers from which so many people were leaving. And something unexpected happened. Because while I was thinking about Ethiopia and looking for a way to express that experience in writing, I wrote my first story almost at a single sitting. "El séptimo trueno" [The Seventh Thunder Bolt] is about the rafters, not about Africa. That was the first time in my life I'd written a piece of fiction, and it was unforgettable. I heard a voice dictating the story to me. Yes, what so many writers say: that's exactly what I felt.

Interviewer: Your first book of short stories, *Tirar la primera piedra* [To Throw the First Stone] came out in 1997, and it was a panorama of a number of social problems that emerged in Cuba during the 1990s. What spiritual, moral, and objective implications did that moment awaken in you for it to become such a central theme in your literature?

Nancy: As I said, the impetus for beginning to write was the 1994 crisis of the rafters. But the social problems and my concerns about them began much earlier.

I went to Ethiopia with the Berlin Wall standing and returned after its demise. That is to say, I belong to a group of Cuban internationalists who experienced that profound change far from home. We were many miles away when we heard what had happened in Eastern Europe and its repercussions in Cuba: that our markets were almost empty, that there was no gasoline, no buses, maybe the U.S. would invade us. In short, total catastrophe. My return was dramatic because of all the scarcity. But the worst thing was a deterioration of values which we know, if we are Marxists—and I continue to be one—is the result of such brutal economic change. Our society was far from perfect, and of course there was no way we could have imagined that sort of intense change wouldn't have consequences. The thing was, I thought it would take more time, and the deterioration of values was heartbreaking for me. The rafters were the last straw. After that first story, I wrote the others in less than a year. I felt a tremendous urgency to talk about what was happening.

I hope Nancy Alonso will write more African stories. Art is often so much more evocative than journalism or speeches or even our history books in transmitting complex events. And the experiences of Cubans on internationalist missions continue to be profound—and complex. Too often, because they are defined by values unfamiliar to most of us, they remain beyond our imagination's reach.

LAIDI IN ZAMBIA

Laidi Fernández de Juan is a medical internist, mother, prize-winning author, and internationalist. She spent two years (1988–89) practicing medicine in Zambia, and because she was already a writer it was logical that she would express that experience in two short story collections.[1] I began by asking Laidi the circumstances surrounding her decision to embark on an internationalist mission, where she was in her professional life at the time, and how Zambia came to be her destination.

> **Laidi Fernández de Juan:** I signed up on one of those lists where they were collecting the names of those willing to volunteer in countries that needed our humanitarian aid. In the context of those years—at the end of the 1980s—it wasn't unusual for a Cuban family to have one or several members who were about to go on a mission or were already offering their services in distant places. I was twenty-six years old when I decided it was time to share what I'd learned at the Piti Fajardo Medical School during my previous six years of study and practice. I'd been a model student. I'd graduated two years earlier, in 1985, with very high grades and the Gold Star distinction, all of which allowed me to choose my specialty.
>
> I immediately began my residency in internal medicine, which would take the next three years. Of my own volition I interrupted that specialization when I was just beginning the second year. I was an R-2 at the time, that is to say a second-year resident, when I got the news that I would be part of the

first Cuban medical brigade posted to the Republic of Zambia, in southern Africa.

I left on February 14, 1988, three months before my twenty-seventh birthday and two before I would have earned the degree of Specialist in Internal Medicine, Grade 1. For my two years there I was the only doctor who had completed his or her degree, and I was later designated floor chief at several Zambian hospitals located in the Copperbelt [Ndola and Kitwe]. I treated patients suffering from AIDS, tuberculosis, and malaria. I returned to Cuba in 1990, and after giving birth to my first child and reintegrating myself into my field by going back to work at the hospital where I'd graduated, I became a specialist in 1992.

Margaret Randall: Can you talk about internationalism in the context of the Cuban process? It seems to me to be an important principle of the Revolution. Its contours have changed somewhat over the years, but the number of Cubans working in different parts of the world remains extraordinary, especially when one compares that number with the size of the population as a whole. Can you tell me about how you see the phenomenon overall as well as what it has meant to you?

Laidi: For me, personally, having gone on that mission when I did was the most traumatic as well as the noblest experience of my life. I suffered as I never had before, and I learned that the suffering of others vastly outweighed my own. This taught me in one dramatic moment that the human condition is simpler when we all share the same helplessness and an identical fear of death. One's only advantage is the knowledge one possesses, and the only way of helping is by sharing that knowledge, putting it at the service of others without expecting anything in return. If I suffered like I never had prior to my African experience, I also gave more selflessly than I have since.

Margaret: As a woman, did you face any special challenges on your internationalist mission?

Laidi: As a woman, none. As a non-African, perhaps. It was understandably hard for my patients to accept that a white-skinned person with no knowledge of the local languages was there to help them and not to exploit the little they had. At the beginning it was difficult to establish relations of friendship, but little by little the cultural barriers broke down and I learned to speak like them, to cook what the women cooked, and sing (more or less) their melodies. And I hope I was able to achieve the miracle of being accepted as a member of the community.

Margaret: Forgive me for not having followed your writing career. Were you a writer before your experience in Africa or, as with Nancy Alonso, did you feel the need to write as a result of that experience? In either case, how did Africa affect your creative life? Was it really a "before" and "after"?

Laidi: Nancy Alonso has publicly stated that she began to write after reading my book *Dolly y otros cuentos africanos* [Dolly and Other African Tales] because it surprised her that someone had put on paper something that reflected her own experiences on that continent, and it made it possible for her to do the same with her time in Ethiopia. That "someone" was me, and I deeply appreciate my colleague's honesty.

In contrast, I've written all my life. I was in boarding school for six years, away from my family from the age of twelve to the age of eighteen, and during that time of my adolescence I wrote to my parents twice a week. Later, when I began studying medicine, I stopped writing for a while. But I started again during my twenty-four months in Zambia. I am drawn to the epistolary genre, although since I became what you might call a serious writer I haven't developed it much.

When I came home from Africa, my parents handed me the bundle of letters I'd written to them and suggested I turn them into a novel. They're both writers, but I didn't think much of the idea. Three years later *Dolly y otros cuentos africanos* was born, and from that moment on I haven't been able to escape the painful and exorcising joy that writing every day produces in me. I've enjoyed this literary fiesta for more than two decades now, and if the gods are merciful I'll continue to write as long as I live and my senses are alert. But I owe Africa much more than having made me the professional writer I am today. I owe it my having learned fundamental concepts I'm not able to reveal. At least not yet.

Laidi's story "Dearest" speaks powerfully of her Zambian experience.[2]

DEAREST

I

I finally got where I was headed. I'm so far away I can't say I've gone. Rather, I feel that I disappeared. If it wasn't like this (and only then) I'd take refuge in the possibility of immediate return, although it would be a difficult goal. Neither do I dare tell them I find myself (like the title of a Lobo Antúnez novel) in the butthole of the world. We were all conscious of how far away we would be, but time's labyrinth surpasses distances, and I have the impression of having moved beyond a dimension that belongs to transient time, not geodesic. I'm simply not among you now, and a proud shudder urges me to tell you this place overwhelms in every way, that I miss you painfully, and that I won't stop sending my circadian rhythm your way. This is how I carry you with me: in the infinite day to day, in the nostalgia of my pulse, in the shadow of a tree of forgetting whose branches I refuse to contemplate.

II

As always, I rise early. I must have been a lark in my bird life. In morning light, any landscape is more appealing. Here flowers are short-lived, most of them mauve colored. When they drop they create a matting upon which it is difficult to walk, as if they were reminding us they are the only proprietors of such furtive beauty. At this hour there is no odor. Nothing is contaminated, and I only occasionally hear unfamiliar sounds resembling women's songs. It must be true: there's not one thing in the world that isn't mysterious, as Borges said. I ask myself why I had to come to this place to discover that. I would like to communicate weighty stories, not these vacuous comments about flowers and longings, but for the moment I beg you to satisfy yourselves with the terrible reality of my orphan's gaze.

III

The grief of separation begins to leave its scars on me. I'd imagined I would be able to avoid that as I discovered the world made of lightning bolts in which I find myself, but there's no consolation possible. The word *ocean* doesn't make me happy, the word *soon*, the word *always*. Words begin to lose their meanings, and I am disgusted at the possibility of becoming a kind of subdued monster, an animal forced to breathe ashes. My fire of longing is so immense that I live within my effort to put it out. Better to assume an insect's watery and dispassionate gaze than to keep on battering myself with my memory of you. I will give up; I have no choice. From this moment on I will talk to you about ordinary subjects. For example, about the misery that surrounds us, the worms in the sores, the hollows in cheeks they call oris cankers.

IV

It may be that the highest form of misery is death. I want to speak to you about it today. Not the casual sort, but the daily one. Not that which happens when you least expect it, but the other. Tonight I have written the number thirty-three on the board where the day's events are recorded, under the heading *Passed away*. My hand didn't shake. I entered the number with an ordinary night's exhaustion, without allowing room for fear. Before sitting down to tell you I had just recorded the age of Christ, I suddenly realized that on this night thirty-three people ceased to exist. Six more than my own age and millions more than those who deserved to find refuge in Copperbelt's red earth. The funeral chants, because one hears them so often, are part of the landscape of this place. They are like timeless trills that announce nothing, nor do they provoke surprise. It is death herself who dominates them, arousing and stilling them as she will. One might almost say the chants are as expected as the fever, the lethargy of hunger and absence of hope. Perhaps tonight their tone is more intense, but I'm not sure. The sound of trees swaying in the breeze somewhat cushions the sound that emerges like birds from the throats of women who, kneeling down, seem to be begging the heavens for answers. Today, for the first time since we arrived, I looked in the mirror and asked myself how I could have been so selfish as to have told you this.

V

A member of the Maasai tribe brought me an unwrapped gift and for a long time waited for my reaction. We've known one another for several weeks and, as often happens, it was my shame that made me approach him. His earlobes hang to his shoulders, with holes so big they could accommodate a fist. I saw him walk by with that pride characteristic of faithful tribal people. With that arrogant look only they have, with their insistence on walking so slowly it seems they crawl. With the harmonious sway of arms of those who don't even hurry when faced with death. With the irritation on his face at having to walk on cement. That's how I met him several weeks ago.

"Who is that *kabualala*?" I asked Lufungulu. "Why the holes in his ears? Has he *tutuma*? Doesn't it look like he has *mpepo*? Will he answer me if I say *Toalá monana*?"

Good morning, he said, coming back to where I stood. *Let me explain that I am a Maasai. My ears are beautiful, like all the Maasai. Nice to meet you. I am Chief Chikola.*

I kept myself from falling to my knees. Completely ashamed, I put myself at his disposal. After a few weeks, he no longer needed my help and disappeared once more into the depths of what appears to be jungle. Today he returned just as I was heading out to visit a nearby village. *This is a present for you,* he said, and held out the day's newspaper. On the front page there is a photograph, the caption of which reads *Kenneth Kaunda said . . .* Like every day: nothing special. Determined not to go through another embarrassing encounter, I looked over at Lufungulo. I interpreted her gesture in time (at least I hope I did) and took the newspaper in my hands as if receiving a bouquet of poppies. Didn't I tell you that Borges was right about life's mysteries? What does one do in such utterly alien circumstances? For the moment, I keep this paper imprinted with news along with the other gifts I've accumulated: a carved cane, a drum without nails, and an ivory bracelet that is beginning to yellow.

VI

After many months without writing, here I am again. I've been moved and now live in a little house whose walls are covered with pictures of you. I feel as if I am surrounded by your rhythmic somnambulist peace. The faces I've most loved in my life are smiling at me, and there is no need to summon them. And so my nights pass: gazing upon the magical beauty of parents I might not have deserved. Despite my black mood, I feel that I've ceased to be completely foreign to this place. Now I am no longer upset by its cries, nor frightened by those sounds that emanate from its depths, nor am I permanently watchful for fear I will be bitten by a snake. It now seems natural to me that the rains last half the year, that light bulbs explode at dawn, that the mail is as erratic as it is expensive and useless, that my longing has given way to a strong will to remain alive. I have suffered two bouts of ma-laria, endowing me with the frivolous air of a survivor. Now I no longer count the days until I see you. I've learned that waiting for news is more painful than pretending to shorten the distance. I'm now able to do without dictionaries. I now know how to say what I must say without feeling ridiculous, do what I came to do without complaining, eat what everyone eats without worrying about such trivial things as a balanced diet. I still don't know how to produce sounds as if I were a bird, but I can dance to the rhythms of the local festivals, moving my hips like the women here do. I'm now able to walk kilometers, keeping my balance with a load on my head, cover myself with *chitendes*[3] more colorful than the rainbow and use san-dals as flat as the dirt paths. A bit of compassion keeps me from being completely calloused, but I'm not afraid. I am strong because I am older.

VII

I don't know when I became obsessed with writing. This little sheaf of news I've prepared, in case a messenger miraculously appears, is but a tiny sample. It consoles me to write irrationally. Knowing how implacably illogical my need to communicate is doesn't stop me at all. During the day my eyes take in everything that could be useful to me: wrapping paper, official bulletins, newspaper pages with empty spaces, the blank side of reports that nobody reads, the back sides of labels, notices that fall from the walls, envelopes, paper bags, proposals, the papers in which bars of soap are wrapped, magazine covers, lists of the dead, invitations to meetings and their minutes, cardboard egg cartons, paper flags. Discovering the broad world upon which I can write is fascinating. In any other circumstance I wouldn't have noticed. Once I have gathered everything that can bear the point of a pencil, I choose what I'll use according to my state of mind. And I give my nights over to the delight of speaking via calligraphic strokes. For fictional stories: newspaper pages, envelopes or bags. For describing what surrounds me: soap papers or lists of the dead. If I indulge in imaginary dialogues, usually brief: labels or proposals. For my darkest thoughts: egg cartons or magazine covers as a way of keeping myself concise, because it's so difficult to write on them.

The notices that fall from the walls and the blank sides of reports nobody reads are the best for writing plain and simple letters. Those that say I'll be leaving this place soon, and I'm amazed at how much I will miss it. The paper flags are ideal for recording my desires. I was never able to identify the countries they represent, so I might have told Switzerland, for example, that I wanted two sons when I grow up. Or Liechtenstein, may hunger disappear. Or Laos about my dream of returning the following morning. Who knows to which country I confessed which desire. There are two flags with lots of white space (maybe Japan and the Red Cross), and those I saved for my most elaborate longings. The ones about world peace, peace for everyone, peace in the morning, peace in the afternoon and peace at night. I haven't gone back and reread my notes because they're all packed now, but how we'll laugh about these things. And at the expressions on some people's faces.

VIII

The messenger never showed up for these brief letters. I carry the lot in my suitcase, although they are no longer necessary. You will have my voice, so you won't miss me anymore; you'll have me, so you will no longer feel my absence. It was hard to choose what to bring home with me. The pain of abandoning objects I treasured for twenty-four long months doesn't allow me to fully experience the satisfaction of the return upon which I embark today. I write you one last time as I wait to hear the loudspeaker call my name. In a few minutes I will put away my notes and submerge myself in the lethargy of the several means of transport I must take over the next two days. Right now I am sorry I left behind the pot in which I prepared *milimili*,[4] the curtain I made from a swatch of mosquito netting, the elephant-hair bracelet I left on the bathroom windowsill, the last orchid that bloomed in my garden, and the red monkey's foot key ring. They say that leaving things behind means you want to return. Who knows. I carry all the rest like proof that I haven't imagined these times: a drum, a cane, a newspaper, the yellow bracelet, photos of women friends, of the dead, of colleagues, of all the dear ones.

I imagine all of you, and start to laugh. If you think I will be the person who left, I should warn you of your mistake, although it may be too late. You won't be welcoming that plump young girl, eager and smiling, of whom you took leave, but a gray-haired woman who walks beneath the weight of a joy briefly delayed. Please don't feel sorry for me; I'm not returning from a punishment, but just the opposite. I'm not strong, just better. You'll see that I've learned fundamental things that would have taken centuries if I hadn't launched myself full force upon the road of distinguishing between what is futile and what is important. Between what is possible and what is unobtainable. Between what is justice and what is fair. Between good and bad, us and the enemy. Between sky and sea. There's no better place than the Copperbelt for these elemental lessons. It's almost a shame they are already announcing my first flight.

Only almost.

EDUCATING NEW MEN
AND WOMEN, GLOBALLY

It goes without saying that education is the basis for raising a country's cultural level, making new achievements possible, and broadening the opportunities for individuals to reach their potential and excel in their chosen fields. Educated people are able to think more critically, and they tend to raise their children to value knowledge—not to accept platitudes or half-truths at face value—and to rise above base instincts and question decisions about the issues that affect their lives.

What does educating a people mean? Can it really mean building an excellent educational system across the board, making it possible for people in all areas and of all classes to get the education they deserve? What, in fact, has happened to class divisions in Cuba?

Although the Revolution has not been able to erase class privilege to the extent hoped, and the distance between those who have more and those who have less sadly has grown in recent years, it has managed to develop the right to a free and excellent education for all its citizens. This has been no small feat.

Educating people in Cuba does not mean putting funding into a few show institutions while abandoning those who live in areas with a low tax base, which is what so often happens in the United States. How important is choice? Is it to the advantage of students to be able to choose between public and private schools, as they do here? And what about charter schools? As good as these have been at providing a better education for some, doesn't their very existence make for an uneven system, limiting the possibility of decent schooling for all?

As with health care, overall excellence in education is only really achievable in a universal system. This is the direction Cuba has taken. In Cuba people understand the social and political forces at work and the interests they represent. They are conscious of what's going on in the rest of the world and can evaluate their place in it.

An overall high level of education has also contributed to Cubans' understanding that they are part of a larger world, that their political system gives them a framework in which to help others achieve the social gains they have prioritized, and to get behind the internationalist commitment that has been such a pillar of their revolutionary process. Conversely, when a government wants to control its population it weakens public education, shifting the emphasis from critical thinking to rote mimicry. Schools in disrepair, poorly paid teachers, an exaggerated emphasis on testing, an overblown sense of patriotism, and overriding social hypocrisy replace the joys of learning.

As I've noted, the Cuban upper-middle class and bourgeoisie had a privileged educational level before 1959, especially compared to other Latin Americans. Not so the laboring classes, peasantry, or those living outside four or five urban areas. In the remote reaches of the eastern mountains and tobacco fields of the west, school attendance was minimal. It is estimated that a mere 50 percent of Cuban children were able to study. Cubans were also overly influenced by popular culture and propaganda from the United States, their most powerful neighbor.

Without a doubt the Revolution's first great effort was aimed at eradicating illiteracy. According to United Nations figures for 1959, Cuba's prerevolutionary literacy rate was between 60 and 76 percent. But these numbers differed dramatically from city to countryside. In 1959, in a population of 5.5 million, 23.6 percent of those older than fifteen were illiterate. And there was a serious countryside-city divide: literacy among city dwellers was 89 percent, compared to only 58.3 percent in rural areas. This meant urban and rural Cubans hardly knew each other; they had little in common, and only a vague idea of how the other half lived or the daily problems they faced.

Educational reform was part of the July 26 Movement's program from the beginning, outlined in great detail in Fidel Castro's defense speech at the Moncada trial. Clearly the first task was to bring basic literacy to every citizen. It is rumored that Che Guevara was the one who suggested to Fidel that 1961 be called the Year of Education. We know he was concerned that the soldiers under his command—often young peasants who hadn't had the opportunity of going to school—learn to read and write; he taught some of them himself.

Throughout 1960 studies were undertaken and an organizational model for a far-reaching literacy campaign devised. The core participants in what would be one of the largest and most successful literacy campaigns anywhere were the *brigadistas*, young people (many of whom skipped school for a year) who did the teaching. Overall there were four categories of involvement. The first was the Conrado Benítez Brigade, made up of 100,000 volunteers between the ages of ten and nineteen who went out for the greater part of 1961 to live and work among students who ranged from young men and women to centenarians. During the day they labored alongside their hosts, usually in the fields. This enabled them to better understand the lives of toil and privation faced in remote regions of the country. It also encouraged their students to respect those who had given up a year of comfortable city life in order to come and teach them. The brigadistas held their classes at night. The disruption of the traditional academic calendar was such that an alternative calendar was established for eight months of 1961.

The second category was the People's Literacy Teachers. These were adults who volunteered to go out each day to teach in the cities or towns. Thirteen thousand factory workers held after-hour classes for their illiterate coworkers. The third group was the Homeland or Death Brigade, composed of fifteen thousand adult workers who were paid to teach in rural areas while their coworkers filled in for them on the job, keeping production at reasonable levels. And the fourth group was the Schoolteacher Brigades, fifteen thousand professional teachers who oversaw the campaign's technical and organizational aspects.

The government provided teaching supplies to all volunteers and literacy workers who traveled to rural locations. Each received a standard gray uniform, warm blanket, hammock, two textbooks (*We Shall Read* and *We Shall Overcome*), and a gas-powered lantern so that lessons could be held after the long day of field work ended in areas that did not yet have electricity. Most of the brigadistas must have brought their own notebooks or diaries as well, in which to record experiences that changed their lives. A half century later stories written by the light of oil lamps after a long day's work are still being retold to children and grandchildren. Without a doubt, having been a literacy teacher remains a definitive moment for tens of thousands of Cubans.[1]

Throughout 1961 there were many incidents of counterrevolutionary terrorism, especially in some of the country's remote rural areas, such as the Escambray Mountains.[2] The counterrevolution attacked the campaign as it would subsequently attack other progressive efforts, always hoping to discourage and destabilize support for the Revolution. These were particularly cowardly and heinous crimes, aimed at young people involved in selfless work. Conrado Benítez was a young teacher murdered in the campaign's first days; his name was immediately given to its most visible teaching contingent.

Apart from these dangers, and despite the fact that many Cuban parents resisted allowing their teenage daughters to spend months away in remote parts of the country, cut off from home, and subjected to illness, precocious sexual activity, or counterrevolutionary terrorism, the revolutionary leadership managed to instill the confidence, skill, courage, and exuberance that got the job done. On December 22, 1961, hundreds of thousands of brigadistas marched euphorically into Havana's Revolutionary Square, carrying giant cardboard pencils and chanting, "Fidel, Fidel, tell us what more we can do!" Fidel's response was "Study, study, study!"

The educational materials used in the campaign stressed the new values the Revolution hoped to instill. Some criticized those materials, claiming they were politicized. Of course they were. All such materials, no matter where they come from, reflect the ideology of those who produce them and thus are politicized in one way or another. But how refreshing the contents of the Cuban workbooks were. Rather than push ideals of national superiority, vain competition, and consumerism, they disseminated knowledge of history and a sense of national pride, justice, and fairness. One of the workbooks posed the following problems:

1. A family's bill for electricity used to be eight dollars monthly, and after the reduction in rates ordered by the revolutionary government it is three dollars less. What is the family's present monthly expenditure for electricity?
2. The Revolution is promoting the raising of goats in the mountainous regions of Cuba in order to increase dairy production. If one goat gives six liters of milk every day, how many liters will four goats give?
3. Cuba's first city and capital was Villa de la Asunción de Baracoa, founded by Diego Velázquez in 1512. How many years ago was that ancient Cuban city founded?[3]

Even back then interest in the rest of the world was on Cuba's educational radar. The literacy materials not only taught those learning to read and write some Cuban history but provided knowledge about other countries with questions such as the following: "The Popocatepetl volcano in Mexico is 5,450 meters high and the Orizaba volcano, which is the highest mountain in that country, is 300 meters higher. What is the elevation of the highest mountain in Mexico?"[4]

In addition to its basic educational achievements, Cuba's literacy campaign also brought important advances in gender equity. This was as true for those, mostly from the cities, who went out to teach as it was for those, mostly in the countryside, who learned. Those who designed the campaign could easily have followed the trend of the times, sending only young boys to the most out-of-the-way and dangerous areas to face the most difficult physical challenges. Instead they enlisted both genders on equal terms. Many young female brigadistas reported having experienced their first menstruation in a rural setting far from home; they became women as they labored on an equal footing with their male comrades.

For peasant women, learning to read and write opened unexpected doors. Many went on to acquire higher educational levels, and their studies put them on a more equal footing with men. This can be seen in their later integration into the country's salaried labor force. In 1959 women made up only 12 to 15 percent of Cuba's economically active population. Most were teachers, nurses, and domestic workers; their numbers among professionals were minuscule. Prostitution was also widespread, with between 90,000 and 100,000 women forced to sell their bodies for a few pesos in a population of six million. Ninety-five percent of these prostitutes came from the countryside.

In the Revolution's first twenty years the female workforce more than doubled. Access to birth control and abortion was eased, day care centers and workers' dining halls were established, women were able to exercise more real choices about their lives, and the fertility rate dropped to approximately half its prerevolutionary level. By 1981 nearly 60 percent of urban women between twenty and forty-five worked outside the home; surprisingly the percentage was even higher for rural women. Between 1970 and 1981 the proportion of city women of childbearing age with a secondary education had doubled, from 30 to 61 percent. And these achievements have held steady through subsequent years. Over 400 million women in the world today are illiterate, but not one is Cuban. Over 100 million children don't begin primary school; none is Cuban.[5]

As an interesting footnote, the Cuban literacy campaign also claimed its oldest successful student, a daughter of slaves who learned to read and write at the age of 106. Although it is doubtful that she was able to continue on to further study, the fact that she wrote her name for the first time at that advanced age was a powerful symbol of female tenacity and determination, an example of what is possible when an entire nation gets behind such an effort.[6]

In the years to come Cuba extended the lessons learned in that first successful endeavor to follow-up educational programs, building and staffing schools, and improving the quality of education. The first great push was for every school-age child to be able to study; numbers were more important than curricula. I lived in Cuba during those first years, and my children's elementary education suffered from some of the weaknesses endemic to the times: teachers who were very young and not well-trained, with considerably more enthusiasm than expertise. Following the victory of 1959 many teachers from the upper and upper-middle classes left the country, and the Revolution had to scramble to make up the deficit. The United States encouraged this exodus, hoping through its concerted brain drain to make the Revolution's educational goals less achievable.

I remember my son, nine at the time, telling me about his homeroom teacher. The young man was fourteen, and doing his absolute best to control and teach twenty-eight students only five years younger than himself. One day he warned his charges that masturbating would burn their brain cells; he'd no doubt been told this by his parents. When a few days later my son brought him a library book discrediting the "theory," he was as relieved as the rest of the class. On another occasion he described an incident in which a teenage teacher berated his entire class for some infringement of rules by calling the students *crepúsculos*. He had searched his own vocabulary for the vilest rebuff he could think of. *Crepúsculo* means "twilight."[7]

Those stopgap teachers of the Revolution's first years were extraordinary. They completed four-month courses to minimally prepare them for the classroom. They were among tens of thousands of anonymous heroes and heroines. Happily they were replaced as soon as possible by teachers with greater preparation, and eventually by those who had earned rigorous five-year teacher-training degrees.

When I was in Cuba in 2011, as a judge at the Casa de las Américas literary contest, I received an unexpected phone call in my hotel room. The caller told me she had been my daughter Sarah's third-grade teacher and had never forgotten that "smart sweet little girl who taught me so much!" The teacher, long since retired, said she remembered one day when the lesson was on the Bay of Pigs invasion. She noticed that Sarah was crying. "What's wrong?" she asked. Sarah vehemently defended the people of the

United States, saying it was only the government that was interested in attacking the Revolution. My caller said she'd incorporated the distinction into her teaching from then on.

By the time my children reached high school and university the quality of education had improved immensely. Advisors from a number of countries had been called in to help develop curricula, which Cuba adapted to its cultural and political requirements. After a couple of decades educational reach and quality were equally high. Today data from the UN Program for Development show that illiteracy has all but been eliminated on the island. Among Cubans twenty-five and older the average educational level is 11.5 years. It is expected that this number will soon be 13.8 years (approximately the second year of university). Out of a current population of 11.25 million there are more than a million university graduates.

It's not always possible to offer meaningful comparative educational data by country, because such data are often given in terms of how much is spent on each child, and what money means in one national context may differ dramatically from what it means in another. Additionally how funds are deployed is as important as how much is spent. For example, in the United States a great deal of money goes into administration at all levels, designing and manufacturing tests, and so forth; a school district may spend a lot on education even as its schools remain run down, its teachers are poorly paid, and its graduation rate is appalling. The most relevant figures I have been able to find indicate that Cuba spends roughly 18.7 percent of its gross domestic product on education, compared with 5.7 percent in the United States.[8] In absolute terms (amount of money spent per student), the United States is almost always at the top of the international list, but that figure is misleading and the results of the expenditure disappointing because our students do less well in almost every category than those in the other developed countries. Nor do such figures reflect the differences: the horrible physical plants, overcrowded classrooms, racist warehousing, and lower expectations suffered by children of color and poor children in so many U.S. inner-city ghettoes. Although residual racism persists in Cuba, the elimination of the institutionalized variety means that all Cuban children receive the same education.

My son Gregory and oldest daughter, Sarah, both won places at the Lenin School, at that time a showcase among Cuban high schools. The Lenin was a boarding school on the outskirts of Havana. It had the best of everything. Admission depended exclusively on previous grades and a desire to attend. Those who studied at the Lenin during my son's and daughter's years there included students whose parents were in prison for political crimes as well as those whose parents were part of the revolutionary leadership. Eventually similar schools sprang up across the country; they remain the flagships of Cuban education. And of course every facet of this education is free, from uniforms, food, and textbooks to the beautiful physical campuses with their cutting-edge laboratories and state-of-the-art sports facilities.

The Cuban Revolution's great emphasis on education brought with it the realization that once it had filled domestic teaching positions, the country could export teachers. Teacher training programs soon graduated many more than those lost through emigration, and once the teacher deficit disappeared, contingents began going overseas. Thousands of Cuban teachers continued to receive their home salaries while serving in nations such as Nicaragua, where liberation movements had been victorious, the language was the same, and eradicating illiteracy and extending opportunities to remote areas became priorities. My youngest daughter Ana's fifth-grade teacher labored for a year in that Central American country. Upon her return she told moving stories of makeshift rural schools with students as eager to learn as those in Cuba had been during the 1961 literacy campaign. She talked about teaching one group of students beneath a tree; they didn't even have the most rudimentary classroom. She had been born long after her country's literacy campaign was history, and this was her opportunity to experience similar sacrifice and satisfaction.

In 2014, interviewing one of Haydée Santamaría's nieces for my book about the heroine, she too mentioned her time as an internationalist teacher in Nicaragua. She told me she had been facing some difficult personal issues at home and didn't know if she wanted to accept the mission. Her aunt told her, "This is your Moncada. You must go and do your best."[9]

These overseas aid workers can be distinguished from their U.S. counterparts in a number of ways. In the first place, their services are never imposed; they respond to an invitation from the country in question. Second, and more important, Cuban overseas personnel in every field are careful to respect local culture, customs, and politics. They don't gather data that will later be used to exploit the lives of their students or patients. They are not there to advertise Cuba's political system but simply to teach or heal. Their moral and political values are implicit in their willingness to go to the most inhospitable places and do the hardest jobs. Their sacrifice and compassion have earned them praise everywhere.

Cuba has placed special emphasis on literacy as the necessary first step toward further education. The country's successful 1961 campaign received international recognition. Based on this, other countries looked to Cuba for help in the area. In 1995 Niger requested Cuban assistance to combat its very high illiteracy rate (over 50 percent). Cuba proposed a program delivered by radio. Niger's president was killed, however, before the new approach could be implemented, so it was tried out instead in Haiti and Nicaragua. This was five years later, in 2000. Originally developed in Spanish, the program was called Yo sí puedo (Yes I Can). It has now been translated into many other languages, including Portuguese, English, Quechua, Aymara, Creole, and Swahili. It is the cornerstone of Cuban overseas educational efforts and a model for people around the world. As of this writing the program has enabled more than six million people in twenty-nine countries to read and write.[10]

The Cuban pedagogue Leonela Relys Díaz developed Yes I Can. She was born in Camagüey in 1947 and was fifteen when she took part in her country's great literacy campaign. It was the experience that would direct her life's work. In 1964 she graduated from the Antón S. Marenko Teaching Institute with a degree that enabled her to work at the primary school level. She participated in several of the Revolution's early dynamic educational programs, among them the night school for domestic workers and a soils and fertilizer school for those in the Sierra Maestra who lacked the appropriate schooling to make their farming more effective. From those early experiences Relys Díaz moved on to instruct teachers, and eventually into positions where she would be called upon to analyze existing educational methods and design creative alternatives. In 1999 she left what she was doing in order to give her full attention to developing a literacy project in Haiti. It was carried out in Creole, disseminated by radio, and proved enormously successful. Relys Díaz also designed the intensive training undergone by all the Cuban teachers involved in the program. By 2001 they had met their Haitian goals.

It was in Haiti that Relys Díaz prepared the first materials for what would later become Yes I Can. As with all Cuba's aid programs, care is taken to respect and preserve local traditions and customs. Native facilitators are trained on site, and they help develop the teaching materials most appropriate to their culture and circumstance. Yes I Can classes are convened by members of the community. They are organized around a discussion topic, which introduces a key letter or word. The facilitator uses a series of prerecorded classes, usually on DVD, and an accompanying workbook. The DVD depicts a small literacy class in which the teacher explains the lesson and exercises, and the students in the film ask questions and make comments.

Watching the video encourages local students to do the same. The facilitator can stop and start the DVD to allow students time to complete the exercises or discuss particular points or to repeat sections if necessary.

Yes I Can has an introductory lesson block designed for people with no prior reading or writing experience, which includes exercises to practice holding a pen and forming simple shapes. Where participants already have some literacy skills, these initial lessons can be skipped. In later classes students work with more complex texts and learn other aptitudes, such as how to fill out forms with basic personal data. They are considered to have successfully completed the program when they can write a simple letter to a friend that includes both description and opinion.

A 2006 UNESCO review of Yes I Can noted strong commitment on the part of local facilitators, but also some problems of consistency. UNESCO's main criticism was that those doing the instruction were facilitators rather than experienced teachers. It goes without saying that for those who have gained rudimentary literacy through such a program, it is up to the country in question to implement follow-up courses in which people can convert basic literacy into ongoing education.[11] Cuba's 1961 campaign was followed by a massive effort to get every adult to acquire a sixth-grade education. Later the goal was a ninth-grade education. For this degree of attention to overall learning a nation must be deeply committed to facilitating meaningful education to all its citizens. To date we have seen this commitment truly prioritized only in countries with some elements of a socialist system.

A particularly interesting aspect of Yes I Can is its alphanumeric approach, which uses a knowledge of numbers to develop a knowledge of letters. It was believed that among illiterate people numbers are more familiar than letters in everyday life. In this approach the vowels, a, e, i, o, and u, are associated with the numbers one to five, and the consonants are associated with numbers that roughly correspond to their frequency of use.

In 2003 Yes I Can was launched in Guinea-Bissau, and for the first time classes were carried out via television.[12] Between 2003 and 2005 it was implemented in Venezuela, where 1.5 million people completed the program. In 2005 the country declared itself an illiteracy-free territory. Hugo Chavez's government followed up by greatly increasing primary school access and instituting other educational reforms.[13] In East Timor the program was begun in 2006, when twelve Cuban literacy advisors arrived in the country, and by the end of the following year literacy classes had commenced in more than four hundred communities. The first materials were printed in Portuguese but soon translated into Tetum, the most widely spoken of Timor's many languages. By 2012 all thirteen districts of East Timor had been declared free of illiteracy.[14]

Between 2003 and 2007 Yes I Can was adopted in Aotearoa, New Zealand, as part of the Maori-led Te Wananga O Aotearoa initiative. Cuban educators worked with their Maori counterparts on a diagnostic stage which resulted in the development of a program appropriate to Maori culture.[15] In 2012 Australia entered into a formal licensing agreement with Cuba, enabling the country's first Yes I Can pilot project. A version of the Cuban program has been implemented since 2007 in Uruguay, where it has enjoyed widespread success.[16] Guatemala adopted the program the same year, and almost twenty thousand people have learned to read and write with its methodology.[17] In Angola 300,000 have benefited.[18]

Illiteracy exists, of course, even in the developed countries. Yes I Can is currently being implemented in Seville, Spain, its first European adaptation.[19] And in the United States the Latino Alliance for Literacy Advancement in my own state of New Mexico initiated four pilot sites in 2015.[20]

To my mind a particularly Cuban contribution to adult literacy lies in its sociopolitical concept. In the Yes I Can method low literacy is not seen as an individual problem but a social one, the solution to which requires a community-wide approach. In relation to this aspect of the campaign, UNESCO has noted that the program "is in fact more than a method. It would be more appropriate to understand it as a literacy training model that goes beyond processes, materials, strategies, etc., as it includes, both explicitly and implicitly, concepts of literacy training, learning, life skills and social mobilization, and involves a wide range of actors with various roles, from the beneficiaries of the literacy training to other stake holders such as state entities and other concerned institutions."[21] In 2006 UNESCO's King Sejong Literacy Prize was awarded to Cuba's Latin American and Caribbean Pedagogical Institute for developing and disseminating Yes I Can. In 2012 the Institute received the Mestres 68 Prize.[22] Leonela Relys Díaz died of cancer in 2015.

In Havana in February 2016 I was able to interview Osvaldo Lara Cruz, whose vast experience in educational internationalism is no less interesting.[23] Lara was Relys Díaz's supervisor; together they brought reading and writing to a number of countries, including Mexico, Haiti, and Venezuela. Lara is a large man with a broad smile and gentle manner. He was both eager to share his history in promoting Cuba's adult literacy program and still so emotionally involved that at times the memories seemed to overcome him.

My involvement with literacy began when I was a boy, in 1960. I was eighteen when the call went out for what was to be the advance contingent in our own literacy campaign the following year. I had to ask my parents for permission. They gave it, but told me to think about what I was getting myself into. They didn't want me turning back.

Those first brigadistas had to find a company willing to sponsor them. I went to the Zenith Radio company outlet and explained the mission. The manager said he'd call his employees together so I could explain it to them as well. The company ended up sponsoring me, and even sent two employees with me into the Sierra Maestra mountains; they donated a generator plant, a television, a radio, and an electric mixer—things no one there had ever seen before.

Lara smiled as he recalled:

The first time I gathered a group of peasants from the area to watch TV, I had a remote control hidden in my hand. Those were the first remotes, unusual at the time. I asked them if they liked the program, and when one of them said, "Not so much," I "told" the television to show us something else. Those people were amazed.

Lara's experiences in the Cuban literacy campaign would determine his life's work. He went on to help design and manage Yes I Can as it evolved through a number of different iterations in dozens of countries. He shared problems and challenges along the way, such as designing the Haitian program in French before realizing that Creole is the language spoken there, and meeting with Catholic bishops in Mexico to (successfully) convince them that the program designed for that country was not a purveyor of materialistic ideology. His description of the work in Mexico was particularly interesting:

We didn't look at the illiterate person as worthless, the way he was too often seen by the rest of society. We stressed his knowledge of the seasons, crops, traditional medicine—all the wisdom that comes from that way of life. In our TV spots and other forms of outreach we said that the only thing the illiterate farmer was missing was that one little detail: how to read and write. This proved to be enormously important in terms of self-esteem.

UNESCO requires that illiteracy in a country or portion of a country be reduced to less than 4 percent for the program to be considered successful. Although we worked in many parts of Mexico, we only achieved this percentage in the state of Michoacán, where we went into the most remote areas. When we started, there was 45 percent illiteracy among the 400,000 inhabitants spread over thirteen different municipalities. It took us months to finish our work there. Today we are able to teach a person to read and write in between three and four months.

I can't tell you how grateful people are when you bring the light of literacy to them. In Mexico everyone respected the Cuban teachers, even in some of the mountainous regions controlled by the drug cartels. Our people would be riding a bus stopped by bandits, where they made everyone get off, including the driver. They'd line them up and take their money and valuables. But when our teachers opened their mouths, and the bandits realized they were Cuban, they exempted them from their criminal demands. It was embarrassing—mortifying even—for those teachers; they didn't want to be singled out that way. But the respect was overwhelming and came from all quarters.

Cuba continues to offer this literacy program to the international community and has suggested that with its implementation illiteracy could be eradicated globally within ten years at a relatively modest cost of approximately $1.5 billion. Will the international community consider such an investment? Probably not. It seems much more important to those who control this level of funding to spend it on conquest, death, and destruction. I can point to other mass educational programs that have failed to achieve worldwide implementation. One originated in the United States, a country equipped to make technology available while Cuba still focuses on the ability and willingness of human beings to make the difference.

In the early 2000s an MIT professor named Nicholas Negroponte spent some time in a remote Cambodian village, where he realized that if every child had access to a computer an enormous unrealized potential could be unleashed. That's where he got the idea for One Laptop per Child (OLPC). He and his colleagues began working on the development of a rugged, solar-powered computer that uses a flash memory instead of a hard drive. Negroponte's dream was that virtually every country would buy into his idea. He would be disappointed.

A number of ways to distribute the initiative were tried, but in most cases each one of the plastic-encased computers could be obtained for between one and two hundred dollars. This would seem to be a minuscule outlay when compared with expenditures in so many other areas. Still the world has mostly failed to adopt the program. There are several reasons for this. One may in fact be the cost. For a developing country, even at such bargain prices, outfitting every child is a challenging goal. Another may be cultural relevancy: some African educators have said that the program is too rooted in U.S. values to be appropriate for their youth. Others have questioned issues of security and control. Nigeria began to buy into the program, but said it found child pornography was involved, and withdrew. Our competitive free market system has also created some unexpected glitches: giants such as Microsoft have tried to capture OLPC's software market and have been accused of subverting the original idea. I believe that any program aimed at providing an education to the 900 million children who do not have access to school is ultimately just too frightening to those who profit from keeping masses of people in ignorance.

Yet a few countries have adopted OLPC. Uruguay was the first and so far only nation to document its purchase of a full order. In 2007 it imported 100,000 laptops, and by the fall of 2009 had completed their distribution. In 2008 the much smaller South Pacific island nation of Niue also claimed to have fully implemented OLPC. The Republic of Nagorno Karabagh launched a pilot OLPC program in 2012. Inside the United States, Birmingham, Alabama, got on board in 2010. Most of these places have reported problems. Even Uruguay, after several years of the program, has not yet recorded great educational benefits. I spoke with a university professor there who told me that expecting an immediate learning improvement isn't even reasonable, but that there are other ways of measuring its success. There has been a marked uptick in social inclusion, he said: members of rural families now apply for courses online and fill out paperwork that once required them to travel long distances to municipal or federal offices. Some students have learned to write software programs, a few even winning internships in programs offered by NASA.[24] Where teachers are able to teach via computer, educational strides have been made. The results obtained through One Laptop per Child have moved Uruguay's president to initiate a program of distributing free digital tablets to all elderly people with limited income. The follow-up must be a global will to prioritize a level of use that would enable all peoples to become agents of their futures.

Teaching literacy is the first step toward teaching basic knowledge, personal and collective history, world events, and critical thinking. The dominant governments understand all too well how dangerous this would be. But Cuba, drawing on its human resources rather than technological invention, has continued to send teachers around the world, often to areas where local educators refuse to work. Some of these teachers continue to volunteer their labor; in countries that are able to pay, their salaries fall far short of the gift they give. Through Yes I Can millions have embarked on the first step toward acquiring an education. The Cuban Revolution's ingenuity and solidarity in this arena is astonishing.

CUBAN HEALTH CARE
A MODEL THAT WORKS

I went to live in Cuba in 1969. I had resided in Mexico for the previous eight years and had four young children and a partner, Robert Cohen, another U.S. poet I'd met a little over a year before. The circumstances of our arrival were complicated; I'd participated in the 1968 Mexican student movement and been forced into hiding by the government repression that crushed it. I'd visited Cuba twice before my definitive move and admired the Revolution. In that difficult personal time the country represented a welcome safety net, but we didn't really know what to expect of life under socialism.

As a family our immediate medical needs were pretty dramatic. My youngest daughter, Ana, was only three and a half months old. Because of having to send her off with her brother and sisters, I had to wean her in a day. She needed everything, from emotional reassurance to a complete physical checkup. My daughter Ximena, who was four at the time, had suffered from an ear infection almost since birth. She needed a complex operation to close and reconstruct the membrane of her eardrum. I arrived on the island exhausted and ill; soon I would discover I had a severe kidney problem and one of my kidneys would have to be removed. Not long after that my partner developed a case of hepatitis serious enough to hospitalize him for a couple of weeks.

I remember being told I would have to lose my kidney and immediately thinking I should get a second opinion. This is what I would have done in my native United States or in Mexico. But when I asked my doctor about this, my question seemed to perplex her.

So I called a friend. He explained, "By the time you receive such a diagnosis here, your case has already been discussed by a panel of specialists. Unless such an operation is absolutely necessary, no doctor would prescribe it, nor would a hospital make one of its precious beds available." I went into the operation convinced it was what I should do, received excellent care throughout, and have never regretted it.

We had been saving for Ximena's operation all through the previous year. For it to take place, her ear needed to be infection-free for a certain length of time. A few wayward drops of bath water, her natural desire to join her siblings in a friend's swimming pool, and my precarious political situation kept getting in the way. By the time we got to Cuba her predicament was dire. Ximena was soon in the care of a Cuban ear, nose, and throat specialist who took a liking to her. In fact he and his wife became our friends. This doctor announced that we were in luck: a Czechoslovakian surgeon who had developed a special technique for dealing with just such a problem as my daughter had was in the country at the time, teaching the procedure to Cuban specialists. He would perform the operation.

It didn't turn out to be that straightforward, however. My daughter was tiny, and an anesthesiologist had to be found who was willing to put her out for the considerable number of hours the operation would take. Once one was on board, a less medically centered issue arose. Ximena woke up one morning with a bad case of head lice; it wouldn't be possible to operate until they were eradicated. Poor Ximena had to have her head shaved. I still remember the variety of whimsical hats nurses and other hospital personnel brought to her room.

Finally it was a go. The operation lasted close to nine hours and succeeded beyond our wildest dreams. The Czechoslovakian surgeon had invented a procedure that used the patient's own tissue to repair the eardrum. He told us he would save Ximena's life, but probably wouldn't be able to restore her hearing in that ear. Only weeks later, back in our apartment, when I noticed my daughter was talking on the telephone and holding the receiver to what had been her bad ear, did I realize that she could hear out of both. More than forty-five years later she still does.

These personal stories give some sense of Cuba's health care. The country coordinates a system of universal attention that has gone through a number of changes: adopting what works and discarding what doesn't. This attention includes dentistry, ophthalmology, and mental health services. The Revolution's great capacity for mass mobilization and educational outreach play their parts. For example, preventative procedures such as vaccinations and Pap smears are organized through the Comités de Defensa de la Revolución (Committees for the Defense of the Revolution, CDR). This mass organization, which has a branch on every block, also holds periodic blood drives. When someone needs an operation, another person in the family is expected to donate a liter of blood. If no family member is able to do so, the CDR finds an outside donor. During periods of economic stress Cuban hospitals have lacked lightbulbs, sheets, and other basic conveniences, and families have often been asked to provide these. The U.S. economic blockade has been responsible for many shortages. I once saw a clothesline with hundreds of washed rubber gloves stretched across the patio of Havana's América Arias Maternity Hospital. But the important elements of diagnosis and healing remain strong. And all health care is free.

Cuba has been no less impressive in the sciences than in the arts, and nowhere has its impact been felt more profoundly—globally as well as throughout Latin America—as in health. Prerevolutionary Cuba had its luminaries in this arena, where a tradition of excellence existed. Carlos Finlay (1833–1915), for instance, was the first to understand that mosquitoes cause yellow fever. But the Revolution changed everything when it came to medicine, medical training, and health care.

The tradition of which Finlay was a part continued to exist among Cuba's elite. Prior to 1959 health services and facilities were considered good but were concentrated in the cities. Havana was home to almost half the country's physicians and contained more than half its hospital beds.[1] This situation was immediately made worse by the United States, as one of its calculated efforts to destroy the Revolution has been focused on luring doctors and other health specialists by offering them instant residency status and high salaries if they defect. Salaries have been kept low in Cuba, including those of medical professionals, and this has been a problem even in a country where the cost of living is so much less than in other places. Salaries were raised in 2015 as part of a gradual overall increase. When these professionals go on international missions, most feel the moral recompense is enough. Some, however, inevitably compare what they earn with the salaries of their counterparts in the countries in which they serve. Some of them decide to defect, and the United States is ready and eager to offer an option that appears luxurious when compared with what they've known at home. And yes, it is considered defection rather than emigration. Ever since the first decades after 1959, when a highly trained professional, whose education had been obtained at no cost, left the country, he or she was thought to have betrayed the Revolution. The United States knows this, and its systematic brain drain is meant to foster social distress as well as rob the country of well-trained people in a variety of fields.

Because it has been consistent throughout the decades of U.S. aggression against Cuba, a few words about this brain drain from the point of view of those doing the luring are in order. In the Revolution's early years great numbers of doctors and other specialized health personnel were promised fast-track residency status and jobs in the United States. Cuba had to prioritize the training of doctors to make up the deficit and eventually graduated so many it could send them on internationalist missions. However, the U.S. government has never put an end to this deceitful policy. According to the U.S. Citizenship and Immigration Services, eleven members of Cuban medical missions abroad were admitted into the United States in 2006; in 2008 the number was 781. These figures diminished somewhat from 2009 to 2012, but then rose again, to 995 in 2013 and 1,278 in 2014. According to Homeland Security statistics, 1,663 Cuban medical professionals posted overseas were accepted into the United States in 2015 alone, a 32 percent increase from the previous year. The number of doctors admitted to the program has more than tripled since 2011. Seven thousand Cubans have been approved for residency since the program to urge their defection began.[2]

This U.S. government program doesn't always fulfill the promise it holds out to those Cubans who defect. Although most are granted residency, they cannot work as doctors until they are able to pass the required medical boards. Many end up struggling in lesser jobs for years; some never again work as the specialists they once were.

The Cuban government considers the U.S. medical defection program to be duplicitous, one more aspect of its many-faceted effort to debilitate and destabilize the Revolution. After all, Cubans study medicine at no cost; in return they are expected to practice at home or, if they choose, volunteer for a while in one of many overseas programs. A certain number of medical professionals, like a certain number of Cubans overall, want to move to the United Sates in search of new horizons. They have every right to want to explore what looks so much like greener grass. But inviting them to defect while on overseas tours goes too far and is one of many U.S. policies that prevent a healthy relationship between the two countries, especially now that diplomatic relations have been restored and good faith on both sides is needed in order to resolve the many outstanding issues. In 2014 even the *New York Times* judged the brain drain to be unfair:

There is much to criticize about Washington's failed policies toward Cuba and the embargo it has imposed on the island for decades. But the Cuban Medical Professional Parole Program, which in the last fiscal year enabled 1,278 Cubans to defect while on overseas assignments, a record number, is particularly hard to justify. It is incongruous for the United States to value the contributions of Cuban doctors who are sent by their government to assist in international crises . . . while working to subvert that government by making defection so easy.

. . . Cuba has been using its medical corps as the nation's main source of revenue and soft power for many years. The country has one of the highest numbers of doctors per capita in the world and offers medical scholarships to hundreds of disadvantaged international students each year, and some have been from the United States.

Havana gets subsidized oil from Venezuela and money from several other countries in exchange for medical services. This year, according to the state-run newspaper *Granma*, the government expects to make $8.2 billion from its medical workers overseas. The vast majority, just under 46,000, are posted in Latin America and the Caribbean. A few thousand are in thirty-two African countries.[3]

I want to talk about what the Revolution did to address its own population's health needs before, in the next chapter, describing in detail several of its overseas medical missions. How bad health care in the Cuban countryside was in 1959, when the Revolution came to power, can be seen in the following fragment of an interview by Conner Gorry and published in MEDICC *Review*: "'I had ten brothers and sisters. We were so poor,' relates Algimiro Ortíz in the honeyed afternoon light flooding the Seniors' Center in Cruce de los Baños. 'School wasn't an option—there wasn't a school here—only work. I began picking coffee when I was eleven. When somebody got sick, we had to carry them on our shoulders to the hospital in Contramaestre, sixteen miles away,' Ortíz, now in his seventies, told MEDICC *Review* [the journal published by the nonprofit organization MEDICC, which works to enhance cooperation among the U.S., Cuban, and global health communities and to provide in-depth information in peer-reviewed articles about health care in Cuba]."[4]

Such a scene is still intimately familiar today throughout the developing world. Gorry goes on to say that Cuba had a single rural hospital at the time. Eighty percent of the country's children suffered from intestinal parasites, which was the number one cause of death, and 60 percent of the population was seriously undernourished. Life expectancy in rural areas was fifty years, and infant mortality was 100 per 1,000 live births.

With the victory of the Revolution Cuba immediately prioritized health, and Cubans of every social class received an education making it possible for those interested to enter the medical professions and advanced scientific research if they were so inclined. Cuba responded to the U.S. brain drain and, more important, to its own needs by creating a system of medical education unlike any in the world. Its several medical schools fulfill domestic needs, and the Latin American School of Medicine continues to attract students from all over the world. Today the country is a leader in biomedical research, with a number of important discoveries. It is also an exemplar in the area of disaster response and in its disinterested health care internationalism in dozens of countries.

When it comes to health, the Revolution has never thought only of its own people. Written into Cuba's 1976 Constitution, as well as its 1983 public health law, is the affirmation that global health cooperation is a fundamental obligation of the country's health system and its professionals.[5] This conviction extends to the Revolution's internationalist work in bringing health care to people where for-profit medicine has priced them out of access.

Inside the country health care has gone through a number of overhauls, becoming better able to meet the needs of a population prone to respiratory ailments, diabetes, and stress.[6] In fact the growing threats to Cuban health today are similar to those in the more technologically advanced countries: heart disease, stroke, and lung cancer.[7] Focused on prevention, Cuban medicine attends to all the usual tropically induced problems and at the same time has honed excellence in complicated procedures used only in the most advanced societies.

The exceptionality of Cuba's system is internationally recognized. Especially when compared to health care in the United States, it often seems too good to be true. Edward W. Campion and Stephen Morrissey write, "The Cuban healthcare system seems unreal. There are too many doctors. Everybody has a family physician. Everything is free, totally free—and not after prior approval or some copay. The whole system seems turned upside down. It is tightly organized, and the first priority is prevention. Although Cuba has limited economic resources, its health care system has solved some problems that [the U.S. system] has not yet managed to address."[8] It is this unique combination of high-level research and universal coverage that makes Cuba's a health care model praised internationally as well as within its borders. But mostly it is the result of right priorities. What can be more important than a healthy population? Or more cost-effective, for that matter? Excellence of specialization and 100 percent coverage are the results of the Revolution having put health front and center. No insurance companies calculating profit against making people well. No voracious pharmaceutical industry fabricating need and making fortunes on medications priced out of the range of most who require them. No medicines with horrendous side effects that continue to be pushed on the population by misleading, often devious advertising. As we in the United States know all too well, for the pharmaceutical companies the bottom line is profit, and if more money can be made by paying out a few legal awards while continuing to sell a medication that causes serious problems, including death, that is the route they will take.

It is unusual that a small country with strained resources places this sort of importance on health care. We expect to find such attention in much wealthier nations, such as Canada, Britain, France, and Sweden, or in those where ideological tradition has led to fulfilling this need, such as Uruguay or Argentina. Many of us are exhausted by trying to get a succession of U.S. administrations to back universal health care, the only model in which everyone is covered.

What is truly extraordinary in Cuba's case is that universal health care has been honed to such excellence and that health care for the world is such a large part of its foreign policy.

The Rural Medical Service was established in 1960, posting hundreds of newly graduated physician volunteers in remote areas over the next ten years.[9] A decade later there were fifty-three hospitals in rural Cuba. This was the beginning of efforts, continually being refined, to distribute personnel and facilities according to the population's proven needs. It has led to the country's current model of embedding health professionals in the communities they serve and combining public health concerns and preventative protocols with the practice of curative medicine.

In health care as in other areas, an assessment of what works best is constantly being revisited. In 1976 the training of health professionals was turned over to the newly established Ministerio de Salud Pública (Ministry of Public Health, MINSAP). Provincial medical and nursing schools were established in order to decentralize training and encourage professionals to practice in the regions where they grew up. Tuition for these schools was and continues to be free, as is all education in Cuba. Vocation and academic achievement are the sole prerequisites for admission.

By the end of the 1970s health services were available nationwide and indicators began to improve. For example, infant mortality was 37.3 per 1,000 live births in 1960; in 2010 it had dropped to 4.5. In comparison, in 2009 U.S. infant mortality stood at 6.42. In 2010 overall life expectancy in Cuba was almost seventy-eight years; in the United States it is only two-tenths of a year higher. Cuba has achieved these and many other improvements in people's health with a doctor-to-patient ratio of 1 to 147, while in the United States each doctor serves 390 patients, though the ratio varies considerably depending on an area's income level.

As the 1980s began Cuba started giving higher priority to tertiary-care facilities and research. It expanded its accreditation of medical specialties to fifty-five fields. It established national institutes as centers of excellence, initiating and quickly accelerating its investment in biotechnology research, programs for prenatal screening, and organ transplantation. It installed the first nuclear magnetic resonance imaging equipment in Latin America. I was surprised to learn that Cuba obtained this equipment before countries such as Mexico and Brazil, with their much greater resources. Once again it's about priorities.

During my time in Cuba (1969–80) I acquired chronic asthma, requiring frequent emergency attention. My children fell prey to the range of minor health problems all kids get. We lived in a Havana neighborhood and visited our local polyclinic when there was a need. As in many other places, we tended to go to an urgent care unit to avoid a longer wait to see a specialist. This tendency, shared by others, was clearly an area where reassessment was in order. So, early in the 1980s, Cuba made the important decision to make family practice the center of its health care program. It was the first nation in the developing world to choose such a course. Teams of practitioners—including a family doctor, a nurse, a gynecology-obstetrics specialist, and often a psychologist or social worker as well—were sent to every neighborhood and rural community. These teams became familiar with the lifestyle, health, and unique problems of those they served. They got to know each family and individual, pinpointing cases of diabetes, alcoholism, domestic abuse, and other special needs. At first each team was responsible for improving and maintaining the health status of six hundred to eight hundred people (120 to 150 families). They generally held office hours in the mornings and made house calls in the afternoons. (Remember when doctors made house calls here in the United States?) On a trip back to the island in the early 1990s I visited a community doctor's office in a small town in the rural province of Camaguey. The young doctor and a group of preteen boys and girls proudly demonstrated their expertise in karate. I could see that their relationship was easygoing and deep, the kind that makes it possible for young people to confide in a professional living and working among them.

Today, because of the continuing improvement in people's health, and with thousands of Cuban family physicians serving abroad, these community teams are able to handle as many as 1,500 people each. In the countryside, however, the doctor-patient numbers remain closer to the original ratio in order to preclude those living in remote areas from having to travel long distances to a doctor's office. Family doctors and nurses are also stationed in large factories and schools, aboard ships, in child care centers and senior citizen residences.

As is true throughout the world, nurses are central to this model. While doctors may rotate to other areas once they complete their two-year family residency (a requirement of their free medical education), nurses often spend years serving in the same neighborhood or rural community. They become part of that community and are the glue that keeps the program working so well. A changed curriculum for both doctors and nurses has introduced an increased proportion of epidemiological and public health sciences (including social communication), community service learning, and problem-based and other active methods as well as clinical skills early in the training process. By 1999 this model had achieved full coverage nationwide. It is important to note that even during the decade-long economic crisis triggered by the collapse of the Soviet Union in 1989, the number of family practice teams continued to increase. In the next decade data also showed the positive impact of universal primary care on hospitals, notably decongesting outpatient and emergency services.

Today anywhere you travel in Cuba you will see a simple, government-built, two-story structure housing at least a physician-and-nurse team (usually mentoring medical and nursing students as well). Either the doctor or the nurse and his or her family live upstairs, a way of providing twenty-four-hour accessibility in the event of an emergency. Downstairs is the clinic, comprising a waiting room, a small office, an examining room, and storage.

Cuba's National Health Service is a socialized system. *Socialized medicine*, that term that is still so scary in the United States. It means that health facilities are government-owned and -operated, and almost all professionals are government employees. They do not earn exorbitant salaries, but they also do not have huge medical school loans to pay off. This does not mean that one size fits all. Health institutions are guided methodologically by MINSAP but supervised by community, municipal, and provincial bodies. The system's principles, policies, and procedures are centrally developed, but local flexibility responds to particular health circumstances that may exist in a geographic area. An analysis of diseases, risk factors, and environmental influences must be updated twice yearly, and findings are used to set local priorities. Much of the information contained in the analysis is obtained from the health team's patient records, still compiled by hand!

A step above these grassroots-level medical teams are the polyclinics: large facilities with more specialized services. Currently there are 488 polyclinics in the country, each serving a population of between twenty thousand and sixty thousand. Supervision for family physician offices is also located in the polyclinics, each clinic supporting some twenty to forty teams.

Socialized medicine in Cuba means everyone is covered. Ninety-eight percent of all children under the age of two are vaccinated against thirteen common illnesses. Ninety-five percent of all pregnant women are seen by a doctor during their first trimester, resulting in the extremely low infant mortality rate already mentioned. Freedom of reproductive choice has been available to Cuban women from the moment the Revolution was victorious, and abortions take place in hospitals with an overnight stay to ensure that any complication is addressed. Abortion is discouraged as a form of population control, though, and the usual range of birth control methods are available. Almost the entire population enjoys chronic disease control, including blood pressure regulation and other preventative tests.

The main challenge facing Cuba, in health care as well as in other areas, continues to be how to do more with even less, as the impact from the global recession and the U.S. embargo continue to make themselves felt. Cuba also has an aging citizenry that is no longer economically productive. In 2014, 12.6 percent of the population was over sixty-five, making it one of the oldest in Latin American. This puts a greater burden on health services, including geriatric medicine, attention to chronic conditions, and resource-heavy rehabilitation.

On the positive side revenues are expected from more exports of biotechnology products and from medical services provided abroad. (Although the country continues to offer free services in poor countries and those experiencing national emergencies, it has begun to charge for them where payment doesn't constitute a hardship or contracts are established with international bodies such as the World Health Organization.) Cuba currently has more than thirty-five thousand medical professionals serving in more than seventy countries and providing care for seventy million people. Cuba's more than $1 billion investment in its pharmaceutical and biotech industry is paying off: new vaccines, diagnostic kits, and therapeutics are provided first to meet domestic needs and then patented and marketed internationally. These sales, along with income from joint ventures with firms in Great Britain, Canada, Brazil, China, and India reached an annual level of $300 million in 2015.

Before describing some of Cuba's internationalist health missions, I want to mention one more domestic effort, the program to contain and cure HIV/AIDS. It is a program that has received both criticism and praise: the first because some believe it unnecessarily quarantines people with the virus, perhaps betraying a heterosexist policy, and the second for its extraordinary success.

In fact the first Cubans to contract the virus were not from the island's LGBTQ population but soldiers returning from foreign battlefields. HIV/AIDS entered Cuba from Africa, so in a reverse journey it bears on the country's medical internationalism on that continent. About a quarter-century ago volunteers returning from internationalist service in Africa showed signs of a mystery illness. According to MEDICC Review's Conner Gorry, "[Cuba's] response was modeled on classic infectious disease control and included an epidemiological surveillance system, contact tracing and screening of at-risk groups and blood donations, accompanied by intensive research and development. The first AIDS-related death occurred in April 1986 and a policy of mandatory treatment in sanatoria was established, thought to be the most effective way of delivering the comprehensive medical, psychological and social care needed, and limiting the spread of the disease. The sanitation policy was harshly criticized by global media, human rights advocates, and some public health specialists."[10]

As the Cuban medical establishment studied the disease, a closed community was established in the Havana suburb of San Antonio de Las Vegas. Soon similar communities were set up in other parts of the country. All those found to be HIV-positive were confined to these localities, which consisted of specially equipped hospitals and private housing; these were pleasant lodgings with all the amenities, the latest medications, and diets rich in the nutrients needed to help people stay healthy—all free. Patients received classes in how the disease does and does not spread, practicing safe sex, and preventing transmission to others. The overall population meanwhile received an education in understanding and accepting those with HIV/AIDS without fear or prejudice. And Cuba began producing zidovudine, stavu-dine, lamivudine, didanoside, and indinavir: the ingredients for the cocktail that has now turned the disease from fatal to chronic.

As patients learned to live with the virus, they were released back into their previous living situations, although many have opted to remain in the communities, which are no longer closed. They can bring their family members. They can also live there and work outside. Mariela Mendoza, a twenty-three-year-old woman living with HIV, said, "Today people with HIV can live in their communities, where they have access to medical attention with doctors and dentists who know about HIV and how to treat patients in a caring, dignified way."[11]

Cuba's success in dealing with HIV/AIDS, and the realization that the original communities were set up to control the outbreak rather than as punishing camps, have lessened criticism. This has been true especially since people outside the country began to understand that the closed communities didn't reflect a homophobic response. Cuba has laws and policies prohibiting discrimination against men who have sex with men and against transgender people. Since 2008 sex reassignment surgery and hormone replacement therapy are offered free of charge, within the context of the country's universal health care system. It is obvious that people are at the center of Cuba's health strategy and AIDS response.

Based on statistics, the Revolution's AIDS program is now considered the most successful in the world. Many also believe it is the most innovative and interesting. Cuba put all its creativity into facing a problem that has stymied many other countries. As of 2015 mother-to-infant transmission of the HIV virus has been eliminated. Statistics for 2014 show seventeen thousand Cubans living with HIV; all are receiving the attention they need to be able to enjoy happy, productive lives. According to UN statistics, only two hundred Cubans have died from the disease.[12]

13

CUBAN HEALTH MEANS
WORLD HEALTH

Enrique Ubieta Gómez, in the prologue to his book about the saga of Cuba's contribution to the eradication of the Ebola crisis in western Africa, sums it up concisely: "In 1959 Cuba had 6,286 doctors and—faced with the tempting job possibilities offered by the United States, that tried by a variety of means to defeat the recently victorious Revolution's economic and social sustainability—3,000 of them emigrated immediately. Nevertheless, in spite of the low number of Cuban doctors, the country's first permanent internationalist medical brigade left for Algiers in 1963. Today Cuba has 85,000 doctors, 7.7 for every thousand inhabitants, the highest per capita ratio in the world."[1]

A book could be written about the dozens of countries and millions of people who have benefited from Cuban medical aid over the past half century. One of the most impressive programs has been its many-faceted project to help people see. The World Health Organization estimates that 314 million people throughout the world are visually impaired, of whom forty-five million are blind. Eighty-five percent of these people live in developing countries, where health care is either inaccessible or too expensive for them to be able to take advantage of it. Cataracts are the leading cause of blindness, and about 85 percent of cataracts are operable. Corrective eyewear, also out of reach for most of the world's inhabitants, could restore normal vision to twelve million children. This is clearly a problem that has a solution if there is political will and if a practical way can be devised. Since 2004 Cuba has found that will and exercised that way.

One of the Revolution's showcase projects is Operación milagro (Operation Miracle), a program that functions in Cuba as well as in a number of other countries throughout the developing world. Since its inception a decade ago it has been dedicated primarily to cataract removal surgery, although it also addresses glaucoma, chronic infections, and other eye problems.

Interestingly Operation Miracle demonstrates what can happen when solidarity in one area leads to solidarity in another. The massive program emerged out of Cuba's adult literacy program, Yes I Can. When teachers realized that an inability to see was preventing students from learning to read and write, they understood the need to attack that part of the problem. Just as Cuba's in-country health system has provided valuable lessons for its international outreach in public health, and just as the country's educational system has taught it what might work or not overseas, experiences in one area are drawn on to strengthen others.

Often large groups from a single country come to Cuba for the operation. Their travel, lodging, food, and follow-up care are covered by the Cuban government. Others have had their sight restored in their country of origin, in assembly-line clinics set up by Cuban overseas personnel. In 2007 Cuba reported having treated more than 750,000 people for eye conditions such as cataracts and glaucoma. The number is now estimated at more than 1.5 million.[2]

Dr. Reynaldo Rios Casas, the director of Cuba's Ramón Pando Ferrer Institute of Ophthalmology, reported that the first days of the in-country program were frantic: "Eye surgeons worked in three shifts, keeping the hospital's operating rooms going all day and all night. It was not uncommon for a single surgeon to perform forty operations in a shift. It was really heroic. . . . Since then [we] have been training new eye doctors at an astounding rate. . . . The hospital's budget has been increased tenfold and its equipment upgraded. It now has thirty-four operating theaters with state-of-the-art equipment, including two outfitted for advanced laser surgery techniques."[3] Some doctors complained about the program's ambitious nature, citing long hours and inadequate salaries. As with all such initiatives, goals often seem exaggerated. But it is no less true that by undertaking such large-scale programs the Cuban Revolution has made so many of its extraordinary advances—in health care, education, and other arenas.

Because Cuba sold a large-scale ophthalmology operation to Venezuela for oil, some accuse the Revolution of trading on its medical services for economic reasons or political goodwill. Such accusations may be partially true, but the recipients of these services—the ordinary people whose sight is restored by Cuban solidarity and professionalism—couldn't care less about the program's political or economic motives. Reina López, age fifty-eight, is from San Vicente, El Salvador, and was interviewed in the Havana Hospital's waiting room. Cataracts had obliterated her sight thirteen years earlier. Her daughter, Adilia Reyes, who is thirty-three, has cared for her mother since she went blind. Their family, including four children, survive on her father's salary of three dollars a day plus whatever homegrown fruit they can sell at a Saturday market. Adilia expressed what many have repeated wherever Cuban doctors have set up these eye clinics: "For the poor, this is a tremendous benefit."

Even some who might have been able to afford the surgery back home have taken advantage of it. Basil Ward said, "I could have had the operation in Barbados, but I couldn't have had it for a year; there's a huge waiting list there." For most, however, it isn't convenience but poverty that has led them to look to Cuba's offering. And for Cuba, although there is no doubt that its aid in this area has earned it much-needed revenue, the primary impetus is its commitment to worldwide health.

To give an idea of the scope of Cuba's solidarity in this respect, I will discuss four more categories of medical aid, each quite different from the others. The first of these is earthquake relief.

The Ancash Earthquake (also known as the Great Peruvian Earthquake) occurred just off the Pacific coast of that country on May 31, 1970. The epicenter was located just where the Nazca Plate is pushed down by the South American Plate. The quake, which had a magnitude of 7.9 on the Richter Scale, caused a landslide of snow, ice, and mud that crashed through the Callejón de Huaylas. This was the worst natural disaster in Peruvian history, and perhaps the world's deadliest avalanche. There were an estimated 66,794 to 70,000 casualties. Sixty thousand people died and approximately three million others were seriously affected.

This was a systemwide disaster, completely destroying regional infrastructures of communications, commerce, and transportation. Economic losses surpassed half a billion U.S. dollars. Cities, towns, and villages as well as homes, industries, public buildings, schools, and electrical, water, and sanitary facilities were seriously damaged or obliterated.

In Chimbote, Carhuaz, and Recuay 80 to 90 percent of all the buildings disappeared. The Pan-American Highway was also damaged, which made the arrival of humanitarian aid extremely difficult. Cuba was one of the first countries to send aid to Peru, and it was pivotal to survivors of the disaster being able to get back on their feet. A well-provisioned medical team set up six rural hospitals that remained on site for months. It delivered 106,000 blood donations.

At 8:50 a.m. on October 8, 2005, in the Kashmir district of Pakistan, an area long in dispute with India, there was an earthquake measuring 7.6 on the Richter Scale, one of the worst in recorded history. Eighty thousand people died; tens of thousands more received serious injuries; and four million were left homeless. Cuba's response was immediate and extraordinary, its largest overall international health effort to that time. Pakistan and Cuba did not even have diplomatic relations, but presidents Musharraf and Castro spoke on the phone. Fidel offered to send medical assistance, and the first Cuban internationalists were on the scene nine days later.

Maj.-Gen. Farooq Ahmed Khan, head of Pakistan's earthquake emergency unit, the Federal Relief Commission, told the press, "[The Cuban aid workers] are respected, and I think people will always remember their contribution. If they had not come, there would have been very large gaps in medical support for the victims." Dr. Juan Carlos Martín, director of the Cuban field hospital in Muzaffarabad, said, "We knew this had to be a closed-loop relief effort. Not only did we have to bring the medicines and the doctors, we had to provide everything—the hospital, the electricity, the plumbing, the beds—to run that hospital."[4]

As Cuba's internationalist aid to Pakistan unfolded, the country sent over 2,400 physicians and paramedical staff and established thirty-two field hospitals and two relief camps in the North-West Frontier Province, Azad Jammu, and Kashmir. A total of thirty-six transport flights were made; the initial two flights were of military-trained physicians, nurses, and paramedics. Tons of medical equipment and medicines were flown in. Some thirty amputees were brought back to Cuba for treatment.

From October 2005 to January 24, 2006, Cuban medical teams in Pakistan performed 601,369 consultations; 5,925 surgeries, including 2,819 major surgeries; and served at forty-four different locations in the quake-affected region. The effort is even more astonishing when one considers that Pakistan is where the Taliban originated, and extreme Islamist factions occupy large parts of the territory. Yet Cuba's help was well received, with no cultural or religious conflicts reported.

Usmani Ramos, a general practitioner specializing in family health care, was part of the Cuban program. Six days a week Ramos set forth with his mobile team from the Muzaffarabad Hospital in Pakistani-administered Kashmir. Because rural women were not accustomed to being treated by male doctors, the teams went out in pairs, a woman and a man in each.

Translators often omitted the intimate details of female disorders, making these doctors' work more difficult. En route, and always on foot, along the narrow walkways and paths through the area of Domel in the city of Muzaffarabad, where the Neelum and Jhelum rivers meet, the duos broke off to treat patients in prearranged spots. People stopped them frequently to greet them and seek their assistance. Before long, Pakistani women were receptive to being treated by male as well as female doctors. Ramos said he was motivated by a basic belief in humanity. "If you help people during natural disasters, in the future, they will help you," he said. "Solidarity is important, because you can help people, you can make friends. And friendship is better than weapons."[5]

As has been the case with many of Cuba's internationalist endeavors, aid to victims of the quake led to the implementation of other internationalist programs. In 2005 and 2006 Pakistan's Higher Education Commission (HEC) sent 354 scholarship students to Cuba to study medicine and surgery, courses offered by the Cuban government. Dr. S. M. Raza of the HEC explained that Cuba had provided Pakistan with a thousand scholarships and that he considered Cuba's health care system to be better than that of the United States.[6] Cuba's ambassador Gustavo Machín Gómez said Pakistani students will receive the best medical education recognized by the World Health Organization and will have complete religious and cultural freedom while studying in Cuba. He also pointed to the fact that it was the first time Muslim students would receive their education in the Caribbean country.

Cuba's aid in the wake of the Pakistani quake was remarkable for many reasons: its enormous scope, all-inclusive nature, and the fact that people from such different religious traditions, social conditions, and political systems managed to give and receive solidarity in a spirit free of conflict. It would set a standard repeated elsewhere in the world in the years to come, but sadly not one that has predominated. While capitalist aid models and militaristic interference overwhelmingly have brought chaos and death, Cuba's more humane protocols have mostly been overlooked as purveyors of peaceful coexistence.

In April 2016 an earthquake measuring 7.8 degrees on the Richter Scale hit Ecuador. Its epicenter almost entirely destroyed the coastal town of Pedernales. A series of strong aftershocks threw survivors into a frenzy of fear and made it difficult for immediate aid to reach the devastated areas. Three Cuban doctors who had been working in the area for several years were among the dead. Like all Cuban internationalists, they had known the risks when embarking on their mission. Their bodies were returned to Cuba for burial, and the Revolution sent more health workers and others to help the South American country recover.

In one of MEDICC's international disaster reports, Gail A. Reed describes Cuba's aid policy: "This theme—the poor helping the poor—is at the heart of Cuba's South-South cooperation with other developing countries today, and permeates much of its disaster relief efforts."[7] Cuban health workers have aided victims of many earthquakes, and no few have died in the line of duty.[8]

The second category of medical aid, and in many ways the one from which the others emerged, came about as a result of the nuclear disaster at Chernobyl, Ukraine. While Operation Miracle was set up to address relatively ordinary eye problems, that accident presented much greater challenges.

On April 26, 1986, the central reactor at the Chernobyl nuclear plant exploded and caught fire. Dozens were killed as an immediate result of the accident; many more died in its aftermath. Plumes of radioactive smoke spread outward, threatening millions. Wind carried the smoke toward Western Europe, where food sources were affected. Eventually thousands who had lived and worked at or near the site died, and 150,000 others were forced to abandon their homes and workplaces. A thirty-kilometer radius from the reactor became an instant ghost town.

The children were the first to be evacuated, and many who had become orphans were adopted by families in Spain, Italy, France, and Germany. Other countries offered recreational programs and group vacations for some of the affected children. But after a few years, and despite the fact that many were still sick or just becoming sick, Chernobyl no longer topped the international news. Other catastrophes had replaced it.

In Cuba, however, the medical establishment was thinking long term. By 1990 victims of Chernobyl had been suffering from the disaster's fallout for four long years. That year a program for the children of Chernobyl was established at the Tarará Pediatric Hospital just outside Havana:

> The idea was to provide free, comprehensive medical care to the most severely affected children from the region, aged five to fifteen. From the first group of 139 severely ill children who arrived in Cuba on March 29, 1990 to the nearly 800 patients—both children and adults—treated in 2004, that idea has blossomed into a concrete reality helping people of many nations get well in the wake of disasters.
>
> The majority of the first young patients arriving from Chernobyl suffered from gastrointestinal, immunological and hematological illnesses.

Endocrine problems, particularly thyroid cancer and hyperplasia, were the most common. In the earliest stages of the Tarará project, Cuban doctors and specialists treated 289 patients with leukemia and performed six bone marrow and two kidney transplants. Ukrainian officials estimate the Cuban government has spent some U.S. $300 million to treat these thousands of children—far and away more than any other country has offered the victims of Chernobyl.

. . . Dr. Julio Medina, Director of the Tarará Pediatric Hospital said "the first cases we saw had thyroid-related illnesses—these were the first effects of the accident. Today, we consider posttraumatic stress disorder the second effect of the accident." Genetic malformations—especially in the kidneys—resulting from radioactive exposure, and skin disorders like vitiligo, are other long-term effects being treated at Tarará.[9]

Officials in Ukraine estimate the number of Chernobyl's victims to be roughly 100,000, but it is difficult to say because the area is still contaminated. Much of the contamination is from Cesium 137, which has a half-life of between twenty and fifty years. After nineteen years away from home some inhabitants of Chernobyl are returning. So it is likely that the doctors at Tarará will continue to treat a fair number of victims into the future. Today they are also attending to a significant number of children of the first victims; the damage caused by radioactivity is rarely confined to a single generation.

As with so many of Cuba's health care programs that have been tailored to meet the needs of people from other places, this one has gone far beyond the issue of immediate aid and rehabilitation:

The working partnership on the Chernobyl project could serve as a model for other countries. In 2003, the Ukrainian Parliament took the Chernobyl Children project under consideration and voted to make it an official government program, earmarking funds for its future development.

As for the Tarará facility, it has branched out from its roots as a hospital for the victims of Chernobyl and been transformed into an international post-disaster medical center, treating children from all over the world. Earthquake victims from Armenia, Brazilian children suffering from Cesium 137 poisoning and traumatized families evacuated from Montserrat when the volcano on that island rendered it almost entirely uninhabitable, all have benefitted from the expertise and solidarity of the Tarará Pediatric Hospital.[10]

A number of aspects of Cuban medical aid abroad made this aid particularly effective. The Cubans are constantly evaluating and reevaluating what has worked best throughout their vast experience in other countries: how to address not only the immediate effects of disaster—the need for shelter, food, sanitation, epidemic control, and providing treatment that may run from dealing with burns and performing amputations to treating PTSD and chronic depression—but also longer-term care involving ongoing physical and psychological rehabilitation, often in the face of serious language barriers and the need to innovate the simplest therapies using only what is available on site.

Cuba has a number of medical schools spread throughout the country, but the Escuela Latinoamericana de Medicina (Latin American School of Medicine, ELAM), based in Havana, is special. It is where young people from all over the world have been studying since 1999. The immense institution currently has close to twenty thousand students and graduates well-trained doctors and other medical personnel from 110 countries. Most are from Latin America and the Caribbean, but there are also some from Africa and Asia. ELAM accepts students from the United States. The Cuban government has offered full scholarships (including room, board, and a small stipend) to up to five hundred U.S. students. By 2010, 122 had enrolled, from twenty-nine states and Puerto Rico. As of this writing thirty-three have graduated, many of them women and almost all from poor and underserved communities. As they pass the U.S. medical board exams and move into areas where they are needed, they are helping to fill the gaps in quality medical care suffered in many parts of this country.

Dr. Brea Bondi-Boyd, ELAM Class of 2009, was the first graduate in decades of a foreign medical program to be accepted into California's Contra Costa County Family Medical Residency program. A native Californian, Bondi-Boyd says she was well received, "but found, sadly, that my idealism, volunteerism and dedication to work with poor people, that I largely learned from my Cuban professors, was not the norm for most U.S. applicants, at least not in the applicant pool I came from."[11]

ELAM's graduates are prepared for circumstances requiring innovation and creativity. They have been particularly useful when working in the medical brigades Cuba has sent to respond to natural disasters throughout the world. Many speak the native language of the recipients of their aid as well as Spanish and can bring firsthand knowledge of home terrains, cultures, customs, religious practices, and other particularities to the sites of earthquakes, floods, and similar tragedies.

Cuba's approach is multidisciplinary. In designing programs to aid victims' survival, addressing immediate needs such as dealing with the wounds caused by the disaster in its first dramatic moments, and looking ahead to long-term rehabilitation, medical programs take a holistic approach. Mental and physical health are folded into a single strategy for healing. Safety and hygiene are seen as fundamental to regaining well-being. Community projects enable local people who have suffered from the same devastating event to help one another. Art, music, theater, and makeshift circus performances play a role. Most important, the Cuban relief teams don't leave disaster-stricken areas after the initial show of international solidarity fades and a new emergency somewhere else dominates world headlines. Cuba is known for transitioning its disaster aid into permanent bilateral programs, which can improve the receptor country's overall health system.

In Havana in February 2016 I spoke with Carlos Mejías Márquez, a maxillofacial surgeon from Banes, Holguín, who did his medical studies in the capital and has been on several internationalist missions. He served in Ethiopia from 1985 to 1987, when Cubans worked in many parts of the world without economic remuneration. From 2008 to 2012 he served in Yemen. By this time Cuba was charging for its services. It was in Yemen that Mejías experienced the challenges of vastly different cultures:

> I worked at a hospital that attended the population as well as soldiers, mostly dealing with traumas to the face and mouth, some caused by war and others by genetic defect. In Southern Yemen (what they called Democratic Yemen back then) we had a three-year contract, but they asked us to stay on for another year and I did. I worked with two female Yemeni doctors, and that's where the cultural challenges arose. We developed a good relationship, and could talk about intimate details of treatment which men and women there generally could not discuss. But those female doctors told me that if we were having such a conversation and a man entered the room I should change the subject immediately. They would also invite me to their homes for dinner. But they remained in the kitchen, out of sight, and I ate with their husbands whom I didn't even know.[12]

My third story is about the earthquake I've left for last, one much closer to home. For thirty-seven seconds on January 12, 2010, the earth shook in Haiti. The magnitude-7.0 quake devastated the small island country, which was already known as a place of poverty, inequality, and desperate need.

Even before the catastrophe, of the 169 countries listed on the United Nations Human Development Index, Haiti was 145th, the lowest in the Western Hemisphere. Eighty-six percent of those in the country's capital, Port au Prince, were already living in slum conditions. Half the people in that city had no access to latrines, and only a third to potable water.[13]

The quake's epicenter was near Port au Prince. Three and a half million people were immediately affected: 220,000 are estimated to have died and another 300,000 to have been injured. A quarter of the capital city's civil servants were killed as a result of the quake, and 60 percent of the administrative buildings were destroyed along with 80 percent of schools in the most severely hit area. A million and a half people became homeless when 105,000 houses were destroyed and another 188,383 were badly damaged. As the crisis reached its peak, those homeless people were living in makeshift camps. Six months after the disaster a cholera outbreak claimed the lives of close to 6,000 additional victims, and 216,000 more were infected with the disease. And these figures continued to grow.

That cholera outbreak bears closer scrutiny. Despite scientific findings throughout the ensuing years, it wasn't until August 2016 that the United Nations finally admitted that its peacekeeping forces, not the earthquake, had been responsible for the epidemic: "The first victims lived near a base housing 454 United Nations peacekeepers freshly arrived from Nepal, where a cholera outbreak was underway, and waste from the base often leaked into the river." For six years UN officials insisted that the origins of the outbreak were up for debate, and in 2011, when families of 5,000 Haitian cholera victims petitioned the United Nations for redress, its Office of Legal Affairs declared their claims "not receivable." Finally, Secretary General Ban Ki-moon has acknowledged that the United Nations played a role in the initial outbreak and that a "significant new set of U.N. actions" will be needed to respond to the crisis."[14] It is especially shameful when a supposedly neutral body such as the UN, in order to protect its liability, fails to admit its responsibility in an international disaster, thus becoming part of the problem rather than the solution.[15]

All these statistics give some sense of the disaster's magnitude but fail at transmitting individual stories of anguish and need. Nevertheless a few more numbers bear repeating. Three hundred thirty-one Cuban health professionals were already working in Haiti when the quake struck; they had been there since 1998, knew the terrain and language, and were among the first responders. The situation demanded an immediate scaling up of specialized personnel. By the first week of February the Henry Reeve Contingent, incorporating some of those already on the ground, had 681 members in the country.[16] By April 2010 Cuba's overall health cooperation in Haiti had 1,491 members. Of these, 730 had been trained at ELAM. They came from twenty-eight countries: Argentina, Belize, Bolivia, Brazil, Chile, Colombia, Costa Rica, Cuba, Dominica, Dominican Republic, Ecuador, El Salvador, Guatemala, Honduras, Lebanon, Mali, Mexico, Nicaragua, Nigeria, Panama, Paraguay, Peru, Saharawi Arab Democratic Republic, Santa Lucia, the United States, Uruguay, Venezuela, and Haiti itself. When people from such a diversity of cultural experience come together to work in one place, all sorts of solutions are bound to emerge—the very essence of what internationalism can be.

By the time the first months following the quake had gone by, the Henry Reeve Brigade was staffing ten hospitals, five of them Cuban field hospitals, and it had set up four medical posts in the tent cities. Almost 300,000 doctor-patient visits had taken place, 7,899 surgeries had been performed, 1,523 births had been attended, 107,094 people had been vaccinated (against diphtheria, pertussis, tetanus, measles, and mumps), and close to 60,000 patients were receiving rehabilitation services in twenty clinics throughout the country. Half of all patients were suffering from infectious diseases and parasites.[17]

When it comes to disaster relief, as I say, Cuba's strategy almost always includes inserting its emergency medical response into a program of long-term public health cooperation. In the case of Haiti this meant staffing twenty new community hospitals established through an agreement with the region's eight-nation Bolivarian Alliance for the Americas: "Patients are treated at no cost to themselves. Members of the Henry Reeve Contingent have been given the opportunity to extend their service in Haiti beyond the emergency phase. Cuban members can transfer into the Comprehensive Health Program, agreeing to the standard two years of service required. In addition, the more than 700 ELAM doctors in the contingent can choose to remain three, six, twelve or twenty-four months. Despite difficult living and working conditions, the majority of health professionals living in the contingent's main Port-au-Prince tent camp have opted to stay a year or longer."[18]

One of the Cuban Revolution's great gifts to people in need, whether dealing with them in Cuba or in their home country, is its extraordinary sensibility toward other cultures and belief systems. This wasn't always so. It took years in Cuba itself for the Revolution to accommodate its own citizens of faith, whether Catholics or practitioners of the African religions Santería, Palo Monte, Spiritualism, or Vodu. It might also be argued that it was slow to listen to feminists, whose philosophy went beyond strict Marxist tenets, or to see gay Cubans as part of the national fabric. But when accommodation was made, it was generally deep and comprehensive.

When Cuban medical personnel, teachers, and other technicians went to other parts of the world with deeply engrained cultures and customs, they found that they needed to understand those cultures and incorporate that understanding into their work—or it wouldn't be effective. Because of the great numbers of Cuban internationalists, I believe this understanding will be a two-way street, influencing attitudes at home as well. This is particularly true in the area of medical aid, since the people needing help have usually suffered extreme trauma, making them more than usually vulnerable. MEDICC's Conner Gorry explains:

> "We take a holistic approach—we don't just treat the medical or psycho-pathological effects of disaster," Dr. Alexis Lorenzo, Director of Services at Tarará Hospital and Coordinator of the mental health group at Cuba's Meteorology Center's Climate Center (CLAMED) told MEDICC Review. "We try to understand each person within a broader context, taking into account all the factors in their lives [that contribute to their mental health]. I think we learned that from the Chernobyl children, and that's the experience we took to Haiti."
>
> The Cuban methodology is based on two fundamental principles: 1. The collective, historical memory of the disaster-stricken area is respected and integrated into the mental health response, taking into account popular knowledge and local beliefs, religious principles, personal experiences, and academic research. 2. Every disaster and every context is different. In designing a program for a specific context, the mental health team relies on knowledge-sharing among actors at all levels—local, regional, and international—and across sectors and mental health disciplines.[19]

When the earthquake struck, the whole concept of rehabilitation was unknown to most Haitians. The Creole word for the discipline is *reyabilitasyon*. Here is Gorry again:

> With a public health system that requires patients to purchase everything from gauze and gloves to syringes and anesthesia before a doctor will treat them, most Haitians have no choice but to withstand chronic or acute pain. Cuban rehabilitation services are helping to change that.

Rehabilitation is a new service for the vast majority of Haitians. "The clinics we've established after the earthquake offer treatments most have not had access to before," Dr. Walter del Río, coordinator of Cuba's rehabilitation program in Haiti, told me. "The day we initiated services, we had two patients," physical medicine and rehabilitation specialist Dr. Alexis Verdecia said. "But people took to the idea fast; once word got around that our services were free, we were flooded."

Art has also become an important component in Cuba's disaster relief programs, especially in its long-term mental health work. The Martha Machado Artists Brigade is made up of painters, musicians, clowns, magicians, stilt-walkers, and puppeteers. It was founded by the well-known Cuban artist Alexis Leyva Machado (Kcho) after a trio of hurricanes hit Cuba in 2008. Children were among its greatest beneficiaries. Using art, music, dance, and play the Brigade helped children in the most heavily affected Cuban provinces to express their fears in an atmosphere of fun.

With the experience they had acquired in Cuba, the Brigade went to Haiti, where they toured the region hardest hit by the earthquake, performing almost daily in field hospitals, orphanages, and tent cities. "At first the kids were quiet, dejected," one of the doctors reported. "But slowly they drew closer and began to participate. If I showed you a photo of these kids laughing and dancing, you would never guess they were earthquake survivors. At these activities they became children again, one hundred percent."[20]

These internationalist artists also provided art supplies and helped the traumatized children explore their feelings through drawing, painting, and collage. They worked alongside the children, offering their artistic expertise. Ernesto Rancaño, a founding member of the Martha Machado Brigade and another of Cuba's most accomplished artists, has said, "Haitian kids have amazing creativity and what they make is incredible. We'll show them a couple of techniques and they'll just run with them. There's a lot of talent, and when they're painting they're in another world."[21]

Ebola, a highly infectious hemorrhagic virus discovered in 1976, saw its most violent outbreak to date in March 2014, principally in three African countries: Sierra Leone, Liberia, and Guinea. My fourth story is about Cuba's response to this crisis. Like HIV/AIDS in earlier decades, in the areas where Ebola was most prevalent a general lack of knowledge about how it spreads and how to treat it kindled superstition and provoked ignorance, shame, and violence. Those young men charged with burning the bodies of the dead, for example, are still experiencing social shunning. The outbreak created serious crises in the countries involved and a threat to the global community.

The international organization Doctors without Borders was the first to sound the international alarm. Like Cuba it already had health professionals on the ground in Africa. They were soon joined by health care specialists from all over the world. Once the World Health Organization (WHO) called for nations to step up with funds and human resources, Cuba was the country that offered the most assistance. It sent 256 volunteers, all with significant international emergency experience: thirty-eight to Guinea, fifty-three to Liberia, and 165 to Sierra Leone, and more stood ready to join them.

Ebola has claimed more than 11,300 lives to date, the vast majority in Africa but also two in the United States (a misdiagnosed traveler returning from abroad, a nurse who had come home after treating victims). Although safety measures are strict, an inordinate number of these deaths are of the health workers in the infected areas. And although the enormous international eradication effort has brought the epidemic mostly under control, new cases continue to appear in small villages in Guinea. Getting to zero—the goal of everyone involved—still seems elusive.

Jorge Delgado, a Cuban internationalist who has worked in Nicaragua, Zimbabwe, South Africa, Guatemala, Honduras, Haiti, Angola, Equatorial Guinea, and Guinea-Bissau, headed the first team of medical doctors who went to combat Ebola in Sierra Leone. They traveled in response to a request from the United Nations. Delgado says:

> The average age of the doctors was forty-seven, and many of them had previous international experience, so we began our work fully aware of the risks. Some of our relatives would tell us we were crazy for going there. It wasn't just my family or the families of the 256 members of the medical team who were scared. The whole of Cuba was scared. Our press had divulged the terrible images of what was going on and the whole of Cuba was on edge throughout the time we were working there. We knew that, in case of death, our remains could not be brought back to Cuba for five years. We knew that if we fell in "combat" we would be left there—that we were at war. We all signed that agreement before leaving and it was absolutely voluntary. Those who didn't want to go on this mission had every right to turn it down and continue where they were or even opt for a different mission abroad. We had thousands of volunteers for the 256 spots on the team.[22]

Dr. Delgado also speaks about losses:

> We lost two doctors in the war against the virus. Jorge Juan Guerra, an economist, contracted cerebral malaria that killed him in three days, and Reinaldo Villafranca, a nurse, also contracted a deadly case of malaria. It was very sad and painful. The other case was that of Félix Báez, who contracted Ebola. It was hard to watch him become ill and see his condition worsen. We tested him for malaria and got a negative. At the British Hospital they tested him for Ebola and it came back positive. They conducted three tests on him. There was no doubt he had Ebola.

Cultural creativity shows up in Dr. Delgado's story, as does solidarity between professionals whose shared humanity defies the stances of their respective governments:

> We planted a tree of life, a small mango tree right outside the center [where we worked]. We would tie a colored ribbon to it every time we saved a patient. [At the center] we worked next to the U.S. non-profit organization Partners in Health . . . exchanging scientific reports every morning after our shifts. This happened despite the fact that the United States offers an express visa program to Cuban medical doctors who wish to leave their teams and emigrate to the United States, where the vast majority aren't allowed to practice medicine. They do it only to try and weaken us, but every medical doctor who joined the Ebola campaign returned to Cuba.

I have often wondered why opponents of the Castro government have so often found it necessary to lie when they attack the Revolution. They would gain credibility by speaking about the experiment's real problems or simply admitting they prefer living under another political system. While researching this book I came across several stories on counterrevolutionary blogs claiming that Cuban internationalists are told that if they contract the disease they cannot return to Cuba. This is such an egregious lie that I won't dignify it by citing sources. Instead I will offer parts of an interview Gail Reed did with Félix Báez, the Cuban doctor infected while serving in Sierra Leone, and Jorge Pérez, director of Cuba's Instituto de Medicina Tropical "Pedro Kourí" (Pedro Kouri Tropical Medicine Institute, IPK). Pérez is affectionately known as Cuba's AIDS doctor. The conversation speaks to how the Cuban internationalists integrate themselves into the communities they serve, one man's personal struggle with the disease, problems that have arisen because of the U.S. Cuba policy (some of which have been resolved), and more. I have transcribed so much of it because I believe it reflects the training, skill, and solidarity of Cuban internationalists throughout the world.

Félix Báez: I was with a Cuban team of forty-two, some British and a number of local health workers, in the Kerry Town Ebola treatment center, run under [the] auspices of the U.K.'s Save the Children. . . . I started with fever and chills, and was classified as a suspected case, until the lab results returned positive. When WHO was informed—all Cuban doctors and nurses are under WHO contract—they decided to transfer me to Geneva University Hospital.

Jorge Pérez: The Cuban health minister asked me to pack my bags, and I flew from Havana to wait for Félix. He arrived in Geneva about midnight in critical condition, not always lucid. . . .

Félix: I remember boarding the plane in Freetown, feeling very alone: I was totally isolated, wrapped up in what looked like a space suit covered with cellophane. I also remember the long trip, arriving in Geneva, and walking down the steps to the ambulance. First I was disoriented, and then I blacked out.

MEDICC: Jorge, tell me what you're learning about Ebola, and how that relates to the care Félix received at the Geneva University Hospital.

Jorge: We've been studying Ebola since the eighties, along with other hemorrhagic fevers like dengue. I also spent the long nights in Geneva reviewing the latest international information. But when it comes to patient care, theory is one thing and practice is another. The first Ebola patient I saw was Félix; he of course has seen more. At the hospital, his care was meticulous and rigorous, performed by highly qualified and trained personnel. People not only with a heart for their profession, but also for their patients. They treated Félix with enormous affection. Of course he was a pretty good patient: doctors can be the worst, you know. But he was very courageous, and once he was on the mend, his sense of humor—that Cuban sense of humor—also came back. . . . On day two, he recognized me. He told me "I'm going to be okay, and I'm going back to Sierra Leone." Those were his first words to me. I have to admit I was very moved.

Félix: When I saw Jorge, it was like seeing light at the end of a dark tunnel. It was tremendous, even though I was able to talk with my family by phone. And my eighteen-year-old son, who is in medical school, had written me a wonderful letter. . . .

MEDICC: Félix, did you ever figure out how you were infected?

Félix: No, we didn't. You know, the biosafety measures are very stringent, and in addition to the training at IPK, we underwent another four weeks of in-country training. I should also say that the courses in Sierra Leone were very important in other ways, because although we all had some knowledge of English, we needed to get used to wearing the protective suits in such a hot climate, needed to know more about people's culture, the way things are done, and above all about what was expected of our work, the protocols. That helped all of us become a real team, international and local health professionals working in a good environment where people were tactful, respectful. And of course we had to be certified by WHO before we were permitted to treat patients. We worked in groups of three doctors and six nurses, in six-hour shifts, seven days a week. And we used the kind of layered garments recommended by Doctors without Borders. But you could only wear the suit for up to an hour, maximum, sometimes less; and you only went into the patient-care unit twice during your shift. There was even a radio system to advise you when you had to be relieved. For suiting up and removing our suits, we used a buddy system, our decontamination was supervised by local hygienists, who were very strict. But of course we didn't live in a bubble: we lived in a hotel, we ate food there, mingled to some extent with others outside the hospital setting. So although we've gone over and over it, we still don't know how I was infected.

Jorge: The international recommendation is for health workers to maintain a distance of 1.8 meters from Ebola patients. That sounds good, but reality is different: they have to find a vein, examine patients, touch patients, help them to the bathroom. So, they go in and out of the recommended distance between procedures, washing and changing gloves between each patient. But it's still possible to become infected. Even a small hole in a glove or the suit can provide a point of entry.

MEDICC: Under what conditions are the Cubans contracted to serve in these Ebola-stricken countries?

Félix: Well, first of all, we volunteer. Each person has to make that decision. For me, my profession is my life. And, like the others finally selected, I'd served abroad in health emergencies before. When I read about Ebola, I decided to sign up because it seemed help was needed right away. WHO contracts us directly and pays us directly, and we are their responsibility if we get sick, as in my case. We also have certain living conditions guaranteed, such as only two people to a hotel room, air conditioning and twenty-four-hour running water. All these things are important in a situation like the one we're facing.

MEDICC: What was it like when you began to see patients?

Félix: When we first arrived, the British hospital wasn't up and running yet; it hadn't been built. The public hospital was overflowing with patients, in the hallways, vomiting, with diarrhea. Children and whole families. The local health professionals and Doctors without Borders were doing everything they could.

When I went to work at the new hospital, the first cases I saw were critical, people who had sought treatment very late. My first three patients died. Then there was a little four-year-old girl, who came in with no pulse, very sick with malaria. We were able to save her. And then a brother and a sister, Cecilia and Daniel, in their thirties. Both had Ebola. He was in fairly good shape, but her case was more complicated, with diarrhea, vomiting and convulsions. . . . Once I got sick, I was in the room across from them, and we'd shout to each other across the hall. Thankfully, both of them recovered, too.

Jorge: And the situation in Sierra Leone is still critical. Where the Cubans are working, the case fatalities have been significantly reduced. At first, as Félix said, people were coming in late, many already with multisystem organ failure. But then, people began to lose their fear, because they could be cured. . . . Without proper conditions, fatalities run from fifty percent to ninety percent. We've now reduced them to about twenty percent where the Cubans are working in teams with others.

Shortage of personnel in Sierra Leone is still very serious. But even if the Ebola treatment centers had enough health workers, the problem of Ebola will only be resolved in communities themselves, with education, local health workers in direct contact with people who live there. So they can recognize the symptoms, know what to do early, learn how to bury their dead in a safer way.

MEDICC: It's been reported that even though Cuban personnel were working under WHO auspices, the U.S. Treasury Department blocked payment to the Cubans for some time. . . . I'm hoping that's resolved now. But more than that, is there other cooperation happening between the United States and Cuba? Do you expect more now with renewed relations in the works?

Jorge: Once we arrived in West Africa, there was cooperation on the ground—that happened naturally. Our people are working in centers built by the USA in Liberia, for example. And also, of course we are working with U.S. NGOs, like Partners in Health. The logical thing would be for all these barriers to come down. We've seen some signs of this: for instance, the CDC [U.S. Centers for Disease Control and Prevention] warned us of a traveler from one of the three affected countries who had entered the USA with the intention of traveling to Cuba. So we had this information when the person flew to Cuba and were able to act accordingly. And then, of course, there is Félix's own case: he was transported by Phoenix Air, a company under contract to the U.S. State Department, which I understand had to give permission to use the aircraft for his transfer to Geneva. In general, I hope greater cooperation will be possible now, for the sake of people in both our countries and in other countries as well.

MEDICC: I understand the WHO contract calls for the Cuban nurses and doctors in West Africa to make a six-month commitment. What is the plan for them on return to Cuba, and in general how is Cuba protecting its own population? . . .

Jorge: We're in the process of setting up the protocols for the returnees, who obviously have to be quarantined for Ebola's twenty-one-day incubation period. Thus far, only a handful, fewer than five, have returned, and they spent that period at IPK. But we don't have room for over 200! So we need to create conditions for them. In terms of Cuba, we can't afford to have Ebola enter the country: it would be too costly from both human and economic points of view. . . .

MEDICC: The latest data show Ebola is still spreading—in countries like Sierra Leone, where WHO says there were only one to two doctors for a population of 100,000 even before the epidemic . . . and very weak infrastructure. Can the epidemic be brought under control?

Jorge: Yes it can, or we wouldn't be there. Ebola brings into terrible relief the difference between robust health systems and ones that are struggling without resources. We see only incipient health systems throughout Africa, with the exception of South Africa. If patients have the right care, supported by decent infrastructure and with sufficient and protected personnel, the disease can be brought under control. This also means having containment facilities, education to refute all the myths surrounding Ebola and helping to stop direct transmission. The whole world is challenged by Ebola, as it was by AIDS. Like AIDS, Ebola isn't Africa's alone: it can reach any part of the world, crossing borders and oceans and airspace.

MEDICC: Félix, why did you decide to return to Sierra Leone? Are you immunized now against Ebola?

Félix: I believe I'm at least partially immunized, against the Zaire strain, which is the one circulating with the highest fatality rates. But it's not entirely clear. And if my blood could help other patients produce antibodies, I'm willing to give it. I think our nurses and doctors have become symbols that will hopefully give confidence to other health workers: you can go, you can serve, and you can survive. It was extraordinary how my case was followed, especially in social media. I think it helped make more people aware that Cubans and others were risking their own lives to save African lives. Because, unfortunately, not everyone in this world cares what happens to people in Africa. But I said to myself: human life began in Africa. Will it end there, because people are abandoned? I decided to go back because people need us, our whole team.[23]

On November 7, 2015, Sierra Leone declared itself free of Ebola. The World Health Organization made the announcement at an official ceremony in the capital, Freetown, after the country had gone for forty-two days (two incubation periods) without a new case. People celebrated in the streets, although many were subdued, remembering lost loved ones or perhaps wondering if the epidemic that had cost them nearly four thousand lives would return. Neighboring Liberia was declared free of the virus two months earlier, but in Guinea, as of this writing, it is still smoldering; international health workers have detected a small cluster of recent cases in several remote villages.[24]

The Cuban health professionals who have given so generously to help eradicate the virus from these three African countries aren't packing their bags yet. Many will remain to set up more permanent medical facilities or work in other ways try to bring the health care systems more in line with Cuba's own vision of what health care should be: accessible, free, and with as modern an infrastructure as possible. Meanwhile Cuban nurses and doctors, as well as those from many other countries who have received their medical training at ELAM, are ready to go anywhere in the world their services are needed.

I'll let these examples of Cuban internationalism in the area of public health speak for themselves and for others I haven't mentioned. The Revolution's doctors and other health personnel receive nothing but praise from all quarters. The programs themselves have been lauded, but are also sometimes criticized as being ways Cuba can advertise its political system by establishing a humanitarian presence felt throughout the developing world. I would ask: Is creating a humanitarian presence really deserving of criticism? Certainly not for the millions who have benefited from Cuban medical aid. What impresses me most profoundly about Cuba's overseas health care programs are their reach, their long-term design, and the profoundly integrated ways in which they reflect lessons learned at home. They involve expert training and professionalism, sacrifice and art, and a deep respect for those served. The part Cuba's international medical school plays in the overall picture is also impressive—and moving: one more piece in a puzzle being put together to make the whole world healthier.

SPORTS FOR EVERYONE

I began writing this chapter as Cubans awaited the first visit of a sitting U.S. president to their country in more than five decades. Havana's Latin American Stadium was getting a fresh coat of paint; Obama would attend a baseball game between the Tampa Bay Rays and Cuba's national team on March 21, 2016. Both nations are fanatical about their favorite sport. I finished writing it during the Summer Olympics in Rio de Janeiro, where Cuban athletes made the uninspired showing that has been characteristic of them in recent years.

When we speak about the Cuban Revolution improving people's lives, we often mention health, education, culture, and sports in a single breath. This is because these are the elements that enable people to live beyond mere survival, and because from its inception the Revolution has considered these four to be rights to which everyone should have full and free access.

I've described Cuba's domestic achievements as well as its internationalism in the first three fields. Because accessibility to and excellence in sports has been one of the Revolution's mantras, I want to mention it as well, although its narrative of the country's internationalism is of a different order. The Revolution's ideas about physical well-being and sports bring up interesting issues with regard to an entire nation's access to fitness, athletic training, the differences between amateur and professional status in the lives of the world's great athletes, how Cuba's athletic greats often dream of leaving their homeland to play in the Major Leagues, and more general issues such as nationalism and internationalism.

Peripherally at least, I experienced Cuba's love of sports from the moment I moved to the island in the fall of 1969. Because of its physical and cultural proximity to the United States, Cuba was more attuned to the sports that are popular here than it was to those that have the most fans throughout the rest of Latin America. In other words, volleyball rather than soccer; boxing and track and field. And as in the United States baseball is the national pastime.

Voluntary work was something most of us did; revolutionary pride enjoined everyone to give a few hours a week to harvesting vegetables in the Havana greenbelt, cleaning up our neighborhood, or participating in whatever big collective project was on the agenda. When my family and I arrived, the big project in the capital city was remodeling and expanding the Latin American Stadium, the same that would host Obama forty-five years later. The stadium had opened in the working-class El Cerro neighborhood in 1946, with a seating capacity of thirty-one thousand. Our 1971 renovation almost doubled that capacity, to fifty-five thousand, modernized the installation, and added gardens and other communal spaces. With many others I did my part on Saturdays, separating what could be reused from what was no longer serviceable, straightening nails, and doing other odd jobs reserved for those who couldn't take part in the heavier work of reconstruction. Those capable of doing more did.

Before 1959 the majority of the Cuban population had no access to sports, as the fields and facilities belonged almost exclusively to upper-class clubs. Access to quality physical education was also very limited. Before the Revolution came to power there were only 951 sport centers and 609 physical education and sports trainers serving a population of approximately six million. Following victory this problem was immediately addressed. Physical fitness was stressed for defense and for well-being and pleasure, and participation in sports from childhood on up emphasized such qualities as teamwork and cooperation. In February 1961 the Instituto Nacional de Deportes, Educación Física y Recreación (National Institute for Sports, Physical Education and Recreation, INDER) was established. It centralized the operation of and access to all sports on the island. Fidel Castro was frequently quoted as saying that sports should be everyone's right, not something reserved for the wealthy.

From the beginning the Cuban Revolution took a position on sports that for several decades would make its athletic programs unique in the Western world, offer the possibility of an athletic career to every young person regardless of social status, and situate the country high on the roster of medal winners at international events such as the Summer Olympics and Pan American Games.

The most important ideological difference between socialist and capitalist countries in this respect was that in the former all athletes were considered amateurs; there was no such thing as a professional in sports. In the latter, attaining professional status carried different rules and increasingly ✓ allowed for the multimillion-dollar salaries and well-paid endorsements Western athletes enjoy. Today such divisions are almost nonexistent in practice: witness the huge earning power of any one of the great "amateur" athletes who take part in the Olympics.

Professional status was what brought with it the intense competition that spawned doping, a problem that has blemished the names of star athletes in both systems.[1] Russia's entire delegation risked being excluded from the Rio Olympiad; just before the games started, and after the revelation of an immense and decades-long state-sponsored doping program, the International Olympic Committee banned that country's entire track and field team from the games. At the last moment, swimmer Yulia Efimova, who had been barred for a time and then reinstated, was allowed to compete. For the first time in Olympic history, this brought public admonishment from some of the other athletes.

The worldwide competition between high-class professional and amateur athletes has been complicated, no matter how fuzzy each category may become. Some would argue that there is no such thing as amateur sports in today's world. In the United States college athletes are technically amateurs, although full scholarships and other perks endow them with privileges often associated with professional players. Cuba, on the other hand, has been ✓ forced to increase the earning capacity of its athletes, even when it continues to call them amateurs.

Doping in sports has been extremely rare in Cuba. Among the long list of athletes across the globe who have been proven to have ingested performance-enhancing drugs, in Cuba only the discus thrower María Cristina Betancourt tested positive and was banned for life, in 1983. In 2001 Cuba opened a state-of-the-art antidoping laboratory.[2] It has been to the Revolution's credit that doping has so rarely tarnished the image of its athletic prowess.

One high-profile, though inconclusive, incident did take place in 1999. Cuba's star high jumper, Javier Sotomayor, who had dominated the sport throughout the 1980s and 1990s, was accused of having tested positive for cocaine and was stripped of the medals he won that year at the Pan American Games in Winnipeg. Cuba claimed the test was rigged by the anti-Cuba mafia, a diverse group of anti-Castro organizations that has attacked or discredited revolutionary Cubans, downed planes, and engaged in other criminal activities. Cuba appealed. The decision went back and forth, but the ban was eventually dropped, and Sotomayor was allowed to take part in the 2000 Sydney Olympics, where he won silver. I cannot prove that the anti-Cuba mafia fabricated a false test result, but it has done much worse in its long history of vicious attacks against the Revolution.

When doping has been revealed, athletes from dozens of countries have lost their medals, often years after the sporting event in question. Recently, with improved testing methods, old blood and urine samples have been retested, yielding different results. This has sometimes resulted in contenders being awarded medals long after they competed. Cuban Yumileidi Cumbá was given a retroactive gold for her performance at the 2004 Athens Olympics, and Yarelys Barrios won the bronze for her showing at the 2012 London Olympics, also retroactively.[3]

The result of the Cuban Revolution's early ideological shift from professional to amateur sports was significant. It created a very different atmosphere from that which existed in the capitalist countries, conducive to different expectations and behaviors. In 1978 the country's athletes were ranked eighth in the world, second on the continent, and first in Central America. By 2003 more than 1,492 gold medals had been won by Cuba in the Central American and Caribbean Games, 649 in the Pan American Games, and forty-six in the Olympics—extremely high numbers for such a small country. On the occasion of the Sotomayor scandal Fidel told his citizens (and the world), "An Olympic athlete is not a lowly instrument used to gain international prestige, an object to be bought and sold on the market, a commodity to be used and then thrown into the garbage. Athletes are first and foremost human beings [with] pride in the recognition they have earned through their efforts and extraordinary merit. They have honor, above all, honor. Those who have never competed for money have competed and triumphed for honor alone. Honor is worth more than life, because life without honor is meaningless."[4]

Approximately two million Cuban athletes since 1960 (twenty-three thousand in the high-performance category) have participated in thirty-eight sports at the national and international levels. There are now 11,523 sport centers in the country and more than 39,000 instructors; in other words, one for every 342 inhabitants. Physical education is compulsory at all educational levels. And this is not only about producing outstanding athletes for international competition. It is first and foremost about producing opportunities for ordinary citizens to improve their physical fitness and practice the sports they love.

When my son Gregory was in fifth grade, I received a call from his school principal. She asked if I was aware that he had decided to leave the school where he had been studying and transfer to a nearby sports school. I was surprised; he hadn't mentioned it at home, although he assured me he'd planned on doing so when we caught up with one another the following weekend. For the next two years Gregory attended a specialized facility where students took all the regular subjects but also received training in a sport of their choice. He chose tennis his first year, swimming his second. At graduation the students with real talent went on to train seriously; the rest would return to a normal course of schooling. The idea was to give those with physical aptitude the opportunity to find out if they had what it takes to become outstanding athletes.

Although he improved dramatically and had a great time, Gregory had no intention of making sports his life. He told me he had felt physically inadequate and thought that studying a couple of different sports for a year or two would increase his overall ability and improve his sense of self. He was right. He also admitted, with a smile, that he liked the idea of the extra yogurt given daily to the students at the sports school.

The Cristino Naranjo School, where Gregory studied those two years, had been an upscale country club before the Revolution; its seaside sports installations were beautiful. I remember an elderly man who told stories of having tended bar at the place when it was an exclusive club; now he worked in the school's cafeteria. Among Gregory's classmates at Cristino Naranjo were a couple of runners who made names for themselves in Cuban athleticism. I remember in particular Ana Fidelia Quirot, who went on to break world records and earn her share of medals. Ana Fidelia, who was called "la Tormenta del Caribe" (the Torment of the Caribbean), has an inspiring story. She'd already won her first of two Olympic medals—a bronze in Barcelona in 1992—when a cooking stove blew up, causing her serious burns and threatening to end her running career. With a painful rehabilitation plan and tremendous personal courage, she got back in shape in record time. Mere months after her accident she went on to win silver at the 1993 Central American and Caribbean Games in Puerto Rico. In 1996 she won silver in Atlanta, and is still considered one of the greatest 800-meter and 400-meter female runners of all time.

For decades the fact that star athletes in the capitalist countries earn exorbitant salaries and enjoy lives of opulence pointed up unbridgeable disparities, and increasingly over the past several decades a number of talented Cuban players have defected to the United States. As it has in other areas, the U.S. government encouraged these defections, with special recruiters and lures of money, women, mansions, and expensive cars. This history of promise and defection has waxed and waned in line with the ups and downs in the lives of Cuban athletes and the antagonism between the two countries. In time Cuba altered its sports strategies somewhat. Today there are Cuban athletes who, with permission from the Cuban government, compete on foreign teams, splitting their salaries with the State.

The reestablishment of diplomatic relations between our two countries at the end of 2014 also brought with it a certain thaw in the mutual attitudes of U.S. and Cuban authorities caused by the five and a half decades of unrelenting U.S. animosity toward Cuba. In December 2015, in that same Latin American Stadium I helped renovate in 1971, 150 children attended a skills clinic with greats who had emigrated, something few sports enthusiasts over this half century dreamed possible. U.S. Major League Baseball and its Players Union were on a goodwill tour of the island that included a prominent Cuban player who defected in 2013 and three others who left the island in less drastic circumstances.

In two seasons with the Chicago White Sox the defector, José Abreu, has become one of the U.S. sport's premier sluggers. Other Cuban players on the tour were Los Angeles Dodgers outfielder Yasiel Puig, St. Louis Cardinals catcher and first baseman Brayan Peña, and free-agent shortstop Alexei Ramírez. Four other major leaguers not from Cuba, the head of the U.S. Players Union, and two advisors accompanied them. The Cubans who had emigrated met with family, former teammates, and friends, as well as a generation of Cuban baseball heroes who had remained on the island. Among this group were Orestes Kindelan and Pedro Lazo, who received a new glove from Puig. "Blue and red, Cuba's colors," observed Lazo with a smile as he accepted the gift. He is one of the greatest pitchers in Cuban history.

A *New York Times* writer who reported on the emotional series of meetings mentioned one of the top young Cuban players, twenty-two-year-old shortstop Lourdes Gourriel Jr., who was also in the stadium's dugout that day. Gourriel said he had never met a major leaguer; he had only seen them on TV. He admitted that one day he would like to play in the United States, against the best players in the world, but only with his government's permission. "Baseball is for the people here, for the community," he said. "We are with them, and that's very important." The comment speaks volumes about the two countries' differing political positions with regard to sports. In the United States sports stars remain inspirations to youth when they are not involved in scandal. In Cuba they inspire by continuing to play in a national program that faces all sorts of privations.[5] Nevertheless, within a few months Gourriel and his brother Yulieski had both gone north.

As of 2014 Cuba had participated in twenty of twenty-seven Summer Olympics, winning a total of 208 medals. The country has never taken part in the Winter Olympics. Its two bids to host the summer games have been unsuccessful. Over the years International Olympic Committee politics have shown bias toward countries willing to pay great sums of money for the privilege of hosting these events, something Cuba would not do. Still Cuban athletes have been enormously successful internationally. Of those nations that have never hosted an Olympics, it has won the fifth highest number of medals.

It may be interesting to look at an Olympic medal breakdown by category and gender. In twenty Summer Games Cuba has competed in twenty-eight individual sports plus the arts competition, entering 1,207 athletes (921 men, 286 women). It has had the most participants in track and field (125 men, 93 women), boxing (86 men), rowing (74 men, 7 women), and wrestling (78 men, 1 woman). It has also taken part in most of the team sports, with 73 men in baseball, 15 women in softball, 44 men and 30 women in basketball, 26 men in soccer, 27 men in handball, 16 men in hockey, 47 men and 49 women in volleyball, and 36 men in water polo. Through 2014 Cuba had won 202 medals in these competitions (sixty-one gold, sixty-five silver, and sixty-six bronze).

The country's greatest international success has been in boxing, with sixty-seven medals, thirty-four of them gold. Since the mid-1970s Cuba has had some of the best amateur boxers in the world. It is also dominant in baseball, winning gold medals in 1992, 1996, and 2004, with silvers in 2000 and 2008—the only five years in which baseball was an Olympic sport.

Since the victory of its Revolution Cuba has also excelled at the Pan American Games. It had never won more than thirty medals in any of those games held in the decade of the 1950s, and never fewer than one hundred medals per game since 1971. By 1980 it ranked second only to the United States.

Revolutionary Cuba emphasizes team effort, but it has also had outstanding individual athletes who have become national heroes and heroines. The same Pedro Luis Lazo who met with members of the December 2015 U.S. goodwill tour was a pitcher on four of Cuba's medal-winning baseball teams from 1996 to 2008. From 1992 to 2004 Driulys González won four medals in women's judo, a gold, a silver, and two bronze. Amarilys Savón won three bronze in women's judo from 1992 to 2004. Elvis Gregory was an outstanding fencer. Cuba's women's volleyball team won three gold medals from 1992 to 2000. In track and field Alberto Juantorena won gold in both the 400 and 800 meters in 1976; he was only the second athlete ever to win both those events in the same year. High-jumper Javier Sotomayor won gold in 1992 and silver in 2000 and is still the only man in the world to have jumped eight feet. Heavyweight boxers Félix Savón and Teófilo Stevenson have each won consecutive gold medals. Stevenson and Juantorena have also contributed to their country's civic life; both have held seats on the National Assembly. After retirement from athletics in 1984, Juantorena served in many official capacities, including vice president of the Instituto Nacional de Reforma Agraria (National Institute for Agrarian Reform); vice minister for sports; and vice president, and later senior vice president of the Cuban Olympic Committee.

Hard economic times have impacted Cuban sports showings at the international level, a reflection of inadequacies, some would say, in concept as well as in terms of the money available for the programs. After its revolutionary victory, 1960 was the first year the country sent a delegation to the Summer Olympics. No medals were won. In 1964 Cuba brought home one silver. The 1970s, 1980s, and 1990s were the nation's glory years, with performances by boxer Teófilo Stevenson and runner Alberto Juantorena, among others. In 1992 the tiny Caribbean country earned thirty-one medals: fourteen golds, six silvers, and eleven bronzes. Then the decline began. In 1996 the Cuban delegation earned twenty-five medals; in 2000, twenty-nine; in 2004, twenty-seven; in 2008, twenty-four; and in 2012, fifteen. This downward trend continued with eleven medals won in Rio in 2016.

Although its waning athletic potency has removed the country from the international spotlight in recent times, the Cuban Revolution continues to believe sports can promote cooperation among nations. This, it is hoped, may lead to increased understanding and to fostering improved relations, something Cuba has sought since 1959. At the same time, it has taken political positions, usually siding with other socialist countries, in boycotting the games to protest apartheid in South Africa and defending positions of solidarity in line with its socialist, anti-imperialist, and antiracist ideology.[6]

In terms of material aid, the country has expanded its internationalist sports programs over the years to include Algeria, Angola, Benin, Brazil, Congo, Guinea, Guinea-Bissau, Iraq, Malagasy Republic, Mali, Mozambique, Nigeria, Panama, Peru, South Yemen, Tanzania, Venezuela, and Vietnam. In 1983 ninety Cuban sports specialists were working in a total of fifteen countries. By 1987 eighteen countries were assisted by forty-eight specialists. In 1990 there were 414 students from thirty-three countries on sports scholarships in Cuba.[7]

The ups and downs of sports brilliance in contemporary Cuba have involved both nationalism and internationalism. Rigoberto Zarza, a Cuban consul in Jamaica, spoke at the media launch in 2015 of the Twelfth Annual Renewal of the Wesley Powell National Track and Field Meet in that country.[8] He touted the number of medals won since 1959 in a variety of sports competitions and the results achieved in different international events, including the Central American and Caribbean Games, the Pan American Games, the Sport Games of the Bolivarian Alliance for the Peoples of Our America, world championships, Paralympics, and Olympics. Zarza emphasized that the main reason for the Revolution's success in sports is the fact that its athletic movement is the result of a process that has placed human development as its main goal. "Our idea of sports," he said, "focuses all attention on the development of the whole human being, assuring the right to comprehensive training, cultural development, recreation and overall health and welfare."[9] Attention to "the whole human being" includes those who are differently abled. Cuba first competed at the Paralympic Games in 1992; it has participated in every Summer Paralympics since but has never taken part in the Winter Games. The country has won a total of twenty-two gold, thirteen silver, and eighteen bronze medals, primarily in track and field, but also in judo and swimming. There are those who would argue that it has been the country's emphasis on its star athletes and consequent failure to strengthen sports from the grassroots level up that has diminished its dominance at international meets.

Yuniry Castillo is a young Cuban woman who lost an arm in an accident. She won the 100- and 200-meter sprints in the Paralympic Games in Beijing, setting new records in those two competitions. Her performance was not by chance; in world tournaments she had won gold medals in the 100-, 200-, and 400-meter sprints and was the Pan American champion. "I have always been active in sports. When I had my accident I felt bad because my body needed something it could do for me to feel useful," she explained. She added that in 2000 the commissioner of judo—the sport she participated in before losing her arm—introduced her to coaches involved in training athletes with disabilities, and her career took off.[10]

Cuba has also taken part in the lesser known Deaf Olympics, or Deaflympics as they are called; its hearing-impaired athletes have represented the country well, winning medals and drawing attention to this category of special Olympians whose needs are often overlooked. As Stuart Harrison, vice chair of UK Deaf Sport, has said, "Deafness is an invisible disability; the casualty of 'inclusion'. The consequences of mainstream schooling of the moderately/profoundly deaf in Western society has led to hearing people often sharing a notion of 'there's nothing wrong with them' when our athletes need lights and flags instead of starters' guns and referees' whistles, which are only the tip of the iceberg when it comes to communication needs."[11]

Cuba, in fact, has moved away from mainstream schooling for the deaf. In opposition to international trends in special education, the country continues to maintain separate facilities for many of its special needs students. The director of the Centro de Referencia Latinoamericano para la Educación Especial (Latin America Special Education Reference Center) in Havana, representing Cuba's official position, asserts that separate special education institutions are the best way to attend to diversity. He criticizes those who advocate integrating special needs children into regular schools as adopting an integrationist façade and denying diversity cultures.[12]

In Jamaica Zarza spoke as well about the obstacles to success in Cuba's sports program, principally the U.S. blockade, which, he said, limits the acquisition of sports equipment taken for granted by athletes in other countries, forces Cuba to buy such equipment at a greater cost on distant markets, prevents Cuba's Institute of Sports from obtaining reagents and chemical substances for its antidoping lab, and often denies Cuban athletes the opportunity of training with their U.S. counterparts.

Referring to women in sports, Zarza said that the country's policies have played a central role in giving Cuban women worldwide prominence. And he spoke about the country's internationalist solidarity. Because he was speaking in Jamaica, he mentioned Cuba's 1980 donation to that country of the G. C. Foster College of Physical Education and Sports. Although Cuba has also donated sports facilities elsewhere and has youth from many different countries studying on sports scholarships in Cuba, I would say the most important examples of its sports internationalism have been its concepts of sports for the masses and sports as an amateur rather than professional field. The first of these concepts got off to a successful start. The second has experienced highs and lows, subject to the balance of powers in global politics at any given time, and now also to Cuba's changing situation as it struggles to adapt, from a position of extreme disadvantage, to its restored place in the community of nations.

It might be argued that amateur athletics in Cuba eventually turned professional in certain ways, since the athletes' careers occupy their entire working lives and they make their living from their sport, albeit a much less luxurious living than athletes in the capitalist countries enjoy.

Perhaps in sports it is the example set by Cuban athletes that has had the most international resonance. But I think it has also been the early example set by the Revolution itself, when it insisted on treating its athletes—from the stars down to the kid on the block—as whole human beings. Balance was important here. The holistic approach avoids the kind of situation we have lately seen dominate U.S. sports programs, such as frequent concussions and other closed-head injuries that come from putting the need to win before a concern for safety. These injuries plague many of our stars, whose families have even donated their loved ones' brains to science so that the ravages of repeated head injuries can be studied. They have caused concern as well among parents of middle school and high school players, who are showing an increased incidence of concussion and even sudden death.

Shifting economics has meant shifting priorities. There is a crisis in Cuban sports today, one the country has not been able to deflect with Band-Aid measures such as raising athletes' salaries or making changes to regulations regarding what its star players are allowed or not allowed to do. This crisis may be best exemplified by what happened at the Pan American Games held in Toronto in July 2015. Cuba's men's field hockey team suffered a mass defection, more than half its players disappearing into the ever-welcoming arms of the United States. Cuba was forced to play its final contest with less than half its team, and consequently lost to low-rated Trinidad and Tobago 0 to 13. In an essay titled "We Have Seven Compañeros in the United States," the social critic Arturo Arango addresses the moment and its deeper significance. The piece is worth quoting at length:

> The changes Cuba is experiencing also involve language, the point of view we bring to disparate realities. Not that long ago those we call "compañeros" today were deemed deserters who betrayed the confidence placed in them. At the very least, the choice of words describes a process: that which has normalized the possibility that anyone could decide to travel to another country and make their life there. The issue, as we know, has two sides: from the perspective of the person emigrating, it's about exercising the freedom to choose where to live; from a geopolitical point of view we are faced with a brain drain and siphoning off of talents that take place when those trained in the third world go to work in developed countries.

But the use of the word "compañeros" also speaks to the continuity and growth of a phenomenon that is daily bleeding our teams dry. By now I imagine every Cuban player has become accustomed to seeing his teammates disappear, or is planning his own exodus. Some news stories report that twenty-eight players took advantage of their visit to Toronto to emigrate. Even if migration has become an everyday occurrence, the truth is that Cuba's sports program itself is in crisis. Total crisis.

I'm not a specialist in the history of Cuban sports, but I remember a time when INDER had "Sports: the people's right" as its motto. Streets were roped off on Sundays to encourage people to exercise ("Plan de la calle" it was called). This was a dream in which Athens and Sparta seemed to fuse (although after 1968 and for many years Sparta took precedence over Athens).

Cuba's great achievements in a number of sporting events (the Central American Games, the Pan American Games, the Olympics) or in world championships in a variety of disciplines were seen as the top of a pyramid, at the base of which thousands of people, especially children and adolescents, practiced the popular game of baseball, or learned disciplines such as tennis that had previously been reserved for the upper classes. . . .

The most important sports acquired their own laws, by which individual talent mattered more than mass participation. Rather than complying with the old maxim of "a sane mind in a sane body," what took precedence were all those medals that caused us to scream with emotion and spur the nationalist pride of a small blockaded country that, at least on the court or playing field, was superior to the great capitalist powers. . . .

Now everything seems to have regained a sort of normalcy. Even that fourth place in Toronto may have been too much for the real possibilities of the poor nation that, according to the demographers, will never have more than twelve million inhabitants. . . .

What I'm saying should not be construed to mean that I am against the great sports spectacle. I love going to a stadium and watching the game that may bring delight or depression to my week. I am fascinated when I see a human being test the limits of his or her physical prowess. Even more, I enjoy *reading* about sports in its cultural dimension. But it is not that sad fourth place, or seeing our star baseball players depart, that causes me despair. I suffer when I see our broken-down basketball hoops, oxidized volleyball posts, and empty swimming pools that are beginning to crack. If we don't have the money to perform as we once did, if that performance corresponds to a reality that no longer exists, perhaps the solution is to begin once again from the bottom up: in the understanding that the basic right is for people themselves to be able to practice sports, regardless of whether they bring their country a medal, a hymn, or tears of joy.[13]

Arango's essay points up one area in which the Revolution's goal of equal accessibility has been tarnished by a new world order and nationalist lust for power. Cuban athletes remain outstanding. Many of them have set records still in effect. But a changing global situation has, in many cases, brought the original ideology to its knees.

One thing I haven't mentioned—and I suspect it may have a special relevance for sports as well as in many other areas of Cuban life—is the Revolution's concept of emulation as opposed to competition. I witnessed this when I lived in the country, and it made a profound impression. Emulation is emphasized in schools and workplaces, and it works like this: rather than pit students or workers against each other, all members of a class or those in an office or factory get together to decide on common goals, then they help each other achieve those goals within a prescribed time frame. In a classroom those good at math help others lacking in math skills; the same goes for all the subjects. In a workplace a similar practice is in place. Thus people compete against their own potential rather than against others.

Just as competition is the bedrock of capitalism, emulation embodies the less adversarial socialist values. Something of this emphasis on competing against one's own best efforts shows up in Cuban sports programs, more easily of course with team sports than with the individual star.

A healthy nation offers accessibility to physical as well as intellectual activity across the board, sportsmanship as an integral aspect of that, and the respect for their sport that athletes must have so that doping or other sorts of cheating remain rare. It is clear that the Revolution must reevaluate its attitude to its most outstanding players in ways that will either make them continue to want to play for the home team or emigrate without shame.

As the country adjusts to a more normal situation within the community of nations, I hope it will be able to combine the best of its socialist ideals with a reasonable investment of resources and a sane (read: less nationalistic) set of priorities, in order to keep sports available to all, continue to provide assistance to less-developed countries, and show the prowess of its athletic potential on both the domestic and international stages.

WHAT I LEARNED

In my research for this book I examined sources produced by the Revolution and those written by some of its opponents (at least those who pose reasonable challenges and are not given to twisting the facts) and its most rigorous defenders. When speaking with supporters and detractors I have been mindful of the need to separate personal bias from overall experience and factual information. As distance from specific events grows, time and an analysis not bogged down in momentary passions may bring issues into clearer focus. But passions too may be important. Certainly there are times when I share and appreciate their rightness.

I have been alternately bemused, bothered, and outraged by experts and commentators who refuse to challenge cold war discourse long after that period has ended, but I have also found among their claims questions that deserve answers. I refuse to be one of those apologists who erase from historical photographs the images of those who have fallen from favor, leaving telltale outlines or shadows as evidence of such crude manipulation.[1]

I have spoken with many internationalists, observed the ways their diverse experiences have affected their lives, and also questioned recipients of their solidarity. I have spoken to young people whose parents left them for several years to serve on dangerous missions in far-off places. I have been attentive to how the attitudes of the Cuban people with regard to international solidarity may have shifted in the context of changing domestic situations, and in what ways they have remained stable, a solid reflection of identity. More than with previous projects, working on this one has moved me to extrapolate from the specific to the general; in some of the events and ideas explored here I have discovered new paradigms that have allowed me to consider the values implicit as they may be relevant to larger ideas about what constitutes otherness, witness, morality, and making choices that matter.

People everywhere are generous when disaster strikes some part of the globe; they understand that others are suffering and they can help in some small way to alleviate that suffering. When the plight of an individual, especially a child, is advertised on television or social media, almost invariably the public responds. But such generosity is frequently expressed as charity, and the response may be overbearing or paternalistic. This is particularly true of the efforts of many churches and religious organizations, independent of their denomination or penchant for proselytizing. Governmental or corporate aid often involves some sort of quid pro quo, generally in the form of information or control. The individual giver, simply wanting to help, may or may not be aware of these hidden motives.

Many governments place international aid prominently within the framework of their foreign policy. The Scandinavians in particular fund important initiatives throughout the developing world. So do the Dutch; one might imagine the latter doing penance for the ravages of their colonialist past. Even when the United States, China, Great Britain, and some of the other more financially robust nations prioritize their own interests, there is no doubt that individuals from these countries give generously of their money and also of their time, expertise, and energy.

Although United States government interests have been paramount when designing its foreign policy, individual U.S. Americans can also be deeply altruistic, as well as dedicated to meaningful long-term aid. And NGOs such as Partners in Health have done extraordinary work in places that have greatly benefited from their principled stance and even-handed attention to all those needing their help. Cuban doctors who went to fight the Ebola epidemic in Sierra Leone spoke appreciatively of working with people from this organization. It is clear that individuals laboring shoulder to shoulder on the ground put politics aside in pursuit of a common goal. Or perhaps I should say that they are guided by a saner politics, one of humanitarian inclusion and betterment. Partners in Health is explicit in saying its work is aimed at social change; it vehemently rejects notions of altruism or charity.

Médecins Sans Frontières (Doctors without Borders) is another such organization. It was created in 1971, in the aftermath of the Biafra secession, by a small group of French doctors and journalists who believed that all people have the right to medical care regardless of race, religion, creed, or political affiliation, and that the needs of these people outweigh respect for national borders. It operates all over the world, often in extremely danger-ous areas. The organization was awarded the Nobel Prize for Peace in 1999. It has a $610 million annual budget, 80 percent from individual donors and the rest from corporations. Its practice of serving the sick and wounded, irrespective of which side they are on, is reminiscent of the work done by the American Friends Service Committee (Quakers) during World War II and the U.S. war in Vietnam.

But Doctors without Borders field hospitals, often the only medical facil-ity in an immense war-torn zone, have lately been the targets of devastating bombing attacks. On October 3, 2015, a U.S. Air Force AC-130U gunship strafed the Kunduz Trauma Center in Afghanistan; at least forty-two people were killed and many more injured. At first U.S. general John F. Campbell stated that the airstrike was carried out to defend its forces on the ground, then that it had been requested by Afghan forces who were being attacked by the Taliban. The Afghan military tried to defend the bombing by claim-ing that Taliban patients were being treated at the facility.[2] Later Campbell changed his story again, admitting that the bombing had been a mistake. The world had not recovered from its shock over that attack when, on De-cember 1, 2015, United Press International reported that a Syrian hospital supported by the organization had been barrel-bombed, causing seven deaths and the partial destruction of the building. Then on January 11, 2016, CNN reported another Doctors without Borders hospital hit by a projectile in Yemen. And in April 2016 the organization's hospital in Aleppo, Syria, was partially destroyed, killing many, including that city's only remaining pedia-trician. These examples smack of a pattern rather than of chance. Indeed, in the Syrian conflict bombing hospitals has become routine. Warmongers now target the destruction of international humanitarian projects, only hoping not to be held accountable.

As I write, the U.S. military's investigation of the Kunduz tragedy has just produced a 3,000-page heavily redacted report. Its conclusion: the attack was unintentional. No criminal charges were brought, although sixteen of-ficers found responsible received minimal punishment in the form of re-ports that will go into their career files. Doctors without Borders continues to demand an independent review of what went wrong; after all, the organ-ization says, the hospital was strafed for an hour and a half despite frantic phone calls to Military Command alerting it to that fact.[3]

Partners in Health and Doctors without Borders have sterling reputa-tions. Unfortunately many other international organizations misrepresent their aid programs, take majority percentages of donations for overhead, and even siphon off funds or otherwise betray the trust of those who contribute as well as those who are supposed to benefit. In many parts of the world aid has become big business and, following some of the most dramatic disasters, has led to large-scale corruption. International disaster aid can be criminally profitable and subject to cruel abuse. It can be paternalistic or frankly opportunistic. Government programs from imperialist nations have even used "humanitarian" aid to facilitate and justify military intervention and occupation.

What sets Cuban aid programs apart? My findings show that within this panorama Cuba is unique: because the small Caribbean country itself is so politically besieged and economically weak, because its outreach has been so extensive, because—by any measure, material or spiritual—it has given so much more than it has gotten in return, because corruption has never soiled its efforts, and because such a large percentage of its population has taken part in internationalist missions. Internationalism has become a pillar of Cuban revolutionary identity, much as the youth initiative Character Counts (trustworthiness, respect, responsibility, fairness, caring, and citizenship) has taken up residence in U.S. public education. But while the latter offers a vague framework that urges good conduct and may be interpreted in different ways, the former involves tens of thousands of people leaving home for two years at a time to offer their services to strangers in desperate need.

Sharing what one has, and often even what one can hardly afford to spare, is a principle that has been incorporated into the life of the Cuban citizenry from the moment of the revolutionary victory of 1959. Most important, Cuba has never used its internationalist outreach to justify interference in other countries. Its help is never touted as special or magnanimous. On the contrary, it is generally carried out quietly, with the added objective of transforming the host countries' health care and education systems over the long term.

The Cuban Revolution's aid programs function in two directions. Its internationalists travel to many parts of the world, and the country also brings the needy to Cuba and invites young people to study on the island free of charge. The victims of the Chernobyl nuclear disaster constitute but one dramatic example of Cuba's receiving a large group of those who need its help and committing itself to offering them high-level long-term care. The country's international medical school, ELAM, is another; thousands have graduated from its well-respected courses of study at no cost to themselves and with no obligation beyond the promise that they will return to their home country to practice medicine among their own neediest citizens.

There is no doubt that Cuba's internationalism has spread goodwill for socialist values and initiated programs that exemplify that system's principles of universal access to the basic necessities. But it has also instilled dignity where dignity could no longer hold up its head, restored hope when hope was battered or dead, and helped fulfill the promise of basic human rights to many who were all but resigned to despair.

Cuba has never pretended aid while establishing beachheads of geopolitical control or launched exploitative industries that siphon off a nation's natural resources while local people provide cheap labor and the profits revert to foreign coffers. It has never employed locals in unsafe working conditions nor paid them inhumane wages. It has never invaded or occupied another country in order to secure geopolitical supremacy or gain control over that country's natural resources. It has never gone to war with an entire nation to avenge an attack by a small terrorist faction—thereby strengthening and enlarging that faction. Independent of your political position, an unbiased examination of a half century of Cuba's gifts to the global community demonstrates a new paradigm of solidarity.

This policy has also had a profound effect on those who have offered it. Roughly a tenth of Cuba's population of eleven million has taken part in some form of internationalism: as soldiers in foreign wars, disaster relief personnel, teachers, doctors, cultural workers, and specialists in a vast variety of fields. Cuba's internationalism is what being the New Man or Woman is about. It strengthens the Revolution internally and also gives it a good name among nations, in that so many countries are indebted to the practice.

The ongoing follow-up policy of Cuba's aid is also impressive. When its internationalists respond to natural disasters, such as earthquakes, floods, and hurricanes, they don't leave the affected area as soon as they've helped ameliorate its most immediate needs. In most instances a core group of specialists stays on, helping local institutions organize, strengthen, and expand their own services.

For decades Cuban aid was given without monetary recompense. As the Revolution consolidated, however, and because the country has not yet managed to industrialize, it began to explore the economic potential of this human resource. That's when it started offering the work of many of its experts in return for convertible currency, split between the individual internationalist and the national economy. But even when the professional quality of their offering is high, Cuban overseas workers still earn considerably less than their counterparts from other countries. And they are known for their expertise and willingness to work in remote areas and under extremely difficult conditions; they routinely go where even many locals are reluctant to offer their services. A large quota of sacrifice is involved.

The vast numbers of Cubans who have taken part in one or another of the country's overseas aid programs has also had an impact on the way the population as a whole sees itself in relation to the world. Internationalist solidarity is a fact of life in contemporary Cuba. There is a sense of connectedness that belies the country's island condition, history of political isolation, and the hardship that has come from so many years of attack, battery, and resistance. Over the past half century several generations of Cubans have incorporated this solidarity into their collective and personal identities.

Think about the hundreds of thousands of middle- and upper-middle-class citizens in any developed country who routinely vacation abroad. Among Cubans tourist travel has been limited, but a tenth of the population has spent two-year stints in other parts of the world—often extremely remote parts—engaging with local people in ways that have allowed them to know how those people think, feel, live, suffer, and hope. This has produced a profound level of sophistication.

When thinking about internationalism, it is inevitable that we look at nationalism, in so many ways its ideological opposite. I've had this duality (dichotomy?) in mind as I have explored each area of Cuban aid outreach; in fact some of the most important things I learned while researching and writing this book have been about nationalism and internationalism as they interact and shape us all.

Nationalism was consolidated in Cuba throughout the nineteenth and twentieth century, reaching its ultimate expression in the thought of José Martí, who—in his vision of continental defense against imperialist designs from the North—also imbued the concept with an internationalist character. From the foreigners who came to take part in the War of Independence to the large contingent that went in the other direction to defend the Spanish Republic or fight in Africa, internationalism has been a familiar part of Cuban life. The nation's island isolation has also undoubtedly played a role in the ways Cubans think about themselves within the global community, their particular mix of nationalism (sense of nationality) and internationalism.

It is easy to appreciate the importance of a nationalist sentiment for those such as Fidel Castro and his July 26 Movement, as they rallied their compatriots to come together to oust Batista and later demonstrate the unity and will needed to construct a new society and resist so many years of undermining and attack. Time and again over the past five and a half decades a sense of uniqueness or national destiny has helped a battered people keep hope palpable.

However, nationalism can be a slippery slope. During the Revolution's first three decades its domestic policies were often extremist and its attitude toward those wishing to leave the country uncompromising and inflexible. While it is understandable that anger and resentment would be unleashed against those exiles in whom the system invested years of superb education, the ugly displays of repudiation aimed at anyone making the decision to emigrate involved a distortion of patriotism lacking in the very dignity for which the Revolution stands.

Class exoduses took place beginning shortly after the revolutionary victory of 1959. The first to emigrate were the truly wealthy, then those who were afraid of a socialist form of government. Mariel in 1980 proved a tipping point.[4] Other mass emigrations followed, and some level of flight has remained a constant. Routine use of the term *gusano* (worm) to describe those fleeing, no matter the circumstance, screamed epithets and rotten eggs hurled at those on the lists of the departing, brought the issue into regrettable focus. This was nationalism spilling over into chauvinism, ideological dogmatism and extremism in a prolonged situation of conflict.

In recent decades rigid emigration policies have eased or been eliminated, the attitudes they encouraged have diminished, and their shameful echoes among the population have almost disappeared. This shift had its roots in the Dialogue of 1978, when Cubans on the island and those of the diaspora came together in a series of meetings aimed at mutual understanding and acceptance.[5] A softening of the harsh rhetoric accompanied de facto permission given to many intellectuals and others over the next decades to live abroad and return to their homeland as they desired. Without much public fanfare people began to come and go. Where it wasn't too late, ruptured family ties could be mended. When Raul Castro assumed the Cuban presidency in 2008, long-awaited policy initiatives institutionalized this change. There is no doubt, however, that years of rigidity have taken their toll.

How has this extreme nationalism affected Cuba's extraordinary record of internationalism? On the one hand, those volunteering for overseas missions carry with them a deep pride of place. They know why they are there, what they are doing, and the exemplary conduct that must accompany the task. They see themselves as representing Cuba, not simply themselves. In a certain sense giving from a position of poverty rather than from one of abundance imbues the gift with even greater value; the gesture stands unencumbered and unique. The vast majority of Cuban internationalists stay the course. On the other hand, the moment they leave the country, for even a brief time, these valuable professionals—whether doctors or baseball players—are subject to a particularly insidious pressure to defect. There is a sharp contrast between the material hardships they face at home and their glimpses of a professional's life in a capitalist country. The latter can be seductive. Long past the December 2014 reestablishment of diplomatic relations U.S. government agencies continue to fund these brain drain programs.

This has been the case with Cuban doctors fighting Ebola in Sierra Leone. Even as they were receiving praise in the U.S. media, our government's ongoing destabilization program was attempting to lure them with offers of immediate residency status and high salaries. Not a single doctor on Ebola's front lines has taken the bait. But over the years a number of other professionals, including well-trained medical specialists, have. To ensure its high standards of service at home, Cuba has had to rethink allowing doctors to travel when they wish. Specialists are now being asked to stagger their overseas vacations so that there are always enough of them working at home. In many of these situations nationalism and internationalism function like two sides of a coin. I have so far seen no official acknowledgment on the part of the U.S. government, much less an apology, for its devious and offensive brain drain policy. In Cuba it was long silenced but now is often in the news.

In the last analysis nationalism and internationalism are values. They must be thoughtfully shepherded in different situations in order to avoid giving way to fanaticism.

Here in the United States, over the past couple of decades especially, we have seen how an exaggerated nationalistic patriotism has precluded the in-depth public conversation that might have produced more rational solutions to ongoing problems of terrorist attack, homegrown violence, racism, and out-of-control racial profiling. Fundamentalist bombast has taken the place of humanity and reason, and we have racist fear, unending war, an increased number of hate crimes, and mounting gun violence as a result. The vast number of people applauding Donald Trump's racist, sexist, and xenophobic rhetoric during the 2016 presidential campaign attests to the seductive power of such orchestrated hate, and his victory has emboldened them.

Many liberal and progressive people have voiced concern about this, and in 2015 a retired high-level U.S. military official added his voice to the chorus. Lt. Gen. Michael Flynn served in the U.S. Army for thirty years. He became the director of the Defense Intelligence Agency, where he was the nation's highest ranking military intelligence officer. Recently he has disgraced himself, but he was right when, in an interview on November 29, 2015, he castigated post-9/11 U.S. foreign policy, calling it tragically nationalistic:

> When 9/11 occurred, all the emotions took over, and our response was, "Where did those bastards come from? Let's go kill them. Let's go get them." Instead of asking why they attacked us, we asked where they came from. Then we strategically marched in the wrong direction. [The Iraq war] was a huge error. As brutal as Saddam Hussein was, it was a mistake to just eliminate him. The same is true for Moammar Gadhafi and for Libya, which is now a failed state. The historic lesson is that it was a strategic failure to go into Iraq. History will not be and should not be kind with that decision.[6]

In the Cuban context nationalism and internationalism sometimes engage in an intricate dance. Each may be engendered, endangered, or thrown off kilter by the other. Perhaps the opportunity to experience difference—other people, other cultures and customs—and knowing that one must function within parameters of respect for that difference, makes Cuban internationalism the best antidote to the sort of extreme nationalism that hovers at the uneasy edge of most modern societies. It is to the Cuban Revolution's immense credit, and reflective of its deep core values, that the vast majority of the country's internationalists complete their mission with honor. And not a single Cuban serving overseas has been charged with the sorts of crime that U.S. military and civilian contractor personnel so often commit against foreign nationals.

Researching Cuban internationalism, thinking about the phenomenon, and listening to people's stories, I was impressed by the pride and sense of satisfaction that almost always accompanies Cubans returning from missions abroad, whether in the areas of adult education, public health, disaster relief, or wars of liberation. The vast majority of the Revolution's internationalists say their mission was the most difficult thing they've ever done, but that it also gave them the most satisfaction. Many volunteer for a second or third tour of duty. Almost all report having come back changed for the better. Unlike U.S. veterans returning from foreign wars, Cubans who fight overseas can count on appropriate care when they come home; they feel they have done something worth the sacrifice, and psychological help is not stigmatized.

I had a very good friend, the South African novelist Mark Behr, who at eighteen and nineteen years of age fought in the South African Defense Force, on the wrong side of Angola's war. I have dedicated this book to him. An Afrikaner from a working-class and unconsciously racist family, Mark enlisted in that war without giving it much thought. If anything, he believed he was being patriotic. Later, upon reaching political maturity, he realized that he had been misled to fight for apartheid, and he devoted the rest of his life to working for the liberation of all peoples from every sort of oppression.

I was about to write to Mark, inviting him to reminisce with me about his involvement in Angola, when news of his sudden death arrived. Sadly I could not engage him in further conversation about the experience; instead I will quote something he told an interviewer in 2011, speaking about the connections he made among a number of personal and political issues having to do with the profoundly nationalistic underpinnings of his youth. I believe what he said goes to the root of this issue, as it may be reflected in any country, any life:

> I was proud of being in the South African Defense Force and then of becoming an officer. The association between "national service" and "doing your part" and the marriage of these ideas with masculine ideals appealed to me. This was also the case when my mother's cousin, who retired as a general in the Security Police, invited me to become a "source" for the South African police. At that point, as a closeted queer man living a secret homosexual life, I was overwhelmingly concerned with "passing" for straight, so being an officer and a gentlemen—and later a secret agent of the South African government—were shields in part because of their markers of privilege.
>
> With that being said, I cannot believe that I am, or my life was or is, anomalous: one need not be a closeted gay white man in Africa to buy hopelessly into threats of communist expansionism or myths of masculinity, heterosexism, and state militarism. One need also not have grown up there to begin apprehending one's world differently, to begin challenging oneself and one's life-lies in a bid to live differently, in part to make one's own life more bearable.[7]

This statement, more than any I have read, speaks of the ways values such as nationalistic fanaticism, racism, homophobia, and militarism feed and are fed by state policies that institutionalize such values. Identity issues play out as attitudes and actions intimately linked to political positions and acts of war. Conversely internationalism can nurture an opposing set of values.

Behr goes further: "The demand for unquestioning loyalty has built into it the likelihood—the requirement—of betrayal, disappointment, exile and dissidence."[8] This statement is remarkable when considered in the Cuban context. It was made by a man speaking from another culture and out of experiences lived halfway around the world. But just as Cuba and Africa have been intimately linked in the context of the internationalism described in this book, I believe Behr's words offer lessons to be learned about the deep links between extreme nationalism and racism, homophobia, self-loathing, and dissidence. Cuba is a country, but it has also shown itself to be a state of mind, and the solidarity expressed by the Cuban Revolution has those values at its core.

I didn't learn this only from working on this book, although working on this book often brought it to mind. I didn't really learn it only from Mark Behr either. I reproduce his language because it is so articulate and because I believe his life experience gives his observations a weight few others possess. I still imagine us talking about these issues, finishing one another's sentences amid laughter or tears, and nodding conspiratorially—something we will never again be able to do.

The African American scholar, critic, and public intellectual bell hooks says the same thing in a different way. When George Yancy asked her why she uses the expression "imperialist white supremacist capitalist patriarchy" to describe the power structure underlying the U.S. social order, hooks responded:

We can't begin to understand the nature of domination if we don't understand how these systems connect with one another. Significantly, this phrase has always moved me because it doesn't value one system over another. For so many years in the feminist movement, women were saying that gender is the only aspect of identity that really matters, that domination only came into the world because of rape. Then we had so many race-oriented folks who were saying "Race is the most important thing. We don't even need to be talking about class or gender." So for me, that phrase always reminds me of a global context, of the context of class, of empire, of capitalism, of racism and of patriarchy. Those things are all linked—an interlocking system.[9]

Researching this book sharpened my thinking, but for the past three decades, at least—like Behr and hooks—I have understood the profound similarities and interactions between what some relegate to an area they call "identity politics" and the ways nations shape themselves and their international as well as domestic policies. Living so many years in Latin America, I learned about imperialism's designs on the countries it considers within its domain. As a survivor of incest I learned about the invasion of a small body by one more powerful. Eventually I was able to link these two crimes. I realized that the invasion of a vulnerable human being and the invasion of a small country obey the same shameful law of "Might makes right."

Nationalism and internationalism are, as I say, a complex dichotomy. In Cuba and elsewhere they beg for in-depth analysis. In this book I have only just begun to explore the ways they may intersect or affect one another in a particular time and place. Aggression at the intimate level mirrors class and racial aggression. The domination of a small country by a more powerful one mirrors the more intimate forms of abuse. Cuban socialism has at its core an immense reverence for life. As Cuban internationalists strive to make the world better, they themselves become the New Men and Women of whom Che spoke when he said that the only way to create a solid base for future evolution is by changing human beings themselves.

The essayist Enrique Ubieta Gómez writes about the relationship between building a socialist society and taking part in the Revolution's overseas missions and explores the connection between the individual and the collective in his essay "El proyecto socialista de una nueva individualidad" (A New Individuality's Socialist Project):

> I don't know how to say this without it appearing exaggerated or chauvinistic, but almost every Cuban living in Cuba has been, or is, a hero. And this reinforces the cultural concept of the new human being. In any other national context their life stories would be amazing. Any one of those over forty, the anonymous people one finds on a city street, might have fought in Angola, taught in Nicaragua, or been an internationalist doctor in a Latin American or African country. They might have participated in four or five sugar harvests, multiple agricultural mobilizations, not out of economic need or because they didn't have a job in their own

profession, but as a revolutionary act, a way of contributing individually to the common struggle.[10]

This is the essence of solidarity: When you change people you change everything. The survival of the Cuban Revolution, indeed the survival of values that ultimately may save our humanity, wherever we are called upon to put them to the test, depends upon our getting it right.

If how deeply those Cubans going on internationalist missions feel the import of what they are doing impressed me, I readily understood why. There is no mercenary edge to what they contribute. They feel privileged to have been able to take their revolution's values of selflessness and sacrifice to people less fortunate. What I was less prepared for was how central the Cuban Revolution's unique understanding of the creative process and its appreciation of art and culture are to its conviction that community means humanity and that it has an obligation to transmit that humanity not only to its own people but to the world.

And this brings me full circle. In unexpected ways, art—writing, the visual arts, theater, and song—can also help us understand this and move forward in our efforts, something else that was reinforced for me during the writing of this book.

Incorporating artistic and other cultural manifestations into their overseas experience has enabled doctors and soldiers, teachers and relief workers to pierce the millennial membranes that so often make it difficult for those from one culture to come to the aid of those from another, with neither objectification nor condescension. Writing this book I have also discovered a whole new literary genre that has flourished in Cuba over the past several decades. It might be described as a genre of internationalist writing, and it includes novels, short stories, poetry, and essays. It may be a while yet before it is viewed as a discrete literary category, but its many voices have already produced a valuable body of texts.

Some may find it difficult to understand the route by which I came to this realization. Others may question its veracity. Many no doubt still wonder why I approached internationalism through poetry's door. Partly because I am a poet, of course, but there is more to it than that. As I researched and wrote, the clues all but grabbed at me, begging to be followed. There were obvious signs, such as the increasing involvement of painters, musicians, clowns, and other performers called upon to help with the mental health aspects of Cuba's internationalist health care projects, from Chernobyl to Haiti, from Angola to Nicaragua. And there were less obvious clues, like

the ways Cuban poetry, art, and music sustain those working in challenging conditions and for long periods of time far from home. Or how Cuban
internationalists often turn to writing and other artistic expression as a way of
sharing experiences that may be hard for others to grasp. There were the
Cuban internationalists themselves, who after serving in Africa returned to
their previous professions but also wrote fiction because there was no other
way they could express how their experiences had changed their lives. In
none of these cases was this a one-time shot. An internationalist literature is
becoming its own rich genre in Cuba.

Fidel Castro, Che Guevara, Haydée Santamaría, and other Cuban leaders
said on multiple occasions and in different ways that "revolutionary" was
the most profound identity to which a person could aspire, internationalism
the noblest form of revolution, and art essential to social change. Cuba's
first minister of culture, Armando Hart, said, "To confuse art and politics
is a political mistake. To separate art and politics is another mistake."[11]
When Fidel sought a metaphorical rank to confer upon Che after his death
in Bolivia, he called his comrade "artist." It was the highest accolade he
could find.

I embarked upon this book because I noticed the impact Cuban writers
and artists had upon their contemporaries in other countries. I came to this
conclusion after preparing a bilingual anthology of eight decades of Cuban
poetry; translating the poems enabled me to enter them in ways I hadn't
before. This led me to look at other creative genres—music, film, photography, dance, theater—and the ways their Cuban practitioners have influenced the wider world.

I had lived in Cuba for eleven years, raised my four children there, shared
in the Revolution's great accomplishments and painful failures. I heard the
pride, and also sometimes the grumbling, when Cubans spoke about their
country giving others what it often could not give its own. Yet even the
grumbling had a different tone than it might have had elsewhere. Grumbling
with an edge of stubborn pride, I called it. Through subsequent decades I
returned often. I have followed the Cuban Revolution as only someone impressed by its sustainability and direction can. I have been both critical and
deeply moved.

The country's internationalism was always there, in times of great hardship as well as times in which such solidarity was easier. The impressive
outreach has been uniformly praised by international agencies. Especially
when considered in the context of an economy that has never really gotten
off the ground, such extreme generosity of spirit—not to mention human

and material aid—also begs some questions to which I have not found complete or satisfactory answers. Many have questions at this moment of Cuba's transition from a socialist society to one that engages with global capitalist markets: Will it be possible to retain the major socialist gains? How does people's participation at home effect their participation abroad? What role does democracy play, and how does the Cuban Revolution define democracy? Will the transition to a mixed economy, with all the shifts in emphasis that may be implicit, have a negative impact on the great solidarity for which the Revolution is known?

In this respect I find Daniel Rafuls Pineda's analysis helpful.[12] He asks how a country like Cuba, classified among the authoritarian states in the fourth and lowest group on the Democracy Index, also figures among the top countries in the United Nations Human Development Index. The Democracy Index is a development metric created by the UN in an effort to rank the degree of democracy in 167 countries. It is based on criteria such as life expectancy, literacy rate, years of compulsory education, and wealth as measured by GDP per capita—in other words, measures that reflect general well-being. As of 2013, out of 187 countries listed on the Human Development Index, Cuba was tied for forty-third place.[13]

To the analyst who sees traditional notions of democracy as indicative of whether or not a nation enjoys social and political health, this would seem to be a contradiction. But Rafuls Pineda goes on to explain that Cuba has one of the most qualified workforces in the underdeveloped world; it dedicates the most resources to education, is among those with the highest number of doctors per capita, and offers the most health and education aid to other nations. Yet according to its critics, it devotes "the least effort to defending the values of liberal democracy—as if social spending and solidarity had no link at all with competition between political parties."[14]

Perhaps we should broaden our ideas about what a people need to live fruitful lives. Perhaps we should revisit our concepts of competition, political organization, and democracy itself. I do not say this to discourage a furthering of across-the-board political representation or mass participation; I believe that we in the United States as well as the people of Cuba need more of both. I do mean to suggest that we might want to look at our vitiated notions about these categories and how well our current definitions serve us.

Cuba's answers are often surprising. For those of us who travel frequently to the country, it is tempting to believe we understand the characteristics of the Cuban people or the Revolution's positives and negatives. But then the Revolution—either its leadership or the ordinary people trained in its values—comes at us from left field with an idea or creative solution we could not have imagined. Often, because of Cuba's situation, the solutions have been geared to survival. Hopefully, as the country is able to act in more equal partnership with the rest of the world, these solutions will be more systemic and lasting.

The way Cuba is presented in our press and even by many of our academics leads us to consider the frustrations that induce so many to emigrate rather than the inventiveness demonstrated each day by the many more who stay. Some cannot look past dilapidated buildings, rutted streets, and failing infrastructure. Many ignore less visible measures such as values and international solidarity. The truth is, what happens in Cuba resists easy analysis. We inevitably judge through our own lens, whatever that may be, considering what we feel are achievements and errors from a point of view that colors our conclusions and renders them less than accurate.

For example, what really does constitute democracy? Certainly not what exists in Cuba at this moment, but not what we have in the United States either. Is Cuban society patriarchal, its political system marred by social paternalism? Yes and, sadly, I do not know of a society or political system that isn't. Yet who could have carried this Revolution to fruition but someone with Fidel's enormous personality and vision? The sometime rigidity, staying power, and control have been natural corollaries to the brilliance and courage. Did the Federation of Cuban Women, with its early antifeminist stance, hold Cuban women back? Of course. But what other than the FMC could have so massively organized the country's women at mid-twentieth century? Have the Revolution's attempts at economic survival contained large doses of volunteerism and wishful thinking? Yes. Have its solutions brought with them the painful corruption that runs through Cuban society today? Undoubtedly. But how could a small island nation have survived on other terms in the world we had and have? This very survival speaks a language difficult to understand for those who have not experienced it in their own lives.

Cuba has resisted unimaginable attacks with a million daily acts of heroism. The overwhelming problems Cuba faces today have their roots in a complex mix of strategic, tactical, and cultural realities. A certain level of coercion and stifling of popular agency is something we do well to criticize, but we cannot possibly know what dangers may have lain in wait had individual freedoms been dispensed more liberally. I think of Sandinista Nicaragua in this regard; it prided itself on the individual freedoms it was able to protect and then caved to external pressure and internal greed. So much of what a people are and do emerges from traditions that have taken root over centuries. One can have one's opinions, but there is always another layer to be understood, an additional complexity to be unraveled.

From the viewpoint of those receiving Cuba's internationalist aid, the benefits of the Revolution have been tremendous. Nelson Mandela said that without Cuban internationalism, apartheid on the African continent would not have been defeated. Angolan and Namibian leaders acknowledged that without Cuba's military missions to their countries and other nations recently freed from colonialism, they could not have preserved their freedom. Public thanks have been expressed by leaders in Nicaragua, Venezuela, Haiti, Chile, Pakistan, Indonesia, and many other nations. I have spoken with dozens of ordinary women and men throughout the Global South whose gratitude to Cuba knows no limits. I have experienced the Revolution's solidarity in my own family.

Without Cuba's Yes I Can adult literacy program, six million fewer of the world's adults, in twenty-nine countries, would be able to read and write. Without Cuba's assembly-line cataract removal in a number of nations, hundreds of thousands who can see today would still be blind. Without the several hundred Cuban doctors and health care workers who went to Sierra Leone, Libya, and Guinea, the 2015 Ebola pandemic could not have been halted. The generosity of this internationalism continues to be felt throughout the developing world. It is one of the Revolution's basic tenets.

Internationalist values are imprinted on the children—those born in Cuba and those from elsewhere who have experienced its generosity for months or years—my own among them. And I have seen how that sensibility has shaped not only their lives but the lives of their children as well. These values are less and less evident in a world beset by intolerance, fanaticism, hatred, and violence. Yet they are absolutely necessary to our survival as a species.

The endurance of this remarkable solidarity is fragile in a world that increasingly favors economic and military strength over basic human kindness. Nurturing and protecting Cuban internationalism behooves us all.

As Che said, "Solidarity is the tenderness of the peoples." Generosity of spirit, whether in an individual, a nation, or a political system, may be the only real antidote to the greed, deception, and violence that are such pandemics in today's world. When the loudest conversation rages between state terrorism, whose currency is absolute control, and the fanatical madness that spawns holy wars reminiscent of the Crusades, we desperately need the quieter, more caring voice embodied in the Cuban Revolution's motto: "We give what we have, not what we have left over."

NOTES

1. HOW THESE IDEAS TOOK SHAPE

1. Reloba, *De/sobre Mario Benedetti*, 128. Unless otherwise noted, all translations are mine.

2. The School of the Americas (SOA) is a combat training school for Latin American soldiers located at Fort Benning, Georgia. It was initially established in Panama in 1946 but was expelled from that country in 1984 under the terms of the Panama Canal Treaty (Article 4). In 2001 it was renamed the Western Hemisphere Institute for Security Cooperation (WHINSEC). The SOA has left a trail of blood and suffering in every country where its graduates have returned. For this reason it has been dubbed the "School of Assassins" and has attracted yearly protest demonstrations. Since 1946 the SOA has trained over sixty-four thousand Latin American soldiers in counterinsurgency techniques, sniper training, commando and psychological warfare, military intelligence, and interrogation tactics. These graduates have consistently used their skills to wage a war against their own people. Among those targeted are educators, union organizers, priests, nuns and other religious workers, student leaders, and others who work for the rights of the poor. Hundreds of thousands of Latin Americans have been tortured, raped, assassinated, "disappeared," massacred, and forced into refugee status by those trained at the School of Assassins.

3. Idea expressed most explicitly in Che's 1965 "Socialism and Man in Cuba."

4. Anderson, *Che*, 392–94.

5. The July 26 Movement, named for the attack on Moncada Barracks on that date in 1953, was Fidel Castro's organization. It gained adepts, went on to win the war of liberation, and eventually morphed, along with members of other progressive organizations, into Cuba's Communist Party.

6. Randall, *Only the Road / Solo el camino*.

7. Federico García Lorca (1898–1936) was a Spanish poet murdered during his country's civil war. César Vallejo (1892–1938) was born in Peru but lived most of his life in Paris, where he died of tuberculosis. Pablo Neruda (1904–73) was a Chilean communist and Nobel laureate who died days after the overthrow of his country's three-year socialist experiment. Uruguay's Mario Benedetti (1920–2009) is one of the most widely read poets on the continent. Octavio Paz (1914–98) was an important Mexican intellectual and poet. All five were radical in their use of language and continue to be major influences on poetry in Spanish and beyond.

8. The filmmaker Sergei Eisenstein (1891–1938), the poet Osip Mandelstam (1891–1938), and the painter Wassily Kandinsky (1866–1944) were Russian artists whose work strained against official rigidity and who were greatly influential in their fields.

9. Walt Whitman (1819–92), Allen Ginsberg (1926–97), Adrienne Rich (1929–2012), Diane di Prima (b. 1934), and Joy Harjo (b. 1951) are U.S. American poets who have written the American identity in an American idiom.

10. Weiss, *The Whole Island*, 1.

11. Víctor Manuel (1897–1969), Wifredo Lam (1902–82), René Portocarrero (1912–85), Mariano Rodríguez (1912–90), Antonia Eiríz (1929–83), and Amelia Peláez (1896–1968) were important Cuban painters whose work was honored during the Revolution.

12. *Media lunas* are half-moon-shaped transoms above doors or windows in which segments of colored glass filter the island's tropical light.

13. Humberto Solás (1941–2008) was an important Cuban filmmaker who embarked on his career at the age of eighteen, just as the Cuban Revolution was about to be victorious. He is best known for *Manuela* (1966), *Lucía* (1968), *Cantata de Chile* (1975), and *Cecilia* (1981).

14. Mario Rodríguez Alemán writing in *Trabajadores*, July 1982, quoted in Chanan, *Cuban Cinema*, 393.

15. Hayden, *Listen, Yankee!*, 136.

16. Castro, *Fidel Castro Reader*, 33.

17. The Council for Mutual Economic Assistance (COMECON) was an economic organization under the leadership of the Soviet Union in existence from 1949 to 1991. It comprised the countries of the Eastern Bloc along with a number of communist states elsewhere in the world and was the Eastern Bloc's reply to Western Europe's formation of the Organization for European Economic Cooperation (EEC). COMECON's founding countries were Bulgaria, Czechoslovakia, Hungary, Poland, Romania, and the Soviet Union. Albania participated until 1961, when the Soviet-Albanian split occurred. In 1950 East Germany joined, in 1962 Mongolia, in 1972 Cuba, and in 1978 Vietnam. Observer status was held at various times by North Korea, Yugoslavia, Finland, Iraq, Mexico, Angola, Nicaragua, Mozambique, Afghanistan, Ethiopia, Laos, and South Yemen. By the 1970s COMECON was no longer geographical but included countries around the world. Wide variations in economic status and level of economic development generated divergent interests. In the 1980s the EEC incorporated the 270 million people in Europe into an economic association through intergovernmental agreements aimed at maximizing profits and economic efficiency on a national and international scale. COMECON, on the other hand, joined together 450 million people in ten countries on three continents, but its effectiveness was not nearly as great.

18. In conversation with the author, October 2015, my translation.

19. The importance of *Pensamiento Crítico* cannot be overstated in the Cuban Revolution's struggle for analysis and freedom of thought. The journal ran from 1967 through 1971, producing fifty-three issues, and published the most important currents of revolutionary thought. From its inception the important Cuban theoretician Fernando Martínez Heredia was its editor in chief; he also headed the University of Havana's Philosophy Department at the time. Others associated with the publication

were Jesús Díaz, Thalia Fung Riverón, José Bell Lara, and Mireya Crespo. During the repressive period that began to exert control over Cuban culture in 1971, both the Philosophy Department and the journal were shut down. Casa de las América's journal, *Revista Casa*, has enjoyed an unbroken run of close to three hundred issues. It too consistently includes diverse voices, but the prestige of its founder, Haydée Santamaría, the eminent poet and essayist Roberto Fernández Retamar, and a roster of Latin America's most outstanding minds (Ezequiel Martínez Estrada, Mario Benedetti, Julio Cortázar, Eduardo Galeano, among others) allowed it to continue through the repressive period, hampered but maintaining an important presence.

20. Fidel Castro, speech at the University of Havana's Aula Magna, November 17, 2005, my translation.

21. From 1971 to 1975, or the mid-1980s, depending on one's point of view. This period, known as El Quinquenio Gris (the Five Gray Years), saw bureaucrats, most of them from the old Moscow-oriented Communist Party, gain control over artistic freedom. Many homosexuals and artists critical of the Revolution were marginalized. Eventually broader minds prevailed and the repression eased.

It wasn't only Cuba's artists and writers who railed against the stagnant art form. In his important 1965 "Socialism and Man in Cuba," Che wrote, "[Socialist realism is] the kind of 'art' that bureaucrats understand. True artistic values were disregarded, and the problem of general culture was reduced to taking some things from the socialist present and some from the dead (and, hence, not dangerous, past). Thus, socialist realism arose upon the foundations of the past century. But the realistic art of the 19th century is also a class art, more purely capitalist than this decadent art of the 20th century which reveals the anguish of alienated people. Why, then, try to find the only valid prescription for art in the frozen forms of socialist realism?" Guevara, "Socialism and Man in Cuba," n.p.

22. This and other opinions by Guanche from a letter to the author in October 2015, my translation.

23. José Martí (1853–95) was a patriot, thinker, writer, and revolutionary considered the father of the Cuban nation. He was imprisoned, exiled to Spain, and spent time organizing Cubans inside the United States in the period leading up to Cuba's last war of independence from Spain. He foresaw future U.S. designs on Cuba and conceived of a single America, which he called "our America." He was killed in the first battle of the War of Independence at Dos Ríos. His thought influenced Fidel Castro's generation of revolutionaries, and thousands of identical plaster busts of Martí can be seen everywhere on the island. Tomás Gutiérrez Alea's 1966 film, *Death of a Bureaucrat*, makes fun of those busts, an example of the ability of Cubans to laugh at themselves.

24. Fornet, *Rutas críticas*, 109–13. I have quoted and also paraphrased Fornet's observations, as I find them pertinent to my argument.

25. Carlos Manuel de Céspedes, a wealthy landowner and patriot, initiated Cuba's Ten Years' War (for independence from Spain) on his sugar plantation, La Demajagua, on October 10, 1868, with what is known as "el grito de Yara," a battle cry that has come to symbolize that war of independence. The Cuban patriots were called

mambises. Independence would not be won until the end of the century, and no sooner was Spain defeated than the United States stepped in and took control of the island.

26. Like all experiences of profound social change, the Cuban Revolution's first decade was rich in creative exuberance and freedom of expression. In 1968 the first glimmers of excessive control could be seen, and by 1971 a group of old-time Moscow-oriented communists dominated the cultural and artistic sphere. Many brilliant talents suffered during this Quinquenio Gris. In 1975, with the inauguration of a Ministry of Culture, the repressive measures were reversed. But it wouldn't be until 2007 that Cuban writers and artists demanded accountability for what had happened and, more important, public discussion of how the marginalization of valuable creative minds had been allowed to take place, with an eye to making sure nothing similar could happen again. For a more detailed description of El Quinquenio Gris, see Randall, *To Change the World*, 171–90.

27. Cubanía, or Cubanness, is an identification as rich as it has sometimes been suspect in speaking of what it means to be Cuban.

28. The first generation of the nueva trova was defined by the singer-songwriters Silvio Rodríguez (b. 1946), Pablo Milanés (b. 1943), Noël Nicola (1946–2005), and Sara González (1951–2012). Rodríguez especially, and to a lesser extent the other three, are known for lyrics that, when they first appeared, were too complex for Cuba's then narrow-minded bureaucracy. The group caught the attention of Haydée Santamaría at Casa de las Américas and people in the country's film industry, enabling them to flourish. At least two subsequent generations of Cuban singer-songwriters followed, and their most important exponents continue to perform throughout the world.

29. Emilio del Junco (1915–74), Antonio "Tonino" Quintana (1919–93), Ricardo Porro (1925–2014), Mario Coyula (1935–2014), and Roberto Segre (1934–2013) were architects, some Cuban and others who worked for long periods in Cuba, who made outstanding contributions to Cuban architecture of the 1960s through 1990s that can still be appreciated in the country.

30. After the collapse of the Soviet Union in 1990, Soviet aid to Cuba was reduced dramatically, practically from one day to the next. Cuba's economic situation became dire. The government pronounced the four or five years beginning in 1991 to be a Special Period in Peacetime.

31. This marginalization affected many artists, writers, and others during El Quinquenio Gris, which actually stretched from 1971 through the mid-1980s. I was only one of many affected. I tell my personal experience of this in my memoir, *To Change the World*, 171–90.

32. I was told that my marginalization was due to the fact that I had a close friendship with a Canadian accused of working for the CIA. I accepted this, although with reservations, since my partner at the time was also a friend of this person and had not been marginalized. I believe my unabashed feminism also may have played a part, as well as the fact that my home was frequented by people from a number of revolutionary organizations, not all of them favored by the Cuban party.

33. Global Exchange is a San Francisco–based international human rights organization dedicated to promoting social, economic, and environmental justice around

the world and bringing attention to domestic problems as well. It sponsors reality tours to several countries, educates to counteract U.S. media distortion, hosts seminars and public actions, and engages in campaigns designed to bring awareness to issues of injustice. www.globalexchange.org.

34. The United Nations Development Program records an average 11.5 years of education for Cubans over twenty-five. The population completes 13.8 years of schooling (almost through the second year of university). The World Bank has Cuba at the top of its list in terms of its investment in education for 2009–13 (13 percent of its gross national product).

35. Cuban National Center for Sex Education. Mariela Castro, who does not identify as gay, has made eradicating discrimination against and improving life for gay and transgender Cubans a serious pursuit. As the daughter of President Raul Castro and Vilma Espín, who founded and for many years was president of the Federation of Cuban Women, Mariela has a voice many others do not have.

36. Gay authors, whose work was not published during the country's repressive years but has since come out in significant editions, include Gastón Barquero, Antón Arrufat, and José Lezama Lima.

37. According to Nick Miroff's article "Despite Changes, U.S. Businesses Still Face a Minefield of Sanctions in Cuba" (*Washington Post*, January 11, 2015), "Not since the early years of Fidel Castro's rule, when his leftist ideals brought home a number of exiles initially sympathetic to the 1959 revolution, have so many Cubans voluntarily returned. The difference is that today's repatriates are not coming back for socialism [but] as capitalists. . . . Prompted by President Raúl Castro's limited opening to small business and his 2011 move allowing Cubans to buy and sell real estate, the repatriates are using money saved abroad to acquire property and open private restaurants, guesthouses, spas and retail shops."

38. Among the books are *Cuban Women Now, Women in Cuba Twenty Years Later, Breaking the Silences, Gathering Rage, To Change the World, Che on My Mind, Haydée Santamaría, Cuban Revolutionary: She Led by Transgression*, and *Only the Road / Solo el camino*.

39. "Sobre José Martí y el equilibrio del mundo," in Fornet, *Rutas críticas*, 108.

40. Letter to the author, summer 2015, my translation.

41. Students studied a certain number of hours a day and also worked on farms or in special factories, putting what they learned into everyday practice. Even in the day care centers very young children tended little vegetable plots, harvested their produce, and ate the results of their labor. By middle and high school their efforts were economically viable. At university the combination of work and study gave students a genuine sense of how their chosen field functions.

2. TALENT AND INFLUENCE BEYOND NUMBERS

1. *El Corno Emplumado / The Plumed Horn* was a bilingual literary journal that appeared quarterly between January 1962 and July 1969. It published vanguard work of the era. All its issues can be accessed at https://opendoor.northwestern.edu/archive/.

2. The Soviet influence in architecture left many heavy blocks of buildings, antithetical to Cuba's tropical climate and exuberant culture, poorly finished and soon in

sad disrepair. Fortunately poetry is made of words, which are less likely to scar a landscape. If the words don't fit, they are exchanged for others or forgotten.

3. "Citas de Fidel Castro sobre Educación," Cumbres Iberoamericanos, http://cumbresiberoamerica.cip.cu/wp-content/uploads/2011/10/Citas_educacion.pdf.

4. Built by three architects, Ricardo Porro, Roberto Gottardi, and Vittorio Garatti, the five schools included Modern Dance, Plastic Arts, Dramatic Arts, Music, and Ballet. Initially called the National Art Schools, they eventually became the Higher Institute of Art. The idea for a national art school was Che Guevara's. The organic Catalan-vaulted brick and terra-cotta structures, built in 1961, seemed to emerge from the lush tropical landscape in Havana's Cubanacán neighborhood. The complex is considered one of the most important examples of Cuban revolutionary architecture. Early on, students were recruited from every corner of the country. Later provincial schools were built, where young people could study closer to home. The art schools suffered during the repressive 1970s but were reenergized in the following decade.

5. Rolando González Patricio, "Cuatro décadas entre las artes," *Granma*, September 30, 2015, online. In 1976 the schools changed their name to Instituto Superior de Arte (Higher Institute of Art).

6. This loosening of travel restrictions, as well as others concerning the buying and selling of property, the ability to own small businesses, and much else, dates to Raul Castro's administration, which began in 2008.

7. See Randall, *Haydée Santamaría*, 126–58.

8. Jesse Maceo Vega-Frey, "The Carlos Vega Collection of OSPAAAL Posters," in Interference Archive, *El diseño a las armas / Armed by Design*, 8.

9. Alonso and Yáñez, *Damas de Social*, 243.

10. The UN called the campaign the world's most ambitious and organized. It is estimated that a million people took part, as either teachers or learners. In a single year the country's illiteracy rate was reduced from approximately 40 percent to around 4 percent.

11. Camnitzer, *New Art of Cuba*, xxii. An excellent resource for Cuban visual expression through the decade of the 1980s.

12. See Camnitzer, *New Art of Cuba*, for an analysis of this movement.

13. Bruguera graduated from Cuba's Higher Institute of Art and received an MFA in performance from the School of the Art Institute of Chicago. She lives in Havana and Chicago. She has frequently suffered repressive measures—for example, being held for several hours or even days after one of her art installations or actions, all of which reference freedom of expression.

14. Hannah Ellis-Petersen, "The Woman Trying to Change Cuba's Cultural Landscape—and Stay Out of Jail," *Guardian*, April 10, 2016.

15. For a view of González's work, see *Q and A with Seven Contemporary Cuban Artists*. Eiríz's *The Baseball Game* is exhibited, along with a great many other of her paintings, at Havana's Museum of Art.

16. Alexis Leiva Machado (Kcho) (b. 1970) was born into a working-class family in Nueva Gerona, Isle of Youth. He began his art career young, has exhibited all over the world, and is the winner of many prizes and honors. In 2008 he was awarded the Order "Julio Antonio Mella," issued by the Cuban Council of State. He was one of the founders of the "Martha Machado" Brigade, which takes artists to sites of national

disasters to help with issues of mental health. Kcho was elected deputy from the Isle of Youth to Cuba's National Assembly in July 2003 and reelected in January 2008.

17. Quoted in Arango, *En los márgenes, acercamientos a la poesía cubana*, 29.

18. Solarizing is printing film at a midpoint between negative and positive, evoking a sense of time hovering between the real and the imagined.

19. In Randall, *Cuban Women Now*, Alicia Alonso discusses at length the achievements of Cuba's National Ballet, including the ways the school has broken with the exclusion of Afro-Cuban dancers and developed places of stardom for them in the company (149–60).

20. Cuba's Catholic Church opposed the Revolution's turn toward socialism, and the state responded by refusing Communist Party membership to believers and relegating the Church to near irrelevance politically. The burgeoning of liberation theology in the 1980s brought those who saw no contradiction between their faith and the Revolution closer, and today there is growing cooperation.

21. Thirty-seven student musicians from Cuba's Higher Institute of Art traveled to Chicago as guests of the Chicago Jazz Philharmonic for a week-long cultural exchange that culminated in a November 13, 2015, performance with CJP at the Auditorium Theater.

22. *Buena Vista Social Club* introduced the wider world to these musicians, many of them now in their eighties, nineties, or older.

23. Fernando Ravsberg, "Silvio Rodríguez: 'Habrá otra revolución en el futuro, pero mientras llega, lo que nos toca es evolucionar,'" *Público*, October 9, 2015, www .publico.es/culturas/silvio-rodriguez-habra-revolucion-futuro.html.

24. Ernesto Guevara, "Socialism and Man in Cuba," *Revista Marcha* (Montevideo, Uruguay), 1965, quoted in Gordon-Nesbitt, *To Defend the Revolution Is to Defend Culture*, 131.

3. CUBA BY CUBA

1. On February 16, 2016, Reuters released an article written by Daniel Trotta and datelined Havana: "Alabama Company Gets U.S. Permission to Build Tractors in Cuba" (http://www.reuters.com/article/us-cuba-usa-tractors-idUSKCN0VO28R). Cleber LLC, based in Paint Rock, Alabama, announced that it had received authorization from the U.S. Department of Commerce and the Office of Foreign Assets Control to build a tractor manufacturing facility in Cuba. Its first Cuba-produced model will be called Oggun (the name of a Santaría deity), and it is advertised as the first in a complete line of agricultural and light construction equipment. In recent years 70 percent of Cuba's land has been returned to the private sector to be worked by small farmers.

2. This book was written before the Trump administration. U.S.-Cuba relations are now subject to new uncertainties.

3. Quoted in Hayden, *Listen, Yankee!*, 190.

4. Fidel Castro died on November 25, 2016, at age ninety. This book was already in production.

5. All statistics according to United Nations country statistics, data.un.org.

6. Although the term *prehistory* is generally accepted as denoting that which took place before history was written, I have never liked its implications. Human history,

whether written in a language we are able to decipher or not, has existed as long as humans have lived.

7. An English translation by W. Nick Hill was published by Curbstone Press in 1994 with the title *Biography of a Runaway Slave*. Miguel Barnet and Esteban Montejo are both listed as authors.

8. Zuleica Romay is the director of the Cuban Book Institute, an umbrella institution for all state-run publishing. She is a member of the Central Committee of the Cuban Communist Party and a brilliant social analyst and essayist.

9. Romay, *Cepos de la memoria*, 8–9.

10. Julio Antonio Mella (1903–29) fought against Machado's government and, in 1925, founded what was known as the internationalized Cuban Communist Party (i.e., recognized by Moscow). Mella died in Mexico City, shot by one of Machado's men. Other founding members of Mella's Communist Party were Blas Roca, Carlos Rafael Rodríguez, and Juan Marinello, all of whom lived to participate in the early years of the 1959 Revolution. Jesús Menéndez (1911–48) was a labor union leader in the sugar industry and a member of the PSP (Cuba's old Communist Party). He was influential among some of the July 26 Movement's early leaders, including Fidel's second in command in the attack on Moncada Barracks, Abel Santamaría, and his sister Haydée. Menéndez was ordered captured in January 1948 by a man named Joaquín Casillas. Menéndez turned his back on Casillas, who then shot him from behind. The murder caused a national uproar.

11. Two attacks took place simultaneously, one in Santiago de Cuba and the other in Bayamo. But Santiago's Moncada garnered far more attention. There is conflicting data on how many took part, with reports ranging from 120 to 165.

12. Randall, *Haydée Santamaría, Cuban Revolutionary*, 77.

13. Quoted in Chomsky et al., *The Cuba Reader*, 330.

14. Castañeda, *Compañero*, 197.

15. The Bay of Pigs attack was a failed military invasion of Cuba undertaken by the CIA-sponsored paramilitary group Brigade 2506 on April 17, 1961. Launched from Guatemala, the invading force was defeated in three days by the Cuban Revolutionary Armed Forces under the direct command of Prime Minister Fidel Castro. Following the debacle some of the invasion's leaders were executed; most were imprisoned. The Kennedy administration and the Cuban government eventually effected the exchange of 1,113 prisoners for US$53 million in food and medicine, sourced from private donations and from companies expecting tax concessions.

16. Latin Americans are not the only ones that have defied U.S. economic sanctions against Cuba; many others are now trading with the socialist nation, and some have recently renegotiated on very favorable terms for the Revolution. On December 15, 2015, *Cuba Journal* announced: "Cuba has concluded a deal with certain of its Paris Club creditors to restructure its debt on favorable terms. . . . Creditors have forgiven $8.5 billion of Cuba's $11.1 billion debt. The deal covers official debt defaulted on through 1986, plus interest, service charges and penalties. . . . According to a Paris Club statement, 'This arrangement offers a framework for a sustainable and definitive solution to the question of arrears due by the Republic of Cuba.'" "Cuba Extracts Favorable Paris Club Debt Terms," *Cuba Journal*, December 15, 2015, http://cubajournal .co/cuba-extracts-favorable-paris-club-debt-terms/.

17. This is a consequence of the 1995 revision of the Cuban Adjustment Act of 1966 that essentially says anyone who fled Cuba and entered the United States would be allowed to pursue residency a year later. After talks with the Cuban government, the Clinton administration agreed to stop admitting people found at sea. Since then, in what has become known as the "Wet Foot, Dry Foot Policy," a Cuban caught on the water between the two nations (with "wet feet") would summarily be sent home or to a third country. One who makes it to shore ("dry feet") gets a chance to remain in the United States and later qualifies for expedited legal permanent residence status and eventually U.S. citizenship.

18. From December 1960 to October 1962 more than fourteen thousand Cuban youths arrived alone in the United States. This was known as the Peter Pan airlift. Rumors had been spread that the Cuban Revolution intended to take children from their parents, and many parents sent their children away, unwittingly achieving the very outcome they feared. The children from the Cuban Refugee Children's Program were placed in temporary shelters in Miami and relocated to one hundred cities in thirty-five states. Many of them grew up in orphanages. This was just one of several mass exoduses provoked by counterrevolutionary propaganda.

19. A few years ago a member of the U.S. Congressional Black Caucus visited Cuba and remarked on the small number of doctors available in black and poor areas in the United States. When Representative Bennie Thompson said his Mississippi district needed doctors, President Fidel Castro announced scholarships for youth from underserved U.S. communities. An unsigned article, "Cuba Offers Free Medical School for Black & Latino Americans!," appeared in the February 10, 2016, online edition of Word On Da Street: "A few years ago member[s] of the USA Congressional Black Caucus visited Cuba and noted the small number of doctors available in Black and poor areas in American [sic]. When Rep. Bennie Thompson said his Mississippi district needed doctors, then President Fidel Castro announced scholarships for youth from under-served communities in the U.S. . . . 47 students have graduated the program and two are residents in USA hospitals currently. This is proof the [program's] credentials are being accepted and honored in USA hospitals, which is a critical step" (http://wordondastreet.com/cuba-offers-free-medical-school-black-latino -americans/).

20. One of the most prolonged and expensive U.S. programs aimed at defeating the Cuban Revolution has been Radio Martí, established in 1983 by President Reagan at the urging of the Cuban exile leader Jorge Mas Canosa. Its studios are located in Miami, and it has a yearly federal budget of $15 million. It disseminates anti-Castro propaganda and frequently hosts Cuban dissidents. Radio Martí broadcasts twenty-four hours over shortwave transmitters in Delano, California, and Greenville, North Carolina, and over a medium-wave transmitter in Marathon, Florida. Television Martí was added in 1990. Cuba routinely jams both broadcasts.

4. THE ISLAND

1. In Trincher, *Biology and Information*, 10.

2. Comas Paret, *La agonía del pez volador*, 7–8.

3. Several women who work at Casa de las Américas, letter to author, November 2015, my translation.

4. These data are mostly from Pilar Montes, "Cuba Faces Climate Change: Nature Strikes Back," *Havana Times*, December 3, 2015.

5. Montes, "Cuba Faces Climate Change."

6. Ratner and Ray, *Guantánamo*, 94.

7. Ratner and Ray, *Guantánamo*, 1.

8. Ratner and Ray, *Guantánamo*, xv.

9. U.S. direct investment in Cuba did not immediately slow; $355 million was recorded in 1959. The book value of U.S. capital in Cuba was over three times that for all the rest of Latin America. U.S. investments included most of the utilities, half the railways, and almost half of the sugar refineries. The United States also held significant portions of cattle, tobacco, timber, banking, oil, and mining assets. According to the U.S. Department of Agriculture (2008), the United States operated 75 percent of the arable land in Cuba at the time of the embargo. Cassandra Copeland, Curtis Jolly, and Henry Thompson, "The History and Potential of Trade between Cuba and the US," *Journal of Economics and Business* (2011), http://www.auburn.edu/~thomph1/cubahistory.pdf.

10. In September 2014, in its annual report to the United Nations, Cuba estimated U.S. economic sanctions had cost it $3.9 billion in foreign trade that year alone, helping to raise the overall estimate of economic damage to $116.8 billion over the fifty-five years of the blockade. In other reports, taking broader ramifications into account, Cuba has claimed the blockade's long-term damage at $1.1 trillion.

11. Nancy Morejón, letter to author, January 2006, my translation.

12. Roberto Fernández Retamar, letter to author, November 2015, my translation.

13. Mirta Yáñez, letter to author, November 2015, my translation. The novel to which she refers is *Sangra la herida*.

14. Kelly Martínez, letter to author, November 2015, my translation.

15. Cuban poet Dulce María Loynaz (1902–97).

16. Alfredo Zaldívar, letter to author, November 2015, my translation.

17. Laura Ruíz Montes, letter to author, November 2015, my translation.

18. Laidi Fernández de Juan, letter to author, November 2015, my translation.

19. Reprinted in Randall, *Only the Road / Solo el camino*, 472–73, my translation.

5. CUBAN SOLIDARITY: AFRICA

1. Nate George, "Cuba and the Revolutionary Option in the Arab World," in *El diseño de las armas / Armed by Design*, 27.

2. Gleijeses, *The Cuban Drumbeat*, 19.

3. In April 1974 a group of Portuguese military officials staged a bloodless coup that was joined by immense popular support, overthrowing that country's dictatorship. It is known as the Revolution of the Carnations because people put carnations in the muzzles of the soldiers' guns and their lapels. The event also led to Portugal's losing control of its African colonies and East Timor.

4. The Communist International, abbreviated as Comintern and also known as the Third International (1919–43), was an international communist organization that advocated world communism. Its branches, the communist parties in most of the other socialist countries, often tended to accept directives from the Soviet party without taking into account local conditions. Some communist parties favored the Chinese line, while

a few maintained real independence. The Fourth International, founded in France in 1938 by followers of Leon Trotsky, accused the Comintern of selling out to Stalinism. Both organizations lost their international influence with the demise of communism in the Soviet Union. Affiliated parties subsequently waned in their respective countries.

5. George, "Cuba and the Revolutionary Option in the Arab World," 25–38.

6. Horace Campbell, "The Military Defeat of the South Africans in Angola," *Monthly Review* 64, no. 11 (April 2013): 5.

7. Campbell, "The Military Defeat of the South Africans in Angola."

8. This and other contacts between Guevara and a number of African leaders, as well as the Cuban Revolution's decision to side with the Soviet Union at the time of the Sino-Soviet split, are documented in Castañeda, *Compañero*. Castañeda presents a notably balanced view, giving equal credence to declassified documents from the United States and the Soviet Union as well as interviews with participants still alive when he wrote his account. An economist, he is heavy on economic analysis. Although I do not always agree with his conclusions, some of his observations, when they coincide with information found elsewhere, bear repeating.

9. Fornet, *El 71*, 271.

10. Guillermo Alvarado, "Operación Carlota, una epopeya military cubana," *Cuba-Debate*, November 5, 2015, http://www.cubadebate.cu/?p=654869#.VjzoDeqerbl.

11. Campbell, "The Military Defeat of the South Africans in Angola."

12. Céspedes Carillo, *Angola*, 274–75.

13. Also called the Tripartite Accord or Three Powers Accord, it granted independence to Namibia and ended the direct involvement of foreign troops in the Angolan Civil War. Signed at the United Nations headquarters in New York City on December 22, 1988, by representatives of the governments of Angola, Cuba, and South Africa.

14. Oscar Sánchez Serra, "Operación Carlota: la más justa, prolongada, masiva y exitosa campaña militar internacionalista de Cuba," *Cuba información*, November 5, 2015, http://www.cubainformacion.tv.

15. Numbers are from secret documents on the history of African involvement released by Cuba and quoted in the National Security Archive Electronic Briefing Book No. 67, edited by Peter Kornbluh, April 1, 2002, http://nsarchive.gwu.edu/NSAEBB/NSAEBB67/gleijeses1.pdf.

16. Carlos Martinez, "The Revolutionary Legacy of Amilcar Cabral," Invent the Future, September 13, 2014, http://www.invent-the-future.org/2014/09/amilcar-cabral/. Amílcar Lopes da Costa Cabral (1924–73) was a Guinea-Bissauan and Cape Verdean agricultural engineer, writer, nationalist thinker, and political leader. He led the nationalist movement of Guinea-Bissau and the Cape Verde Islands and the subsequent war of independence in Guinea-Bissau. He was assassinated on January 20, 1973, about eight months before Guinea-Bissau's unilateral declaration of independence.

17. Nelson Mandela, recently released from prison, was a guest of honor at Cuba's July 26 celebration, held in 1991 in the city of Matanzas. My transcription from radio broadcast. His full speech can be found at http://db.nelsonmandela.org/speeches/pub_view.asp?pg=item&ItemID=NMS1526&txtstr=Matanzas.

18. Quoted in Céspedes Carillo, *Angola*, 131–32. I recommend this book for its detailed account, complete with documents, of all phases of Cuba's participation in Angola.

19. Cuban government official Jorge Risquet (1930–2015), at the time of Cuba's Third Party Congress when there was a call for the party and all organizations to place more emphasis on promoting qualified women, blacks, and youth, indicated it is very hard sometimes to know what someone's ethnic or racial background is. When they made the first attempt to say how many in each category were members of the Central Committee and of the Political Bureau, he was listed as white. But one of his grandparents was Chinese and he still had his grandmother's certificate freeing her from slavery. See Piero Gleijeses, "Risquet, Jorge," in *Encyclopedia of African-American Culture and History* (New York: Macmillan, 2006), 1958–59, http://www.encyclopedia .com/article-1G2-3444701092/risquet-jorge.html.

20. Fornet, *El 71*, 261.

21. Romay, *Elogio de la altea o las paradojas de la racialidad*, 187.

22. Masetti, *El furor y el delirio*, 238–39. The book is available only in Spanish.

23. Ventura Carballido Pupo, "Operación Carlota: Meditación del combatiente número 54295," *CubaDebate*, November 5, 2015, http://cubadebate.cu/?p=654529#.Vjzm _eqerbl.

24. Laura Prada, "Angola y Cuba: Historia de una Amistad," *Granma*, November 10, 2015, http://www.granma.cu/mundo/2015-11-10/angola-y-cuba-historia-de-una -amistad.

6. CUBAN SOLIDARITY: LATIN AMERICA

1. Much like the European Union, throughout the 2000s a number of Latin American countries joined together to promote regional integration. The Unión de Naciones Suramericanas (South American Community of Nations, UNASUR) includes Argentina, Bolivia, Brazil, Colombia, Ecuador, Guyana, Paraguay, Peru, Suriname, and Uruguay as full members. Venezuela, Panama, and Mexico hold observer status. UNASUR grew out of the South American Community of Nations, established in 2004; it united two trade groups, the Andean Community and Mercosur, which continue to exist in their own right. Several countries now permit their citizens to travel between them without passports. Among the alliance's long-term goals are to create a continental free trade zone, a single currency, and an interoceanic highway.

2. During the dirty wars of the 1970s and 1980s, thirty thousand Argentineans were disappeared, forty thousand Guatemalans, and thousands in other Latin American countries.

3. Ratner and Smith, *Che Guevara and the FBI*, "Excerpts from the declassified documents," xxi.

4. Beverley, *Latinamericanism after 9/11*, 121.

5. Fidel defended himself at the trial following the 1953 attack on Moncada Barracks. His defense speech, which he managed to sneak out of his prison cell and which came to be known as "History Will Absolve Me," included a detailed program for a free nation (Castro Internet Archive, 2001, https://www.marxists.org/history /cuba/archive/castro/1953/10/16.htm). Che's statement is from the 1965 letter he left for his parents when he departed Cuba to follow his dream of leading the liberation struggles in other lands (my translation).

6. The Organization of Solidarity with the People of Asia, Africa and Latin America was founded in Havana in January 1966 as a Cuban political movement with the stated purpose of fighting globalization, imperialism, and neoliberalism and of defending human rights throughout the developing world. It came into being as a result of the Tricontinental Conference, a meeting of delegates from Guinea, Congo, South Africa, Angola, Vietnam, Syria, North Korea, the Palestine Liberation Organization, Cuba, Puerto Rico, Chile, and the Dominican Republic. It published the magazine *Tricontinental*. It still exists as a support for movements of liberation, although, in tune with the times, they may not necessarily be engaged in armed struggle.

7. Manuel Piñeiro (1933–98) was an important member of Cuba's revolutionary leadership. He fought in the mountains with Fidel, spent time in prison, and after victory held a number of positions, all having to do with state security. From 1961 on, as deputy minister of the interior, and especially after 1975, when he was made head of the Cuban Communist Party's Americas Department, he oversaw the training of foreign guerrilla fighters. He was married to a Chilean economist, political analyst, and writer, Marta Harnecker. In 1997 Piñeiro resigned his government positions and devoted himself to writing an analysis of the Cuban Revolution. In 1998 he was killed in an automobile accident.

8. The *foco* theory was publicized by Che himself and by the French revolutionary intellectual Regis Debray in his treatise *Revolución en la revolución*.

9. Taylor Clark, "USAID in Cuba: The Latest U.S. Program to Create Political Dissent," Latin America Working Group, August 9, 2014, http://www.lawg.org/action-center/lawg-blog/69-general/1361-usaid-in-cuba-the-latest-us-program-to-create-political-dissent#sthash.Z8SdEuhT.dpuf.

10. The Peredo brothers—Inti, Coco, and Chato—were founders of the Bolivian Communist Party and fought with Che. Inti inherited what was left of the decimated guerrilla force until his own death in battle several years later. In 1997 a much younger brother, Antonio, joined the Movement for Socialism and worked for the election of Evo Morales. In 2006 Antonio was elected alderman on the Municipal Council in Santa Cruz de la Sierra.

11. Randall, *Che on My Mind*.

12. I recommend the description of this conversation, as seen from afar, by Dariel Alarcón Ramírez (Benigno) in his memoir *Memorias de un soldado cubano*. Alarcón Ramírez knew both men for many years. Although he eventually left Cuba and his words are at least publicly ignored by the Revolution, his interpretation makes sense.

7. INTERNATIONALISM, CUBAN STYLE

1. Ansel Herz, "The Clinton Bush Haiti Fund Is Lying to You," *Huff Post*, *World Post*, November 4, 2010, http://www.huffingtonpost.com/crossover-dreams/the-clinton-bush-haiti-fu_b_778503.html.

2. Biz Carson, "Mark Zuckerberg Says He's Giving Away 99% of His Facebook Shares—Worth $45 Billion Today," *Business Insider*, December 1, 2015, http://www.businessinsider.com/mark-zuckerberg-giving-away-99-of-his-facebook-shares-2015-12.

3. Javier de Miguel, "Author Tells Story of Cuban Volunteers in Spanish Civil War," *Latin American Herald Tribune*, August 16, 2016, http://www.laht.com/article.asp?CategoryId=13003&ArticleId=419355.

4. Alberto Bayo (1892–1967), a Cuban veteran of Spain's civil war who had settled in Mexico after the loss of the Republic, trained Fidel's July 26 members when they were regrouping in that country prior to returning to Cuba on the *Granma*. After the Cuban victory, Bayo immigrated to the island, where he died a general in its revolutionary army.

5. March, *Evocación*, 107.

6. Hayden, *Listen, Yankee!*, 125.

7. Gleijeses, *The Cuban Drumbeat*, 23.

8. Ricardo Alarcón (b. 1937) joined the July 26 Movement early on and has been active in a number of important revolutionary venues. He was Cuba's permanent representative to the UN for almost thirty years, foreign minister from 1992 to 1993, and president of the National Assembly from 1993 to 2013. Significantly he is one of the architects of the evolving relations between Cuba and the United States.

9. Isle of Youth is the name the Revolution gave to Isle of Pines, a large island off the Havana coast. It was the site of the prison where Fidel and others were held following the 1953 attack on Moncada Barracks. After the revolutionary victory of 1959 it was where dozens of special schools received thousands of foreign students from a number of countries at war.

10. Quoted in Hayden, *Listen, Yankee!*, 142.

11. This was reported on October 5, 1973, by various newspapers, including Meriden, Connecticut's *Morning Record*.

12. Ubieta Gómez, *Cuba*, 167.

13. The kidnapping of Charles Burke Elbrick, U.S. ambassador to Brazil, was one among several. He was kidnapped on September 4, 1969, by that country's October 8 Revolutionary Movement and held for seventy-eight hours and was eventually released in exchange for the government's release of fifteen political prisoners. The operation brought attention to the repression, imprisonment, and torture of Brazilian citizens by the military regime. In this case, as in others, the freed prisoners demanded safe passage to Cuba. The film *Four Days in September* tells the story of Elbrick's kidnapping. Alan Arkin plays the ambassador.

14. Macarena Aguiló, who spent part of her childhood in the Chilean Building, made the 2010 film of the same name. It follows the experiences of the twenty adults and sixty children who lived in that building. For the men and women in the Chilean Building, patriotic duty took an unusual turn: from warfare to child care. Cuba encouraged and supported such innovative projects.

15. The first Fair Play for Cuba Committee opened its doors in New York City in 1961. Eventually several dozen chapters existed throughout the United States and Canada. The organization counted Truman Capote, James Baldwin, Allen Ginsberg, Lawrence Ferlinghetti, and LeRoi Jones (later Amiri Baraka) among its early supporters. It rallied support for the Cuban Revolution, particularly after the Bay of Pigs attack and the Cuban Missile Crisis.

16. The Venceremos Brigade was founded in 1969 by members of the U.S. group Students for a Democratic Society and the Cuban government. That year the first trip numbered 216 and had to travel to Cuba via Czechoslovakia. Members worked in agriculture or construction, met members of revolutionary organizations from throughout the Third World, and toured places of interest. As of 2010 the yearly Brigade trips had brought more than nine thousand people to the Island. They continue today, coordinated by Pastors for Peace.

17. The Antonio Maceo Brigade, named after a general in Cuba's 1895 War of Independence from Spain, took its first contingent of sons and daughters of exiles to the island in 1977. Other contingents followed. The Brigade also sponsored what would come to be called the Dialogue between the Cuban government and representatives of the exile community in November 1978, which decreased tension and improved relations between the two sides.

18. Francisco Morales is the author of definitive texts on psychology. From 1975 to 1996 he coordinated all the psychology services for the city of Havana. He lives in Cuba but is currently a professor of community health at the University of the Republic in Paysandú, Uruguay.

19. I owe these observations, in part, to a discussion with the cultural analyst Mary Louise Pratt.

20. Cubana de Aviación Flight 455 was on its way from Barbados to Jamaica on October 6, 1976, when it was brought down by a terrorist bomb attack. All seventy-three people on board were killed. Evidence implicated several CIA-linked anti-Castro Cuban exiles and members of the Venezuelan secret police. Four men were arrested in connection with the bombing and tried in Venezuela. All were sentenced to long prison terms but eventually released. Two later took refuge in the United States.

8. EMILIO IN ANGOLA

1. Comas Paret, *Desconfiemos de los amaneceres apacibles*, my translation.

9. NANCY IN ETHIOPIA

1. Haydée Santamaría's letter to Che Guevara after his death, quoted in Randall, *Che on My Mind*, 85, my translation: "At your wake, when our great people wondered what rank Fidel would confer upon you, he said 'artist.' I felt that any rank would have been too low, inadequate, and Fidel as always found the right one."

2. My translation.

3. Alonso, "May Allah Protect You," translated by Anne Fountain, in *Disconnect/Desencuentro*. Reprinted by permission of Cubanabooks Press, California State University at Chico, California.

4. The interview with Nancy Alonso is from Hernández Hormilla, *Palabras sin velo*, my translation. The book includes interviews with Cuban writers and a story by each.

5. Throughout the half century of the Cuban Revolution there have been periodic mass exoduses. Nancy refers here to the exodus of rafters in the summer of 1994. Thousands of people took to the sea in makeshift rafts; some made it to the United States, while others perished.

10. LAIDI IN ZAMBIA

1. Fernández de Juan, *Dolly y otros cuentos cubanos* and *Sucedió en Copperbelt*.
2. "Todos queridos," in Fernández de Juan, *Sucedió en Copperbelt*, my translation, revised by Fernández de Juan.
3. *Chitendes* is a local word for rags, or cloth coverings the women wear on their heads.
4. Milimili is a local porridge of white rice, eaten daily.

11. EDUCATING NEW MEN AND WOMEN, GLOBALLY

1. Those early mass efforts are being referenced today by a number of men and women now in their late fifties, who weren't old enough to have fought in the mountains but nevertheless responded to the Revolution's call in subsequent years, participating in great missions such as the literacy campaign. Some feel they have not been recognized as they should and were never able to achieve the trust those slightly older, who did participate in the war, were granted automatically. They claim this unfair lack of recognition can be seen in their generation's being given fewer positions of responsibility.

2. From 1960 to 1965 it is reported that at least 681 acts of terrorism were committed against the Cuban people. Throughout the year of the literacy campaign several teachers, students, and peasants were tortured and murdered in order to terrorize farming communities and reduce support for the campaign. Young teachers were shot, lynched, or stabbed. There is documentation showing that the U.S. government backed many of these attacks; for example, the CIA sponsored Operation Mongoose, through which it attempted to defeat the Revolution.

3. Chomsky et al., *The Cuba Reader*, 387.
4. Chomsky et al., *The Cuba Reader*, 387.
5. Maria López Vigil, "Cuban Women's History—Jottings and Voices," *Envío* (Central American University, Managua, Nicaragua), no. 208 (November 1998), http://www.envio.org.ni/articulo/1391.
6. Rebecca Herman, "An Army of Educators: Gender, Revolution and the Cuban Literacy Campaign of 1961," *Gender and History* 24, no. 1 (2012), http://www.maestrathe film.org/activos/reviews/Gender%20&%20History%20Journal%20An%20Army%20 of%20Educators%20.pdf.
7. Personal conversation, Havana, 1970s.
8. NationMaster figures for 2000–2002, www.nationmaster.com.
9. The 1953 attack on Moncada Barracks in Santiago de Cuba was the action that initiated the Cuban Revolution. Fidel and his comrades lost that battle, but it sparked the war that in 1959 would defeat the Batista dictatorship. This story is told in my book *Haydée Santamaría, Cuban Revolutionary*, 111.
10. Bob Boughton and Deborah Durnan, "Cuba's Yo Sí Puedo: A Global Literacy Movement," *Postcolonial Directions in Education* 3, no. 2 (2014), http://www.um.edu .mt/pde/index.php/pde1/article/view/57.
11. UNESCO Executive Board, "Study on the Effectiveness and Feasibility of the Literacy Training Method *Yo Sí Puedo*," August 25, 2006, http://unesdoc.unesco.org /images/0014/001468/146881e.pdf.

12. "Leonela Inés Relys Díaz," *EcuRed*, October 30, 2015, http://www.ecured.cu/index.php/Leonela_In%C3%A9s_Relys_D%C3%ADaz.

13. Ewan Robertson, "Venezuela's Mission Robinson Literacy Program at 9 Years," *Venezuela Analysis*, October 29, 2012, http://venezuelanalysis.com/news/7402.

14. Bob Boughton and Deborah Durnan, "Cuba's 'Yes I Can' Mass Adult Literacy Campaign Model in Timor-Leste and Aboriginal Australia: A Comparative Study," *International Review of Education* 60, no. 4 (2014): 559–80, http://link.springer.com/article/10.1007/s11159-014-9421-5#page-1.

15. Bob Boughton, Donna Ah Chee, Jack Beetson, Deborah Durnan, and Jose Chala LeBlanch, "An Aboriginal Adult Literacy Campaign Pilot Study in Australia Using 'Yes I Can,'" *Literacy and Numeracy Studies* 21, no. 1 (2013), http://epress.lib.uts.edu.au/journals/index.php/lnj/article/view/3328.

16. "En el país de Varela: Yo, sí puedo—Education Programme for Young People and Adults," UNESCO, http://www.unesco.org/uil/litbase/?menu=4&programme=93.

17. "Cuba Teaches Nearly 20,000 Guatemalans to Read," *Telesur*, August 28, 2014, http://www.telesurtv.net/english/news/Cuba-Teaches-Nearly-20000-Guatemalans-to-Read-20140828-0039.html.

18. Cuban News Agency, "Over 300,000 Angolans Benefited from Cuban Literacy Method," JSC: Jamaicans in Solidarity with Cuba, October 2, 2013, https://youthandeldersja.wordpress.com/2013/10/02/over-300000-angolans-benefited-from-cuban-literacy-method/.

19. "Yo sí puedo Sevilla (Parte I)," YouTube, May 27, 2008, https://www.youtube.com/watch?v=Q1uzflvrkLU.

20. "Yo Sí Puedo," Latino Alliance for Literacy Advancement de New Mexico, https://thelalagroup.wordpress.com/yo-si-puedo-program/.

21. UNESCO Executive Board, "Study on the Effectiveness and Feasibility of the Literacy Training Method *Yo Sí Puedo.*"

22. Cuba has received many prizes over the years for its internationalism in literacy, among them the Krupskaya Prize for the Battle for Sixth Grade (1964), the Pavlevi Prize for its Adult Education Model (1968), and the Krupskaya Prize for its Literacy Campaign for the Blind (1990).

23. Interview with Osvaldo Lara Cruz, Havana, Cuba, February 28, 2016, my translation.

24. Conversation with Gregory Randall, professor, University of the Republic, Uruguay, February 2016, my translation.

12. CUBAN HEALTH CARE: A MODEL THAT WORKS

1. C. William Keck and Gail A. Reed, "The Curious Case of Cuba," *American Journal of Public Health* 102, no. 8 (2012): 13–22.

2. U.S. Citizenship and Immigration Services; Victoria Burnett and Frances Robles, "U.S. and Cuba at Odds over Exodus of the Island's Doctors," *New York Times*, December 19, 2015.

3. Editorial Board, "A Cuban Brain Drain, Courtesy of the U.S.," *New York Times*, November 16, 2014.

4. Conner Gorry, "Over the Hills and Far Away: Rural Health in Cuba," MEDICC *Review* 14, no. 1 (January 2012): 6.

5. Keck and Reed, "The Curious Case of Cuba."

6. Dangerous numbers of Cubans also smoke, despite propaganda aimed at reducing the rate. Cuban sociologists have been studying the phenomenon.

7. Richard Horton, "Offline: Four Principles of Social Medicine," *Lancet* 382, no. 9888 (July 20, 2013): 192.

8. Edward W. Campion and Stephen Morrissey, "A Different Model—Medical Care in Cuba," *New England Journal of Medicine* 368, no. 4 (January 24, 2013): 297–99.

9. This and subsequent information on Cuba's health care system is from Keck and Reed, "The Curious Case of Cuba."

10. Conner Gorry, "Cuba's National HIV/AIDS Program," MEDICC *Review* 13, no. 2 (2011): 5.

11. Gorry, "Cuba's National HIV/AIDS Program," 5.

12. "HIV and AIDS Estimates (2015)," UNAIDS, http://www.unaids.org/en/regions countries/countries/cuba.

13. CUBAN HEALTH MEANS WORLD HEALTH

1. Ubieta Gómez, *Zona roja*, 11, my translation.

2. The information on Operation Miracle comes from James C. McKinley Jr., "A Health System's 'Miracles' Come with Hidden Costs," *New York Times*, November 20, 2007; Michael Voss, "Cuba Pushes Its 'Medical Diplomacy,'" BBC *News*, May 20, 2009, http://news.bbc.co.uk/2/hi/americas/8059287.stm; and my observation of this program both in and outside Cuba.

3. McKinley, "A Health System's 'Miracles' Come with Hidden Costs."

4. Connor Gorry, "Cuban Health Cooperation Turns 45," MEDICC *Review* 10, no. 3 (2008): 46–47.

5. Zulquernain Tahir, "PMDC, HEC in Row over Cuba Scholarships," *WayBack Machine*, April 24, 2008.

6. "Thank You Cuba (The Friend of Pakistan)," Suffa Project, July 13, 2010, http://alsuffa.blogspot.com/2010/07/thank-you-cuba-friend-of-pakistan.html.

7. Gorry, "Cuban Health Cooperation Turns 45," and Gail A. Reed, "International Cooperation Report: Cuban Medical Teams in Global Disaster Relief," MEDICC *Review* 17, no. 3 (2015), http://www.medicc.org/publications/medicc_review/1204/pages /international_cooperation_report.html.

8. Three Cuban doctors already working in the country died in Ecuador's 2016 quake. *Havana Times* reported that 59 of the 742 Cuban collaborators working in Ecuador were providing service in the disaster area. "Three Cuban Doctors among Earthquake Victims in Ecuador," *Havana Times*, April 18, 2016.

9. Conner Gorry, "Cuba Marks 15 Years Treating Chernobyl Victims," MEDICC *Review* 7, no. 5 (2005), http://www.medicc.org/publications/medicc_review/0505 /top-story.html. Information about the Chernobyl nuclear disaster and Cuba's ongoing program to treat the children who are its victims is from this source.

10. Gorry, "Cuba Marks 15 Years Treating Chernobyl Victims."

11. Conner Gorry, "Cuba's Latin American Medical School: Can Socially-Accountable Medical Education Make a Difference?," *MEDICC Review* 14, no. 3 (2012): 5.

12. Interview with Carlos Mejías Márquez, Havana, Cuba, February 18, 2016, my translation.

13. Information on Cuba's response to the Haitian earthquake is from Connor Gorry, "Once the Earth Stood Still (Part I): Cuban Rehabilitation Services in Haiti," *MEDICC Review* 12, no. 2 (2010): 44–47, and Connor Gorry, "Once the Earth Stood Still (Part II): Mental Health Services in Post-Quake Haiti," *MEDICC Review* 12, no. 3 (2010): 44–47.

14. Jonathan A. Katz, "U.N. Admits Role in Cholera Epidemic in Haiti," *New York Times*, August 17, 2016, http://www.nytimes.com/2016/08/18/world/americas/united -nations-haiti-cholera.html?rref=collection%2Fsectioncollection%2Fhealth&action =click&contentCollection=health&region=stream&module=stream_unit&version =latest&contentPlacement=6&pgtype=sectionfront.

15. "Philip Alston's Draft Report on the U.N. and the Haiti Cholera Outbreak" is reproduced in the *New York Times Magazine*, August 19, 2016, http://www.nytimes.com /interactive/2016/08/19/magazine/document-Alston-Haiti-Cholera-Report.html.

16. Henry Reeve was rumored to have been born in Brooklyn, New York, in 1850. Very young, he fought in his country's Civil War. In 1868, upon learning of the uprising at La Demajagua, Cuba, he showed up at New York's Cuban Council and volunteered to fight. He was twenty-seven when he died in battle on Cuban soil. The Henry Reeve Brigade was established in 2005 with more than 1,500 Cuban health professionals trained in disaster medicine and infectious disease containment. The all-volunteer brigade built on forty years of Cuban experience in disaster areas around the world. It offered to deploy to the United States following Hurricane Katrina but was rejected by the Bush administration. It has subsequently served in China, Pakistan, Guatemala, Indonesia, Bolivia, Haiti, and elsewhere.

17. *Brigada Médica Cubana en Haití*, press bulletin no. 9, April 13, 2010.

18. *Brigada Médica Cubana en Haití*.

19. Gorry, "Once the Earth Stood Still (Part I)," 44–46.

20. Gorry, "Once the Earth Stood Still (Part II)," 46.

21. Quoted in Gorry, "Once the Earth Stood Still (Part I)," 44–46.

22. Fernando Ravsberg, "Cuban Doctors: The Soldiers Who Defeated Ebola," *Havana Times*, November 26, 2015, http://www.havanatimes.org/?p=115179&print=1.

23. Gail Reed, "Meet Cuban Ebola Fighters: Interview with Félix Báez and Jorge Pérez, A *MEDICC Review* Exclusive," *MEDICC Review* 17, no. 1 (2015): 6–10.

24. Dionne Searcey and Sheri Fink, "Sierra Leone Declared Free of Ebola Transmissions," *New York Times*, November 7, 2015.

14. SPORTS FOR EVERYONE

1. Rebecca R. Ruiz, "A Secret Soviet Doping Plan from 1983 Reverberates in Rio," *New York Times*, August 13, 2016, details the Soviet Union's state-sponsored doping program that continued into post-Soviet Russia.

2. Mario Granda, "Cuba in the World's Tough Battle for Drug-Free Sport," *MEDICC Review* 11, no. 2 (2009): 6–8. Cuba's antidoping laboratory received a $2.7 million

government investment, and technicians were largely trained in Barcelona, Madrid, Lisbon, and Cologne. In 2003 Cuba's lab received dual certification from the World Anti-Doping Agency and the International Olympic Committee.

3. Nicole He, K. K. Rebecca Lai, and Paul Murray, "Athletes Who Were Denied Their Olympic Medal Moments Because Others Were Doping," *New York Times*, August 14, 2016.

4. Fidel Castro, remarks made on the second Special Program on the National and International Sports Movement, Cuban TV, September 3, 1999.

5. Information on the U.S. Major League Cuban trip is from Ben Strauss, "M.L.B.'s Good-Will Tour of Cuba Is Hardly the Last Word," *New York Times*, December 17, 2015, http://nyti.ms/1mbrWAf. The status of star Cuban athletes remains fickle. Osmel Ramírez Alvarez, "Cuba's Latest Sports Defectors," *Havana Times*, February 10, 2016, reported that brothers Yuliesky and Lourdes Gourriel opted to leave Cuba for the United States. Interestingly, while previous defections were not reported in the Cuban media, these were.

6. Cuba boycotted the 1984 and 1988 Summer Olympics. A summary of political boycotts and bans of the Olympic Games by a number of nations, including Cuba, can be found in Jaime Fuller, "A Not-So-Brief History of Politics and the Olympics," *Washington Post*, February 5, 2014.

7. Chomsky et al., *The Cuba Reader*, 479.

8. Rigoberto Zarza, "How the Revolution Transformed Sports in Cuba," Friendship First, Competition Second: An Amateur Sport Website, December 11, 2014, https://amateursport.wordpress.com/2015/07/08/how-the-revolution-transformed-sports-in-cuba/.

9. My retranslation.

10. Fernando Ravsberg, "Cuba's Champion in the Paralympic Games," *Havana Times*, August 23, 2012.

11. Heather Elgar, "Raising the Profile of Deaf Sport and the Deaflympics," Sport and Dev, September 7, 2012, http://www.sportanddev.org/en/newsnviews/highlighted _initiative/social_legacy_of_london_2012_olympics/?4890/1/Raising-the-profile-of -Deaf-Sport-and-the-Deaflympics.

12. Lavinia Gasperini, "The Cuban Education System: Lessons and Dilemmas," *Country Studies: Education Reform and Management Publication Series* 1, no. 5 (2000), http://siteresources.worldbank.org/EDUCATION/Resources/278200-1099079 877269/547664-1099080026826/The_Cuban_education_system_lessonsEnoo .pdf.

13. One in a series of columns Arango writes for OnCuba.com. Arturo Arango, "Tenemos siete compañeros en Estados Unidos," On Cuba, July 31, 2015, my translation, http://oncubamagazine.com/sociedad/tenemos-siete-companeros-en-estados-unidos/.

15. WHAT I LEARNED

1. Throughout the first half of the twentieth century it was common for political figures who had fallen from favor to be removed from official photographs, leaving crude outlines where they originally appeared. Although this is no longer so common, a whitewash of events or the refusal to mention the names of individuals about

whom uncomfortable questions might arise occasionally continues to take the place of a truthful telling of history. Such dismembering of reality serves no one.

2. Gen. John. F. Campbell is commander of the Resolute Support Mission and U.S. Forces—Afghanistan, a post he assumed on August 26, 2014.

3. Matthew Rosenberg, "Mistakes from the Start in U.S. Strike at Afghan Hospital," *New York Times*, April 30, 2016.

4. The Mariel boatlift was a mass emigration of disaffected Cubans who departed from Mariel Harbor for the United States between April 15 and October 30, 1980. There had been a sharp downturn in the economy that led to internal tensions and a bid by some ten thousand citizens to gain asylum in the Peruvian embassy. The Cuban government subsequently announced that anyone who wanted to leave could do so, and an exodus by boat started shortly afterward. The exodus started to have negative political implications when it was discovered that it included some people released from prisons and mental health facilities. The boatlift was ended by mutual agreement between the two governments in late October 1980. By that point as many as 125,000 Cubans had made the journey to Florida.

5. In 1978 members of the Cuban government and members of the diaspora, the latter led by Lourdes Casal and Marifeli Pérez Stable of *Areito* magazine, came together in a series of meetings to discuss solutions to the widening breach between Cubans who had left the island and those who stayed. These meetings resulted in policy changes by the Cuban government that propitiated a thaw.

6. Matthias Gebauer and Holger Stark, "Ex-U.S. Intelligence Chief on Islamic State's Rise: 'We Were Too Dumb,'" *Spiegel Online*, November 29, 2015, http://www .spiegel.de/international/world/former-us-intelligence-chief-discusses-development -of-is-a-1065131.html.

7. Andrew van der Viles, "Interview with Mark Behr," *Safundi: The Journal of South African and American Studies* 12, no. 1 (2011): 3–4.

8. Van der Viles, "Interview with Mark Behr," 3.

9. George Yancy and bell hooks, "bell hooks: Buddhism, the Beats and Loving Blackness," op-ed, *New York Times*, December 10, 2015.

10. Enrique Ubieta Gómez, "El proyecto socialista de una nueva individualidad," in *Cuba*, 167.

11. In Gerardo Mosquera, "El conflicto de estar al día," *Revolución y cultura*, October 10, 1984, 39–45.

12. Daniel Rafuls Pineda, "Cuba's Electoral System and the Dilemmas of the Twenty-First Century: Between the Liberal-Democratic Tradition and True Participation," *Socialism and Democracy* 30, no. 1 (2016): 91–104.

13. Human Development Index (HDI), United Nations Development Programme, Human Development Reports, accessed August 16, 2016, http://hdr.undp.org/en /content/human-development-index-hdi.

14. Rafuls Pineda, "Cuba's Electoral System and the Dilemmas of the Twenty-First Century," 91.

BIBLIOGRAPHY

Alarcón Ramírez, Dariel (Benigno). *Memorias de un soldado cubano: Vida y muerte de la revolución*. Barcelona: Tusquets, 1997.

Alonso, Nancy. *De piedras, reparaciones y desencuentros*. Havana: Ediciones Unión, 2013.

———. *Disconnect/Desencuentro*. Translated by Anne Fountain. Chico, CA: Cubanabooks, 2012.

Alonso, Nancy, and Mirta Yáñez. *Damas de Social: Intelectuales cubanas en la Revista Social*. Havana: Ediciones Boloña, Publicaciones de la Oficina del Historiador de la Ciudad, 2014.

Anderson, Jon Lee. *Che*. New York: Grove Press, 2010.

Arango, Arturo. *En los márgenes, acercamientos a la poesía cubana*. Matanzas, Cuba: Ediciones Matanzas, 2014.

———. *Terceras reincidencias: La historia por los cuernos*. Havana: Ediciones Unión, 2013.

Barnet, Miguel, and Esteban Montejo. *Biography of a Runaway Slave*. Revised edition. Translated by W. Nick Hill. Evanston, IL: Curbstone Press, 1994.

Behar, Ruth. *Bridges to Cuba / Puentes a Cuba*. Ann Arbor: University of Michigan Press, 1995.

———. *An Island Called Home: Returning to Jewish Cuba*. New Brunswick, NJ: Rutgers University Press, 2007.

Beverley, John. *Latinamericanism after 9/11*. Durham, NC: Duke University Press, 2011.

Camnitzer, Louis. *New Art of Cuba*. Austin: University of Texas Press, 2003.

Castañeda, Jorge G. *Compañero: The Life and Death of Che Guevara*. New York: Random House, 1998.

Castro, Fidel. *Fidel Castro Reader*. Vol. 1. Edited by David Deutschmann. Melbourne: Ocean Books, 2008.

———. *History Will Absolve Me*. Translated by Pedro Álvarez Tabío and Andrew Paul Booth. Havana: Ciencias Sociales, 1975.

Céspedes Carillo, Alicia. *Angola: Tortuoso camino hacia la independencia*. Havana: Editorial Universitaria Felix Varela, 2013.

Chanan, Michael. *Cuban Cinema*. Minneapolis: University of Minnesota Press, 2004.

Chomsky, Aviva, Barry Carr, and Pamela Maria Smorkaloff, eds. *The Cuba Reader: History, Culture, Politics*. Durham, NC: Duke University Press, 2003.

Comas Paret, Emilio. *La agonía del pez volador*. Havana: Letras Cubanas, 2008.

———. *De Cabinda a Cunene*. Havana: Ediciones Unión, 1983.

———. *Desconfiemos de los amaneceres apacibles*. Havana: Ediciones Unión, 2012.

Debray, Regis. *Revolución en la revolución*. Translated by Bobbye Ortiz. New York: Grove Press, 1967.

El diseño a las armas / Armed by Design. Brooklyn: Interference Archive, 2015.

Fernández de Juan, Laidi. *Dolly y otros cuentos africanos*. Havana: Letras Cubanas, 1994.

———. *Sucedió en Copperbelt*. Havana: Ediciones Unión, 2013.

Fornet, Ambrosio, ed. *Bridging Enigma: Cubans on Cuba*. Special issue, *South Atlantic Quarterly* 96, no. 1 (1997).

———. *Narrar la nación*. Havana: Letras Cubanas, 2009.

———. *Rutas críticas*. Havana: Letras Cubanas, 2011.

Fornet, Jorge. *El 71: Anatomía de una crisis*. Havana: Letras Cubanas, 2013.

García Luis, Julio, ed. *Cuban Revolution Reader: A Documentary History of Fidel Castro's Revolution*. Melbourne: Ocean Press, 2008.

Gleijeses, Piero. *The Cuban Drumbeat*. Chicago: Seagull Books, 2009.

Gordon-Nesbitt, Rebecca. *To Defend the Revolution Is to Defend Culture: The Cultural Policy of the Cuban Revolution*. Oakland, CA: PM, 2015.

Guevara, Che. "Socialism and Man in Cuba." Montevideo, Uruguay: Revista Marcha, 1965.

Hayden, Tom. *Listen, Yankee! Why Cuba Matters. Based in Part on Conversations with Ricardo Alarcón*. New York: Seven Stories Press, 2015.

Hernández Hormilla, Helen. *Palabras sin velo*. Havana: Editorial Caminos, 2013.

Jordan, Rosa. *Cuba Unspun*. Fernie, Canada: Oolichan Books, 2012.

———. *The Woman She Was*. Edmonton, Canada: Brindle and Glass, 2012.

López Vigil, María. *Cuba: Neither Heaven nor Hell*. Washington, DC: Épica, 1999.

March, Aleida. *Evocación, mi vida al lado del Che*. Mexico, DF: Espasa, 2008.

Masetti, Jorge. *El furor y el delirio: Itinerarios de un hijo de la revolución cubana*. Barcelona: Tusquets, 1999.

Q and A with Seven Contemporary Cuban Artists. Washington, DC: Inter-American Development Bank, 2016.

Randall, Gregory. *Estar allí entonces: Recuerdos de Cuba 1969–1983*. Montevideo, Uruguay: Trilce, 2010.

Randall, Margaret. *Breaking the Silences: 20th Century Poetry by Cuban Women*. Vancouver: Pulp Press, 1982.

———. *Che on My Mind*. Durham, NC: Duke University Press, 2014.

———. *Cuban Women Now*. Toronto: Women's Press, 1974.

———. *Gathering Rage: The Failure of 20th Century Revolutions to Develop a Feminist Agenda*. New York: Monthly Review Press, 1992.

———. *Haydée Santamaría, Cuban Revolutionary: She Led by Transgression*. Durham, NC: Duke University Press, 2015.

———, ed. and trans. *Only the Road / Solo el camino: Eight Decades of Cuban Poetry*. Durham, NC: Duke University Press, 2016.

———. *To Change the World: My Years in Cuba*. New Brunswick, NJ: Rutgers University Press, 2009.

———. *Women in Cuba Twenty Years Later*. New York: Smyrna Press, 1981.

Ratner, Michael, and Ellen Ray. *Guantánamo: What the World Should Know*. White River Junction, VT: Chelsea Green, 2004.

Ratner, Michael, and Michael Steven Smith, eds. *Che Guevara and the FBI: The U.S. Political Police Dossier on the Latin American Revolutionary*. Melbourne: Ocean Press, 1997.

Reloba, Xenia, ed. *De/sobre Mario Benedetti*. Prologue by Caridad Tamayo Fernández. Havana: Casa de las Américas, 2015.

Romay, Zuleica. *Cepos de la memoria, imprenta de la esclavitud en el imaginario social cubano*. Havana: Ediciones Matanzas, 2015.

———. *Elogio de la altea o las paradojas de la racialidad*. Havana: Casa de las Américas, 2014.

Rubiera, Daisy, and Sonnia Moro. *MAGIN Tiempo de contar esta historia*. Havana: Ediciones Magín, 2015.

Trincher, Karl S. *Biology and Information: Elements of Biological Thermodynamics*. New York: Springer US, 1965.

Ubieta Gómez, Enrique. *Cuba: ¿Revolución o reforma?* Havana: Casa Editorial Abril, 2012.

———. *Zona roja: La experiencia cubana del ébola*. Havana: Casa Editorial Abril, 2016.

Urcelay-Maragnes, Denise. *La leyenda roja: Los cubanos en la guerra civil Española*. Barcelona: Ediciones del Lobo Sapiens, 2011.

Weiss, Mark, ed. *The Whole Island: Six Decades of Cuban Poetry*. Berkeley: University of California Press, 2009.

INDEX

art and artists: artistic experimentation, 30, 36, 38; capture of memory through art, 31, 35–36; cartoon, 33; Casa de las Américas as a source of support for, 27–29, 40, 224–25n19, 226n28; challenge in obtaining materials during times of shortage, 34–35; Che Guevara's observations regarding in "Socialism and Man in Cuba," 40, 225n21; circus performers, 33, 179; contributions of to Cuban internationalist mental health work, 33, 183, 217; Cuban achievements in architecture, 14–15, 25, 32–33, 40, 226n29, 228n4; Cuban achievements in dance, 37, 54, 229n19; Cuban achievements in music, 6, 14, 37–38, 229nn21–22; Cuban achievements in photography, 14, 31, 33–34, 35; Cuban achievements in poster art, 14, 28, 31–32, 228n8; Cuban achievements in visual arts, 6, 32–33, 228n15; Cuban internationalist orientation toward, 26–29, 105, 183, 217–18; Cuban singer-songwriters, 14, 37–38, 40, 226n28; Cuban support of refugee, 89; damaging effects of Soviet Stalinism on, 14–15, 16, 40, 226n26, 227–28n2; Five Gray Years (El Quinquenio Gris), 31, 39, 225n21, 226n26, 226n31; function of as a society's conscience, 5, 30–32, 33, 41, 105, 224n8, 226n26; graffiti, 31; influence and outstanding quality of Cuban, 14, 22, 32, 41, 54, 217, 218; Martha Machado Artists Brigade, 183, 228–29n16; National Art School (Escuela Nacional de Arte, ENA), 25–26; painters, 15, 33, 34, 183, 217, 224n11; performing arts, 14, 28, 29, 109, 179; periodic repression of in Revolutionary Cuba, 13–15, 38–39, 40, 225n21, 226n26; as political victims, 10, 31, 225n21, 226n31; prominence of Cuban in Latin America, 14; revolution as inspiration for creativity of, 6, 38, 39; singer-songwriters, 14, 37–38, 40, 226n28; support and promotion of by Cuban government, 24–31, 34, 39–40; urban planning and preservation in Havana,

32–33; Vigía publications, 17; zarzuela performances, 7. *See also* creativity; intellectuals; poets; writers
artistic genres, 6, 14–15, 32–34, 35–36, 37, 218
athletes: access of to high-quality sports equipment, 201; amateur versus professional, 192, 194, 201–2; Ana Fidelia Quirot, 196; competition among, 194; Cuban, 192, 195–202, 204; Cuban physical education programming, 195–96; defection of Cuban, 196–97, 242n5; with disabilities, 200–201; doping among, 194–95, 242n3; earning capacities of, 194, 196–97, 201–2; Fidel Castro on, 195; holistic management of in Cuba, 202, 204; Javier Sotomayor, 194–95, 199. *See also* sports

Báez, Félix, 185–90
baseball, 52, 61, 192–93, 197–98, 203
Behr, Max, 214–16, 243n7
Benedetti, Mario, 1, 5, 27, 223n7, 224–25n19
Beverley, John, 87, 234n4
blockade: breaking of diplomatic relations by U.S. with Castro's Cuba, 51, 55; cultural of U.S. against Cuba, 24, 27, 32; defiance by U.S. nationals of its against Cuba, 79, 94, 230n16; economic of U.S. against Cuba, 42, 64, 79, 161, 201, 230n16, 232n10; U.S. brain drain of Cubans and its anti-Cuba, 42; U.S. trade embargo against, 17–18, 24, 43, 51–52, 64, 163, 168, 232n9
Bolívar, Simón, 83–84, 86, 93
Bolivarian Alliance, 181, 200
Bolivia: Che Guevara in, 95–97, 105, 218; Cuba as a refuge for rebels from, 89; Cuban medical assistance in, 241n16; Cuban military assistance to rebels fighting for liberation in, 89–90; great literary heritage of, 15; membership of in UNASUR, 234n1; Peredo brothers (liberators) in, 235n10; President Evo Morales, 86, 95; Simón Bolívar (early rebel), 84; socialism in, 86, 235n10; training of Bolivian nationals at ELAM, 181

brain drain: Cuban policies and actions to counteract effects of, 164; of Cuban sports talent by U.S., 202–4; exodus in 1959 of schoolteachers from Cuba, 149; U.S. attempts to lure Cuban doctors from Ebola epidemic sites, 52, 185, 212; U.S. policies designed to attract talented Cubans, 42–43, 52, 161–63, 212, 239n3. *See also* emigration

Brazil: Cuba as a refuge for rebels from, 89; Cuban cultural activities with nationals from, 28, 35, 169; Cuban internationalist sports programs in, 199; Cuban medical internationalism in and for, 54, 177; landmass and population of, 44; membership of in UNASUR, 234n1; politics in, 95, 236n13; socialism in, 95; training of Brazilian nationals at ELAM, 181; U.S. intervention in, 95

Bruguera, Tania, 31, 228n13

bureaucracy: criticisms and repudiation of Stalinist in Cuba, 30–31, 39, 225n23; repressive effects of, 6, 11, 16, 24, 225n21, 226n28

Cambodia, 102, 156

capitalism, 33, 53, 109, 157, 204, 216

Carballido Pupo, Ventura, 80–81, 234n23

Caribbean: as an aspect of Cuban identity, 3, 4–5, 7, 22, 43, 53, 60, 65; Caribbean Games, 195; climate change in, 60; colonialism in, 2, 63; emigration of islanders from, 14; intervention by U.S. in, 46, 51, 64, 85; islands of, 63, 64, 83; languages of, 28, 152, 155; rebellious spirit of Caribbean peoples, 85; separateness of Caribbean from Latin American character, 83; use of pseudonyms among writers of, 29; West Indies islands, 63. *See also* islands

Carpentier, Alejo, 29

Casa de las Américas: function of as an international cultural exchange institution, 16, 27, 28–29, 149, 226n28; oversight of by Haydée Santamaría, 27, 40, 224–25n19, 226n28; rejection of Stalinism at, 12; *Revista Casa*, 28, 224–25n19

Castro, President Fidel: 1957 interview of by *New York Times* reporter Herbert Matthews, 49; 1959 reinstatement of 1940 Cuban Constitution by, 50; 1959 victory of, 3, 225n37; accusations against as being an exporter of revolution, 3; on the athlete as an embodiment of honor, 105, 242n4; Bay of Pigs attack, 50, 54, 90, 91, 230n15, 236n15; on close ties between politics and art, 218; death of, 43, 229n4; decision of to send disaster relief aid to Pakistan, 174; decision of to send military aid to Angola, 74–76; denials by that he was a communist, 3–4; false rumors regarding death of, 44; gestures of friendship toward U.S. by, 101, 231n19, 241n16; historic sensibilities of, 46–47; "History Will Absolve Me" speech of, 48–49, 145, 234n5; ideas of José Martí as an influence on, 225n23; on importance of being a revolutionary, 122, 218; influence of pre-Revolutionary Orthodox Party on, 48; initial changes made by in Revolutionary Cuba, 50; internationalism of, 122, 231n19; July 26 Movement of, 49, 109, 145, 210–11, 223n5, 235n7, 236n4, 236n9, 238n9; literacy and education as a major concern of, 25, 39, 145, 147, 228n3, 231n19; meeting of with U.S. vice president Richard Nixon, 3; parenting of orphans by, 103, 122; relationship of with Che Guevara, 86, 87, 96, 123, 145, 218, 235n12, 237n1; on rights and revolution, 39–40; on sharing, 8, 102; on shortcomings of Stalinist socialism, 12, 225n20; on sports as a human right, 193, 242n4; "Words to the Intellectuals" speech of, 39–40

Castro, President Raul, 3, 4, 18, 42, 52, 211, 227n37, 228n6

censorship, 6, 38–39, 41

Central American and Caribbean Games, 196, 200

centralism, 10–11, 25, 29, 193

charities, 98, 99, 206

Chávez, Hugo, 86, 93, 153

communism: Comintern, 70, 232–33n4; Cuban Communist Party, 12, 111, 230n8, 230n10, 235n7; Latin American versus Soviet practices of, 11–12, 73; Marxism, 3–4, 43, 71, 134, 181–82, 234n5; Sino-Soviet split, 233n8; Stalinism, 10–12, 24, 41, 73, 232–33n4. *See also* socialism

Congo: assassination of Prime Minister Patrice Lamumba, 72; Cuban internationalist sports in, 199; Cuban military aid in war for independence of, 70–71, 72, 106, 114; membership of in OSPAAAL, 235n6

Costa Rica, 51, 90, 181

Council for Mutual Economic Assistance (COMECON), 9, 224n17

counterrevolutionary terrorism: acts of in and against Cuba, 146–47, 238n2; School of the Americas, 90, 223n2

creativity: as an initial product of revolution, 6, 23–24, 30, 38–39, 226n26; Casa de las Américas as an international hub fostering, 16, 27–29, 40, 149, 224–25n19, 226n28; economic stress as a challenge to, 34; far-reaching impact of Cuban, 14, 54; fundamental role of to internationalism, 217; importance of musical to Cuban Revolution, 28; importance of to mental health, 183; influence of experiences on personal, 137; need as a challenge to, 152, 170, 178; sheltering and nurturing of foreign architects by Cuba, 89; stifling and rebounding of in Cuba, 11–14, 31, 38–41; transgression as a value in artistic, 30, 38. *See also* art and artists; poets

Creoles, 14, 84–85

Cuba: 1968 Cultural Congress of Havana, 105; accusations against Cuba as being an exporter of revolution, 2, 70, 71, 92–93; Afro-Cubans, 37, 46, 61, 70, 229n19; as an anomaly on worldwide development indexes, 219; anti-Stalinism in, 11–12, 73; architectural blight left by Stalinist aesthetics in, 14–15, 227–28n2; atmosphere in 2015–16 of, 17–18; Bay of Pigs (Playa Girón) attack on, 50, 54, 90;

91, 230n15, 236n15; biotechnology and pharmaceuticals as sources of income for, 3, 109, 166, 168–69; brain drain of talent from by U.S., 54–55, 151, 161–62, 185, 197, 202–4; *brigadistas*, 146–47, 148, 155; Catholic Church in, 37, 181, 229n20; censorship in during times of communist ascendency, 6, 38–39, 41; Chinese contribution to culture of, 14, 234n19; Cuban Communist Party, 12, 111, 230n8, 230n10, 235n7; Cuban Environmental Agency, 59; Cuban *nueva trova* music, 37–38; Cuban sense of humor, 33, 186, 225n23; Cuban *vieja trova* (veteran troubadours) musicians, 6, 37, 229n22; diasporic Cubans, 29, 211, 243n5; dictatorship of Fulgencio Batista, 48, 50, 85, 86, 100, 210–11, 238n9; dictatorship of Gerardo Machado, 48, 230n10; economic dependency of on Soviet Union, 12, 50, 55, 73, 167, 226n30; efforts by to promote peaceful coexistence with U.S., 52, 101; equal opportunity racial categorization as a challenge in, 234n19; expressions of thanks to for its aid, 221, 240n6; factories in, 5, 27, 146, 167, 204, 227n41; farms in, 5, 27, 43, 99, 152, 227n41, 229n1; gender equity as an element of Revolutionary policies in, 148; as a global leader in medical research, 164; housing shortage in, 103–4; illiteracy in pre-Revolutionary, 145; impact of disintegration of USSR on, 10, 18, 43, 123, 167, 226n30; imposition of socialist realist aesthetic in, 12, 14–15, 40–41, 227–28n2; Independent Party of Color, 46; influence of Soviet socialist doctrine on culture in, 11 12, 14 15, 39; as an international leader in education, 18, 54, 55, 150–51, 227n34; as an international leader in medicine, 3, 18, 52, 109, 161–70, 171–72, 185, 212; LGBTQ individuals in, 18, 29, 181–82, 227nn35–36; life expectancy in, 148, 164, 166; literacy campaign in, 145–47, 149; loan of experts and specialists as a source of income for, 3; mass emigrations to U.S. from, 66,

a negation of socialist centralism, 11; participatory, 11

diasporic Cubans: 1978 meeting of with Cuban government officials, 211, 243n5; Antonio Maceo Brigade to foster relations between Cuba and, 104, 237n17; literary works by, 23; poets among, 5, 29; U.S. policies designed to attract talented Cubans, 42–43, 52, 161–63, 185, 202–4, 212, 239n3; work of Radio and Television Martí against revolutionary Cuba, 90, 231n20. *See also* emigration

Díaz, Leonela Relys, 152–54

dictators and dictatorships: 1974 Revolution of Carnations in Portugal, 70, 232n3; Cuban military assistance to liberate other countries from, 1, 14, 73, 89–90, 100, 101; Cuban rebel defeat of Fulgencio Batista, 2, 48–50, 238n9; Cuban rebel defeat of Gerardo Machado, 47–48; of Latin America, 1, 73, 85–90, 94, 101, 103; succession of in Haiti, 53, 101; torture and murder of Cuban rebels at hands of Batista, 48–49; torture, murder, and disappearances perpetrated by, 48–49, 85, 89, 103, 236n13

disaster relief: as a component of Cuban internationalism, 100, 208–9, 213, 241n16; as a component of Cuban solidarity, 1, 2, 8, 21, 53–54, 95, 175; Cuban in Haiti following 2010 earthquake, 179–81; Cuban in Pakistan following 2005 earthquake, 174–75; Cuban in Peru following 1970 Ancash Earthquake, 173–74; Cuban in Ukraine following 1986 Chernobyl nuclear disaster, 176–77, 208–9, 240n9; Cuban response to military disasters, 74; Cuban response to natural disasters, 63, 164, 173–79, 241n16; Cuba's holistic approach to, 178–79, 182; Cuba's ongoing evaluation and assessment of its programs, 178; deaths of Cuban workers on missions, 175–76, 240n8; mental health work as an element of Cuban, 33, 177–79, 182–83, 228–29n16; motivations that can underlie individual and

governmental, 206–8; offered by other countries, 100, 179, 206; ongoing care programs in Cuba for victims of foreign disasters, 101, 176–77, 208–9; ongoing post-disaster on-site assistance by Cuba, 179–81, 209; poor helping the poor theme underlying Cuban, 100, 108, 176, 179, 180–81, 240nn7–8; specialized care in Cuba for victims of foreign disasters, 174; vulnerability of poor populations to natural disasters, 100; work of Henry Reeve Brigade, 180–81, 241n16. *See also* internationalism

disease: chronic, 168; Cuba's work to control and eradicate, 54, 122, 168–70; epidemic, 180; global attempts to eradicate, 99; infectious, 169, 181, 190, 241n16; parasite-induced, 163, 181; radioactively induced inherited, 177

doctors. *See* brain drain; disaster relief; education; health care; internationalism; medical aid; medical care

Doctors without Borders, 184, 187, 188, 206–7

Dominican Republic: Cuban international assistance to, 89–90; dictatorship of Leoncio Trujillo, 85, 103; education of nationals of at ELAM, 181; landmass shared by with Haiti, 64; membership of in OSPAAAL, 235n6; relationship of with Haiti, 64; U.S. intervention in, 83, 91

earthquake: Cuban disaster response to 1970 Ancash in Peru, 173; Cuban disaster response to 2005 in Pakistan, 174; Cuban disaster response to 2010 in Haiti, 19, 179–83, 241n13; Cuban disaster response to 2016 in Ecuador, 175–76; deaths of Cuban workers on disaster missions, 175–76, 240n8; earthquake relief as a primary category of Cuban medical aid, 173; ELAM contributions to Cuba's response efforts, 178–79, 181; ongoing post-disaster on-site assistance by Cuba to foreign victims of, 209; post-disaster medical relief in Cuba for foreign victims of, 177

East Timor, 153–54, 239n14

Ebola: case of Dr. Félix Báez, 184, 185–88, 190; Cuban doctors working with or contaminated by the virus, 184–90, 241n23; Cuban mission against in Sierra Leone, 184, 188–90; Cuba's response to international epidemic, 19, 52, 171, 184–88, 206, 221, 241n22; importance of educating public in fight against, 183–84, 188, 190; medical protocols for treating, 187–89; mortality rate from, 184; nature and symptoms of the virus, 183, 188–89; presence of in Guinea, Liberia, and Sierra Leone, 184, 189–90, 221, 241n24

Ecuador: Cuban medical internationalism in, 175–76, 240n8; earthquake of 2016 in, 175, 240n8; education of Ecuadorians at ELAM, 181; great literary heritage of, 15; membership of in UNASUR, 234n1; Simón Bolívar (early rebel), 84

education: 1961 literacy campaign of Cuba's Year of Education, 145–47, 151–53, 238n6; adult in Cuba, 8, 19, 152–53, 239n22; art in Cuba, 228n4, 229n21; as a basic human right in Cuba, 26, 50; Cuban hosting of international conferences in, 105; Cuban internationalist outreach in, 19, 41, 81, 93, 95, 122, 151–58, 160–61, 208, 213, 219; Cuban National Center for Sex Education, 18, 227n35; Cuban policy on mainstreaming deaf students, 201, 248nn11–12; Cuba's reputation for excellence in, 18, 54, 55, 150–51, 227n34; cultural awareness and sensitivity as fundamental elements of in Cuba, 25–27, 30, 144, 147–48, 154; as factor that defines defectors who emigrate from Cuba, 161, 211; Fidel Castro on, 25; free as a goal of rebels and revolutionaries, 46, 94, 145; free as a goal of pre-Revolution Independent Party of Color, 46; free for foreign students in Cuba, 69, 88, 150–51, 164, 175, 191, 208–9, 231n19, 236n9; free in Cuba, 26, 144, 149–50, 161, 164; health, 160–61, 169–70, 188, 190; higher in Revolutionary Cuba, 24–26, 30, 148; humanities in

Cuba, 25–26; implications of a government's policies toward, 92, 144, 145, 150; lack of access to in some countries, 88, 99, 120, 157; Latin America Special Education Reference Center (Centro de Referencia Latinoamericano para la Educación Especial), 201, 248nn11–12; medical in Cuba, 54, 101, 161–67, 178, 241n11; National Institute for Sports, Physical Education and Recreation (Instituto Nacional de Deportes, Educación Física y Recreación, INDER), 193; needs of a country as an influence on its system of, 25; nursing, 165, 167; physical, 193, 195; preference for emulation over competition in Cuban system of, 204; in pre-Revolutionary Cuba, 30, 145, 163; presence of Soviet educators following Cuban Revolution, 10; primary in Cuba, 24, 148, 153, 239n22; as a priority of Revolutionary Cuba, 20, 22–26, 50, 53, 148–51, 153, 164; "selective" versus "exclusive," 26; sociopolitical impact of on a country, 25, 144–45, 148, 192, 219; special, 200–201, 242n12; teaching of critical thinking as a responsibility of a system of, 92, 144–45; theory and practical learning as basic elements of Cuban, 122–23, 152, 227n41; worldwide rankings of Cuban system, 227n34; Yes I Can literacy program as a cornerstone of Cuban overseas, 152–56, 158, 238n10, 239nn14–16. See also internationalism; literacy; schools

ELAM (Escuela Latinoamericana de Medicina; Latin American School of Medicine), 164, 178, 181, 191, 208–9

El Salvador: Cuban assistance to rebels fighting for liberation in, 89–90; Cuban medical internationalism toward nationals of, 173; Farabundo Martí National Liberation Front (Farabundo Martí para la Liberación Nacional), 93; training of El Salvadorians at ELAM, 181; U.S. intervention in, 49–50

embargo. See blockade

Hart, Armando, 13, 40, 103, 218

Havana: attacks in harbor of, 33, 46, 47; flood threats to areas of, 59; function of as an educational center, 25, 29, 102, 108, 123, 150–51, 201; function of as Cuba's cultural center, 7, 31, 37, 40, 105, 109, 228n15; *Havana Times* news coverage, 232n4, 240n8, 241n22, 242n5, 242n10; medical care in, 88, 161, 163, 166, 169–70, 173, 176–78, 237n18; receipt of refugees through, 88, 89; as site of mass public rallies, 87, 147; streets, spaces, and architecture of, 15–16, 17, 32–33, 193, 228n4

Hayden, Tom, 8, 101

health care: availability of to visitors seeking medical help, 18; challenges to Cuban system of, 160–61, 168; Cuban internationalist, 8, 13, 15, 19, 21, 53, 101, 105, 164, 190–91, 240n4; Cuban internationalist in Africa, 81, 184, 190–91, 221; Cuban internationalist in Latin America and Caribbean, 93, 95, 181; Cuban internationalist in Middle East, 174–75; Cuban professionals, 161–62; dental care, 160, 170; dynamic quality of Cuban, 160–61, 164, 165, 168, 191; family practice as basic to Cuban, 164, 166; hearing care, 159–60; as a human right in Cuba, 26, 50, 161, 165, 240n9; inaccessibility of in many countries, 171; long-term, holistic treatment as a feature of Cuban, 101, 122–23, 182, 190–91, 240n9; long-term treatment for child victims of Chernobyl, 176–77, 182, 208, 240n9; mental health as an element of Cuban, 101, 108, 182, 217–18; nurses, 160, 166–67; Operation Miracle (Operación milagro) to address eye problems, 171–72, 176, 240n2; in pre-Revolutionary Cuba, 161, 163; preventative medicine as a basis of Cuban, 160–61, 164, 165, 168, 169; surgical procedures, 159–61, 170, 172–73; universal in Cuba, 15–16, 18, 92, 108, 145, 164–65, 170. *See also* medical aid

Honduras, 51, 83, 181, 184

hooks, bell, 215–16, 243n9

hospitals: absence of rural in pre-Revolutionary Cuba, 163–64; AIDS-HIV specialist, 169; construction and renovation of as a priority following Cuban Revolution, 17, 18, 165; creation of as a goal of Mexico's Zapatistas, 94; creation of as an element of Cuban disaster relief, 173–74; Cuban missions at foreign, 136, 179, 181, 188; Cuban missions at foreign teaching, 123–24; Cuban service in disaster zone field, 174, 181, 183; demands placed on Cuban, 160–61; shortage of throughout developing world, 163–64; Tarará Pediatric Hospital (Havana), 176–77, 182. *See also* medical care

human development, 180, 192, 200, 219, 243n13

humanitarian aid: Cuban as an outgrowth of Revolution, 1, 8, 71, 135, 173–74; differences between charity and, 98, 99, 206; Doctors without Borders as exemplars of, 206–8; hidden motives underlying some actions presented as, 8–9, 206, 208; Partners in Health as exemplars of, 206–8

human rights, 26, 50, 62, 169, 209, 226–27n33, 235n6

identity: Caribbean, 12, 83; collective of the Cuban people, 8, 14, 15, 61, 101, 205, 208; Cuba's political, 2, 4; culture and national, 88; factors that shape individual, 214–16, 218, 224n9; island, 9, 10, 56, 61, 64, 68; Latin American, 12, 13, 83–84

illiteracy. *See* literacy

immigration: attempted of Haitians to Dominican Republic, 64; to Cuba, 14, 64, 236n4; from Cuba to U.S., 18, 42, 52, 162, 239n2; slavery as forced, 61. *See also* emigration

imperialism: anti-imperialism, 87; Cuban anti-imperialism, 2, 92, 199, 210; imperialist powers, 8, 21, 57–58, 208; by U.S., 32, 71, 210, 216, 235n6

independence: 1868 bid for Cuban led by Céspedes, 13, 225–26n25; 1902 mediated

independence (*continued*)
of Cuba, 63; 1908 Cuban war for, 46;
achievement of versus sense of nationhood, 13; Cuban assistance to movements fighting for, 1–2, 12–13, 69–71, 74,
77, 87, 93, 101; Cuban policy of troop removal at end of its military missions, 70;
Cuban revolutionary ideology regarding,
11, 12–13, 92; Cuban training of foreign
liberation fighters, 72, 87, 97; Cuba's fight
to preserve its, 50–51, 63; Cuba's wars for
from Spain, 36, 46–47, 225n23; liberation
and achievement of as necessarily homegrown in nature, 70; liberation versus,
63; Mapuche wars for from Chile, 84;
wars for waged in Africa, 70; winning of
by Haiti, 63; winning of by Namibia, 106;
winning of by Nicaragua, 151; winning
of by Philippines, 47; Zapatistas' war for
within Mexico, 94–95
indigenous peoples: cultures of, 28, 45, 53,
83, 84, 105; uprisings by, 45, 84–85, 86,
92, 94–95
infrastructures: coincidence of inadequate
and epidemic disease, 189–90; coincidence of inadequate and poverty, 54;
damage to by natural disasters, 173; damage to national by corrupt politicians,
99; damage to national during military
occupations, 20
intellectuals: bell hooks (U.S.), 215–16;
cosmopolitanism of Cuban intellectual
life, 14, 15, 23–24, 27–28, 54; Cuba's
intellectual heritage, 6–8, 12–13, 15, 29,
40–41, 96; Fidel Castro's "Words to the
Intellectuals" speech, 39–40; functions of
as a society's social conscience, 5, 10–13,
96, 215–16; lasting influence of José
Martí, 12–13; manual and intellectual
labors as complements in Cuba, 20, 23,
122–23; Mario Benedetti (Uruguay), 1–2,
223n7; opposition of Cuban to Stalinism,
10–13; repression and survival of during
Cuba's periods of repression, 13–14, 15,
211; Revolution and Cuban, 23–24, 38,
40–41, 85, 101; sports and sportsmanship

as complements to intellectual life, 204.
See also art and artists; writers
internationalism: as a force underlying
Cuban disaster relief, 100, 208–9, 213,
241n16; as an element of Cuban identity,
101; areas of Cuban outreach, 15, 19,
54; creative arts as an aspect of Cuban
mental health outreach, 33, 179, 183,
217–18; Cuba as sanctuary for rebels
from other countries, 87, 88; Cuban
educational, 2, 175, 178, 181; Cuban ideology of poor helping the poor, 101, 102,
110, 165; Cuban medical, 171, 174–75, 178,
181; Cuban sports, 208; Cuban support
for liberation struggles throughout
the world, 13, 71; of Doctors without
Borders, 184, 206–7; educational, 154–58;
host country culture as a framework
for implementing Cuban, 154; impact of
foreign mission experiences on Cuba's
populace, 122–23; medical, 184; mission
of Carlos Mejías Márquez in Yemen,
179; mission of Laidi Fernández de Juan
in Zambia, 135–43; mission of Nancy
Alonso in Ethiopia, 123–34; missions
of Cuban nationals in other countries,
122–23; of Partners in Health, 185, 189,
206, 207; politically disinterested nature
of Cuban, 100; work of Martha Machado
Artists Brigade, 183, 228–29n16; Yes I
Can literacy campaign, 152–55, 158, 172,
221, 238nn10–11, 239nn14–15. *See also*
disaster relief; education; medical aid;
military aid; solidarity
International Monetary Fund (IMF), 81, 91
islands: Caribbean, 60, 62, 63–64, 83, 85,
179–80; Cuban landmass, 44, 53, 60;
Cuba's cosmopolitanism despite its
poverty and smallness, 26–27, 88–89, 102,
103–4, 181, 208, 237n16; Cuba's international influence despite its size, 4, 6, 15,
31–32, 54, 70, 72, 87–89, 110, 210; Cuba's
island environment as a unique influence
on residents, 6, 9, 19, 57, 64–68, 210,
224n12; Cuba's sociopolitical situation as
a small island nation, 1–4, 10, 24, 29, 47,

50–51, 61–63, 64; ecological, geological, and climatic threats to, 58, 59, 177, 179–80; England, 57–58; European colonialism and U.S. imperialism on Cuba, 44–47, 83, 85, 225–26n25; Galápagos group, 60; geopolitical situation of Cuba, 53, 64, 70, 83–85, 89, 162–63, 210–11, 220–21, 237n7; Greenland, 56, 59; Iceland, 59; introduction of African slaves on Cuba, 45, 61–62, 78; island landmasses, 56–57; island nations, 56, 57–58; isolation as an influence on islander sensibilities, 56, 57, 64, 66–67, 210; Japan, 57–58; Madagascar, 58; origin of *mestizaje* population on Cuba, 45; Pacific, 58, 60, 157; pre-Columbian indigenous cultures on Cuba, 44–45; remote and inaccessible areas on Cuba, 35, 61–62; as unique ecological environments, 58, 60. *See also* Caribbean

Isle of Youth, 88, 102, 228–29n16, 236n9

July 26 Movement: early bourgeois support for, 11; as Fidel Castro's program for change in Cuba, 87, 145, 210–11, 223n5; July 26, 1953, attack on Moncada Barracks in Santiago de Cuba, 48, 49, 223n5, 230nn10–11, 238n9; Mexico's support and protection of leaders of, 85–86, 236n4; relationship of with PSP, 4; revolutionary leadership of, 11, 41, 48, 230n10, 236n4, 236n8. *See also* Cuban Revolution

language: architecture as, 14; as a challenge for Cuban internationalists on mission, 119, 123, 124, 127, 129, 136; Creole, 152, 155, 182; cultural thought and, 28; literary accomplishment in Spanish-speaking countries of Latin America, 5, 6, 7, 14, 223n7; as a means of acquiring knowledge and a sensitivity to other cultures, 44, 70, 178; of poster art, 32; reinvention of through poetry, 5, 22, 223n7; translations, 7, 45; translations in support of Yes I Can literacy program, 152, 153–54, 155; use of gestures to pass barriers of, 119;

use of students' native in Isle of Youth schools, 88; variety of contained within countries, 10, 45, 83

Laos, 102, 142, 224n17

Lara Cruz, Osvaldo, 154–56

Latin America: Bolivarian Alliance, 181, 200; Cuba as a refuge for rebels from throughout, 89; Cuban military assistance to rebels fighting for liberation in countries of, 89–90; domestic national resistance against imperialist incursions in, 86; education of children from throughout at Cuba's Isle of Youth, 88; education of nationals from throughout at ELAM, 181; great literary heritage of, 15; indigenous resistance to European colonial incursions against, 84–85

Lenin, Vladimir, 4, 10, 11

LGBTQ individuals, 18, 29, 170, 182, 214, 227nn35–36

liberation. *See* freedom; independence; internationalism

Liberia, 183–84, 189, 190

literacy: alphanumeric approach to teaching, 153; as an element of Cuban internationalism, 2, 53, 72, 151–56, 221; eyesight as a factor in learning to read and write, 172; illiteracy in pre-Revolutionary Cuba, 145; nationwide campaign of 1961 in Cuba, 24, 30, 145–52, 228n10, 238n1, 238n6; One Laptop per Child (OLPC) campaign, 156–57; as a powerful first step toward critical thinking and knowledge acquisition, 157–58; promotion of as a goal of Mexico's Zapatistas, 94; promotion of in Mexico, 155–56; as a social rather than individual problem, 154; teaching materials used to promote in Cuba, 146–47; UNESCO program ratings of, 155–56; work of Conrado Benítez Brigade to teach in rural Cuba, 146, 154–55; work of Cuba to promote among blind persons, 239n22; work of Homeland (or Death) Brigade to teach to Cuban factory workers, 146; work of People's Literacy Teachers to teach adult Cubans, literacy (*continued*)

146; work of Schoolteacher Brigades in overseeing Cuba's program for domestic, 146; worldwide illiteracy rates among women, 148; Yes I Can (Yo sí puedo) campaign to promote worldwide, 152–54, 155, 158, 172, 221, 238nn10–11, 239nn14–22. *See also* education

market economy, 33, 35, 55, 109, 157, 219

Martí, José, 13, 30, 46, 83–84, 210, 225n23, 227n39

Martínez, Kelly, 66

Marxism, 3–4, 43, 71, 134, 181–82, 234n5

Matthews, Herbert, 49

medical aid: assembly-line cataract removal, 54, 172, 221; four categories of Cuban, 173; high incidence of inadequate infrastructures in countries that require, 190; inaccessibility of for-profit, 164; medicines and equipment provided through Cuban, 174; mission of Carlos Mejías Márquez in Yemen, 179; mission of Laidi Fernández de Juan in Zambia, 135–43; mission of Nancy Alonso in Ethiopia, 123–34; nursing assistance, 33, 106, 123–24, 174, 185, 186–87, 189–91; Operation Miracle (Operación milagro), 171–73, 176, 240n2; Pedro Kouri Tropical Medicine Institute (Instituto de Medicina Tropical "Pedro Kourí," IPK), 185, 187, 189; surgical procedures, 54, 171–74, 176, 181, 240n2; vaccinations, 169, 181. *See also* health care; internationalism

medical care: abortion policies and procedures in Cuba, 168; access to emergency in Cuba, 166, 167; access to in pre-Revolutionary Cuba, 161, 163; cataract removal, 54, 171–73, 221; for cholera, 99, 180, 241nn14–15; Cuban model for, 164–65, 167–68; eye care, 54, 172–73, 176, 221; family practice teams, 164, 166–67, 168; HIV/AIDS management in Cuba, 169–70, 240nn10–12; for malaria, 136, 185, 188; medical vulnerabilities of Cuban populace, 164, 240n6; Ministry of Public

Health (Ministerio de Salud Pública, MINSAP), 165, 168; National Health Service, 167; Operation Miracle (Operación milagro), 171, 172, 176, 240n2; polyclinics in Cuba, 166, 168; for posttraumatic stress disorder (PTSD), 107, 177, 183; preventive medicine, 160–61, 164, 165, 168, 169; as a priority of Cuban Revolution, 17, 18, 164; Ramón Pando Ferrer Institute of Ophthalmology, 172–73; Rural Medical Service, 165; smoking as a chronic problem among Cubans, 240n6; socialized medicine as defined in Cuba, 160, 167–68; for trauma, 88, 179, 182; universal primary in Cuba, 167; vaccinations, 160–61, 168, 169. *See also* hospitals

MEDICC (Medical Education Cooperation with Cuba): health care in rural Cuba, 163, 240n4; holistic medical approach of, 182, 240n9; *MEDICC Review*, 163, 169, 182, 186–90, 240–41nn9–11, 241–42n2, 241n23; mission of, 163, 176, 240n4, 240n7, 240n9, 241n13

Mella, Juan Antonio, 48, 228–29n16, 239n8

memory, 31, 35–36, 46, 85, 139, 182

mental health: as an element of assistance offered to foreign nationals in Cuba, 88, 182; as an element of Cuban long-term internationalist assistance, 101, 182–83, 241n13; as a standard element of Cuban health care, 160; work of Cuban artists in countries hit by natural disaster, 33, 183, 217; work of Martha Machado Artists Brigade in promoting, 183, 228–29n16

mestizo (*mestizaje*), 14, 45, 83, 84

Mexico: Aztec heritage of, 84; Cuba as a refuge for rebels from, 88–90, 94, 159–60; Cuba's Yes I Can literacy program in, 154–56, 239n20; drug cartels and gang warfare in, 93; great literary heritage of, 5, 22, 27, 223n7; historic ties between Cuba and, 14, 45, 84–85, 86, 94, 236n4; landmass and population of, 44, 53, 83; membership of in UNASUR, 234n1; Mexican-American War, 83; Mexican

Revolution, 85–86; Octavio Paz (poet), 5, 223n7; President Lázaro Cárdenas, 85–86; as a refuge for Cuban rebels, 86, 236n4; Spanish colonialism in, 84; training of Mexican nationals at ELAM, 181; Zapatistas, 89–90, 94–95

military aid: Cuban assistance in wars of liberation, 1–2, 12–13, 69–71, 74, 77, 87, 93, 101, 213; Cuban to assist African anticolonialist freedom fighters, 71, 75, 76, 81, 221; Cuban to end apartheid in southern Africa, 70–78, 106, 111–13, 121, 199, 214, 221; idea of "enemy," 119–20, 214. *See also* internationalism

Moncada Barracks, Santiago de Cuba, 48, 49, 223n5, 230nn10–11, 238n9

Morejón, Nancy, 5, 65

Mozambique, 71, 106, 199, 224n17

Namibia: Cuban military aid to, 106, 221; education of Namibian children at Isle of Youth in Cuba, 88; experiences of Ricardo Alarcón in, 101–2; liberation of as a by-product of Angola's independence, 74–75, 77; New York Accords, 75, 233n13

nation: as constituting all of humanity, 13; government actions versus attitudes and actions of a national populace, 104, 149–50, 206, 236n15; origins of Cuba's identity as a, 13, 61

nationalism: Cuban, 12–13, 203, 210–11; Cuban reactions to its emigrants, 211–12; fear, hatred, and, 212, 213, 215, 216; internationalism versus, 200, 210–13; loyalty to homeland as, 212, 214–15, 216–17; as a lust for power, 204, 212, 216; nationalist movements and nation-building, 30, 210, 233n16; nationalist pride, 203, 210–11, 213, 216–17

Negroponte, Nicholas, 156–57

neoliberalism, 85, 86–87, 91, 95, 235n6

Netherlands, the, 46, 83, 206

New Zealand, 154, 239nn14–15

Nicaragua: Contras, 91; Cuba as a refuge for rebels from, 89; Cuban internationalist contributions in, 90, 93, 106, 151, 152, 184,

216, 217–18; dictatorship of Anastasio Somoza, 85; education of Nicaraguan children at Isle of Youth in Cuba, 88; education of Nicaraguan nationals at ELAM, 181; implementation of Cuba's Yes I Can literacy program in, 152; membership of in COMECON, 224n17; Sandinistas, 50, 86, 90, 220–21; training of Sandinista liberation fighters in Cuba, 2, 89–90; U.S. intervention in, 50, 83, 90, 91

Niger, 152

Nigeria, 157, 181, 199

nonaligned nations, 12, 15, 72

Núñez Mosquera, Pedro, 76–77

Olympics: case of Javier Sotomayor (high jumper), 194–95, 199; Cuban medalists, 194, 195, 196, 198; Cuban participation in Summer, 193, 198, 199, 242n6; Cuban winnings in, 198, 199–200, 203; doping violations at, 194–95, 241–42nn2–3; Fidel Castro on the athlete as an embodiment of honor, 105; professional versus amateur athletes, 194

Organization for European Economic Cooperation (EEC), 224n17

Organization of American States (OAS), 23, 51, 52

Organization of Solidarity with the People of Asia, Africa and Latin America (Organización de Solidaridad con los Pueblos de Asia, África y América Latina, OSPAAAL), 28

outreach. *See* internationalism

Pakistan: Cuban disaster response to 2005 earthquake in Kashmir, 174–75; Cuban humanitarian aid to, 71; Cuban medical internationalism in, 174–75, 241n16; public thanks by to Cuba for its aid, 221, 240n6; training of Pakistani medical students in Cuba, 175

Panama: Cuban internationalist sports programs in, 199; education of Panamanian nationals at ELAM, 181; liberation of by Simón Bolívar, 84–85; membership

Panama (*continued*)
of in UNASUR, 234n1; U.S. intervention in, 91, 102

Pan American Games, 193–95, 198, 200, 202, 203

Paraguay: dictatorship of Alfredo Stroessner, 85; education of Paraguayan nationals at ELAM, 181; membership of in UNASUR, 234n1

Partners in Health, 185, 189, 206, 207

Pereira Dos Santos Van Dumen, Cándido, 81–82, 233n24

Pérez, Jorge, 185–90, 241n23

Peru: Ancash Earthquake of 1970 (Great Peruvian Earthquake), 173–74; Cuban assistance to following Ancash Earthquake, 174; Cuban assistance to rebels fighting for liberation in, 89–90; Cuban internationalist sports programs in, 199; education of Peruvian nationals at ELAM, 181; great literary heritage of, 5, 15, 223n7; Hilda Gadea (revolutionary), 86; José de San Martín (early rebel leader), 84–85; José Gabriel Túpac Amaru (early rebel leader), 84; membership of in UNASUR, 234n1; President Juan Velasco Alvarado, 93; U.S. intervention in, 90–91

poets: as commentators on human condition, 22–23, 25; Cuban on living in an island environment, 65–68; Cuba's heritage of great, 5, 6, 14, 27, 28–29, 30; far-reaching impact of, 5–6, 23, 41, 65, 223–24nn7–9; function of as a society's conscience, 1–2, 5, 33, 38, 65, 223n7; great Latin American, 5; intellectual nurturing of in post-Revolution Cuba, 25, 26–27, 40; powerful role of poetry in Cuba, 14, 27; in repressive environments, 24; revolution as inspiration for, 6, 23. *See also* art and artists; creativity; writers

Portugal: 1974 Revolution of the Carnations in, 70, 232n3; Cuban assistance in liberating colonies of, 70, 116; loss of colonies by following Revolution of the Carnations, 70, 72–73, 232n3

poster art: Cuban poster artists, 28; influence of OSPAAAL on worldwide revolutionary activism, 28, 228n8; liberation struggles as a major subject matter for, 31; protest song, 14, 32; worldwide culture-building impact of, 31–32, 34

poverty: compounding effects of, 100; Cuba's assistance to other poor countries, 2–3, 19, 53–54, 72, 110, 168–69, 173, 176; housing for poor in Angola, 117; as an incentive for rebellion, 93–94; populist governments that have fought, 93–94; in pre-Revolutionary Cuba, 163–64; race and, 19, 64; traits of in most poor countries, 8, 19, 89, 94, 99–100, 120, 173; in U.S., 18, 150, 178, 231n19; violence against poor and those who assist them, 77, 223n2

prisoners and prisoner exchanges, 51, 63, 91, 103, 124, 136n13, 230n15

propaganda: anti-Castro by U.S., 18, 54–55, 194, 231n20, 237n20; anti-Cuba by U.S., 44; by U.S., 71, 85, 92–93, 145, 231n18

PSP (People's Socialist Party), 3, 4, 41, 48, 230n10

publishing and publications: in Cuba, 24, 28–29, 224–25n19, 227n1, 227n36, 230n8; use of opposite-gender pseudonyms among writers, 29; Vigía publishing collective, 17

Puerto Rico: African influences on culture of, 37; as a U.S. territory, 47, 63, 83; membership of in OSPAAAL, 235n6; training of Puerto Ricans at ELAM, 178

racism: apartheid in Africa, 70–78, 106, 112, 113, 121, 199, 214, 221; bell hooks on, 215–16; in Cuba, 23, 46, 78, 150; as an element of attitudes toward neighboring countries, 61, 64, 86, 216; as an element of colonialism, 44–45, 46; institutionalized, 212, 214–15; racial categorization, 234n19; segregation, discrimination, and prejudice, 50, 78, 120, 150; in U.S., 150, 212

radio: as a medium for delivery of *Yes I Can* programming, 152–55; Radio and Television Martí, 90, 231n20; *Voice of Vietnam*, 108

refugees, 62, 69, 71, 89, 104, 223n2, 231n18

rehabilitation: as a challenge to Cuba's domestic health care system, 168; concept of, 182–83; ongoing on-site post-disaster foreign assistance by Cuba, 100–101, 177–79, 181–83, 241n13

religion: African religious practices in Cuba, 7, 37; as an area of internationalist cultural respect, 128–32, 155, 182; Catholic Church in Cuba, 37, 181, 229n20; and creativity in Cuba, 7–8, 30–31; reconciliation of Cuban Revolution to popular practice of, 181–82; religious freedom for guests in Cuba, 175; Santería, 6, 7, 181

repression: as a by-product of Stalinism, 10, 12, 225n21; children as victims of, 88–89, 103; of creativity and freedom of expression, 6, 38–39, 224–25n19, 225n21, 227n36, 228n4, 228n13; damaging effects of, 38–39, 225n21, 226n26, 236n13; emigration as a response to, 38, 88; fear, censorship, and self-censorship as products of, 38; Five Gray Years (El Quinquenio Gris) in Cuba, 13–14, 31, 39–40, 73, 226n26; hiding as a response to, 88, 159; as a product of revolution, 6, 38; rebellion and revolution as responses to, 70, 93–95; repressive periods, 13–14, 16, 38–40, 54; survival of creativity through periods of, 17, 31, 38, 224–25n19, 226n13; as a topic of creative work, 31; U.S. support of repressive political regimes, 85

revolution: in Africa, 70–74, 101–2, 106–7, 233n16; Bolivarian, 86, 93; Che Guevara's dedication to, 70–72, 87, 95, 96, 101, 115, 218, 233n8, 234n5, 235n10; in China, 10, 12, 38, 39, 53; as collaborative product of multiple, differing political interests, 11, 48; concept of "exporting," 1–3, 53, 70–72, 90–93, 96, 105; Cuban military

aid to foreign liberation movements, 1, 64, 70–74, 97, 100; as an impetus to creativity, 6, 17, 23, 32, 38–39; as an inherently homegrown phenomenon, 70; internationalism as a moral virtue of, 3, 13, 53–54, 89, 100–107, 122, 145, 208; José de San Martín's accomplishments, 83–85; José Martí's ideas concerning, 13, 225n23; in Latin America and Caribbean, 2, 45, 49–50, 64, 85–86, 93, 101–2, 236n13; liberating, emancipating goals of, 11, 45, 48–50, 53–54, 70–72, 85–87, 91, 101, 236n13; in Middle East, 71, 232n1; as mission of OSPAAAL (Organization of Solidarity with the People of Asia, Africa and Latin America), 28, 87, 235n6; nation as a product of, 13; Portugal's 1974 Revolution of the Carnations, 70, 232n3; as possibility and transformation, 1–2, 64, 85, 87; pre-twentieth-century revolutionary leaders, 46–47, 73, 83–85, 225–26n29; revolutionary sentiments as inherent to Cuban cultural tradition, 11–12; rights and, 39–40; Russian Revolution, 6, 9, 38, 39, 53, 70; Simón Bolívar's accomplishments, 83–85, 86, 93; as social change, 1, 4, 7–8, 10–12, 53, 105, 216–18, 224–25n19; socialist, 4, 8, 9–12; Spanish Civil War, 100; in Vietnam, 2, 12, 53, 87, 108–9. *See also* Cuban Revolution

Revolution of 1959: and Cuban culture, 30, 33, 41; as an impetus underlying Cuban internationalism, 4, 12–13, 108; as a turning point in Cuban history, 9

rights: acquisition of as a goal of rebellions and revolutions, 39, 85–86, 94–95; basic human, 26, 50, 62, 169, 192; basic human as a goal of Cuban Revolution, 26, 50, 192, 209; defense and promotion of human, 226–27n33, 235n6; denial of human, 62, 223n2; Universal Declaration of Human (1948), 62; within context of revolution, 39–40; women's, 32

Roca, Blas, 4, 230n10

Rodríguez, Carlos Rafael, 4, 230n10

Rodríguez, Gilda, 33, 34

Rodríguez, Mariano, 6, 224n11
Rodríguez, Silvio, 37–38, 40, 226n28, 229n23
Rodríguez Gutiérrez, Milena, 29, 68
Romay, Zuleica, 46, 78, 230nn8–9, 234n21
Ruíz Montes, Laura, 67
Russian Revolution, 6, 9, 38, 39, 53, 70

sacrifice: Cuban sense of necessary, 23–24, 100, 121, 122, 151, 191, 210, 213–14, 217; effects of on recipients, 75; patriotism as, 93, 107; sense of underlying Cuba's July 26 Movement, 49
salaries: in Cuba, 148, 161, 167; of individuals on internationalist missions, 122, 123, 151, 158, 172, 212; of international athletes, 194, 196–97, 202; low as a cause of corruption in modern Cuba, 17–18; as a tool of U.S. brain drain of Cuban talent, 52, 161
Santamaría, Haydée: as a Cuban revolutionary, 17, 49, 238n9; internationalism of, 103, 122, 218; leadership of Casa de las Américas by, 27, 40, 224–25n19, 226n28, 227n38
Santería, 6, 7, 181
Santiago de Cuba, 25, 48, 49, 230n11, 238n9
schools: agricultural in Cuba, 152; Antón S. Marenko Teaching Institute, 152; attendance and graduation rates in Cuba, 24; boarding in, 137, 150; construction and renovation of as a priority of Revolutionary Cuba, 17, 24, 228n4; construction of as an element of Cuban internationalism, 72; Cristino Naranjo School, 196; Cuban attitudes regarding schools for students with disabilities, 201; Cuba's funding of its, 144–45; Cuba's national ballet school, 37, 229n19; Higher Institute of Art (ENA), 25, 228n5; international in Cuba, 88, 101, 102–3, 150–51, 191, 208; on Isle of Youth, 88, 102–3, 236n9; Latin American School of Medicine (Escuela Latinoamericana de Medicina, ELM), 101, 164, 178, 181, 191, 208, 241n11; Lenin School, 150–51; National Art School

(Escuela Nacional de Arte, ENA), 25–26; Piti Fajardo Medical School, 135; "selective" versus "exclusive," 26; special for deaf individuals in Cuba, 201; sports in Cuba, 196. *See also* education
Sierra Leone: Cuban medical aid during Ebola pandemic in, 183–90, 206, 208, 212, 221, 241n24; Cuban military assistance to, 72
slavery: runaway slaves (maroons), 45, 230n7; slave rebellions in Cuba, 7, 45, 46–47, 73; in Spanish colonial Cuba, 13, 45, 73, 76, 78; use of island of Cuba as a way station for mainland-bound slaves, 61
social change: Cuba as a new model for implementing, 32, 53–54, 93, 105, 226n26; experimental, culture-specific nature of, 11, 15, 16, 23, 28, 53, 105; medicine and health care as bases for, 206; new kinds of human beings as products of revolutionary, 3, 209; as practical enactment of sociopolitical discussions, 8; roles of art and culture in achieving, 28, 218, 226n26
socialism: 1917 Russian Revolution, 9, 70; access to opportunities and services as an element of, 3, 153, 167–68, 243n12; African practices of, 73, 121; amateur status of athletes in socialist countries, 194, 204; capitalist fear and stereotyping of, 92, 167–68, 211; Che Guevara's reservations concerning Stalinist, 12, 40, 223n3, 225n21, 229n24; Council of Mutual Economic Aid, 9; Cuban Revolution interpreted as a socialist revolution, 4, 8–9, 87; democratic elections that have installed socialist governments, 89; dogmatic approach to by Soviet proponents, 10–12, 225n21, 232–33n4; egalitarian orientation of, 3, 199; emergence of a unique Cuban, 43, 204, 216, 218–19, 227n37, 229n20, 230n16; environment, culture, and tradition as factors that shape practice of, 10, 46, 229n20, 229n24; Fidel Castro on construction of a socialist society, 12; influence of on national cultures, 10–12; internationalist

orientation of, 9, 10, 70, 100, 209, 216–17, 243n10; Latin American practices of, 64, 86, 89–90, 95, 223n7, 235n10; opposition of to apartheid and racism, 199; persistence of racism and sexism within Cuba's system of, 78; revolution in Vietnam as a socialist process, 12; socialist realism, 12, 40, 223n3, 225n21, 227–28n2; Soviet versus Chinese, 9–10, 43, 233n8. *See also* communism

social justice, 2, 13, 32, 54, 73

Solás, Humberto, 7, 224n13

soldiers: Cuban sent on internationalist missions, 54, 72, 75, 92, 122, 125, 209; Cuban training of revolutionary of other countries, 2, 69, 74, 87, 89, 92, 97, 235n7; humanitarian activities of Cuban serving overseas, 72, 217; of July 26 Movement, 49; PTSD among returning, 107–8

solidarity: antidictator, anticolonial attitudes as forces that unify oppressed peoples, 14, 75, 76, 89, 94, 199; concept of human community that underlies, 13, 41, 106, 109, 111, 131, 158, 185, 217–21; Cuban domestic initiatives that have influenced its internationalist, 20, 53, 172–73, 178–79, 239n18; Cuban international outreach as a model of, 1, 4, 8, 13, 15, 41, 53–54, 102–4, 209–10; as an element of revolutionary mindset, 9, 108–9, 215–19; as a force underlying Cuban disaster relief, 2, 8, 21, 53–54, 95, 173–77; geopolitical logic underlying Cuban in Africa, 73; integrity and ingenuity as unifying values of, 35, 43, 49, 87, 95, 218–20; OSPAAAL (Organization of Solidarity with the People of Asia, Africa and Latin America) initiatives and events, 28, 235n6; Sister City initiatives to promote, 104–5; U.S. organizations that participate in international, 104; Venceremos Brigade, 104. *See also* Cuban Revolution; internationalism

Somalia, 124, 125

South Africa: collaborations of pro-apartheid with colonial and imperial powers, 70–75; Cuban military support of African peoples fighting apartheid, 70–77, 102, 106, 120; experiences of Mark Behr, 214–15, 243n7; membership of in OSPAAAL, 235n6; military incursions into other countries by apartheid, 70–74, 77, 106, 233n6; military presence in Angola of apartheid, 72, 73, 74–75, 77, 214, 233n6; New York Accords, 72, 233n13; Olympic Game boycotts to protest apartheid in, 199; President Nelson Mandela, 75–76, 77, 221, 233n17; pro-apartheid South African Defense Fund (SADF), 74, 214–15

South American Community of Nations (Unión de Naciones Suramericanas, UNASUR), 234n1

South West Africa. *See* Namibia

Soviet Union: Comintern, 70, 232–33n4; Council for Mutual Economic Assistance (COMECON), 224n17; Cuban economic dependency on, 12, 14–15, 18, 41, 50, 55, 79, 123; Cuba's move into political orbit of, 9, 12, 50; disintegration of, 10, 43, 55, 79, 123, 167, 226n30; dogmatic approach to socialism of, 11, 70; internationalist tradition of, 10, 74, 80, 100; response of Khruschev's to Cuban Revolution, 3–4; Russian Revolution, 6, 9, 70; socialism of, 9–11; sports doping practices of, 195, 241n1; Stalinism versus Trotskyism and Leninism in, 10–11; years 1917–1925 as a period of artistic innovation in, 6

Spain: as a colonial power in Latin America and Caribbean, 36, 45–47, 83, 84–85, 225n23, 225–26n25, 237n17; Spanish American War, 47; Spanish Civil War, 10, 76, 100, 108, 210, 236n3

Special Period in Peacetime (El período especial en tiempo de paz), 55, 226n30

sports: access to as a human right, 26, 55, 193, 203–4; amateur versus professional participation in Cuban, 193–95, 197, 201–2; baseball, 52, 61, 192–93, 197–98, 203; boxing, 193, 198; crisis in Cuban

violence (*continued*)
103, 236n13; attributed to U.S. personnel, 2, 63, 72, 90, 91–92, 97, 223n1; Convention against Torture, 62; disappearances, 85, 89, 95, 223n2; illegal imprisonment, 62, 63, 89, 91–92, 225n23, 230n15, 236n13; kidnapping, 76, 78, 94, 124, 236n13; murder, 48, 49, 72, 85, 103, 105, 147, 223n7, 230n10, 238n2; rape, 223n1; terrorism, 110, 146–47, 221, 237n20, 238n2; torture, 2, 48, 49, 63, 85, 89, 91–92, 238n2
volunteers. *See* internationalism

women: in Angola, 119; antifeminist Federation of Cuban Women, 220, 227n35; as *brigandistas* in Cuba's 1961 literacy campaign, 146, 148, 238n1, 238nn5–6; Cuban Revolution as a redefining influence on, 23, 24, 61, 148, 227n38, 229n19, 238n6; discrimination against, 23, 119, 128, 131; employment for in Cuba, 148, 234n19; in Ethiopia, 128, 131; feminists and feminism, 16, 29, 31, 181–82, 215, 226n32; gender inequality and stereotyping of, 29, 32, 61, 78, 94, 148; literacy rates among Cuban, 24–25, 148; medical care targeted for, 148, 168; Muslim, 131, 132; in Pakistan, 174–75; participation of in Cuba's military aid missions, 80; participation of in July 26 Movement, 41, 49; school attendance among Cuban girls, 24; slave rebel, Carlota, 46–47, 73; world-class Cuban athletes, 194, 196, 198–99; worldwide literacy rates for, 148; worldwide participation of as freedom

fighters, 89, 105; in Yemen, 179; in Zambia, 139, 141, 143, 238n3
World Bank, 91, 227n34
writers: *Cecilia Valdés* (novel, 1839), 7–8; challenge to in obtaining materials during times of shortage, 34–35; Cirillo Villaverde, 7; essayists and essays, 30, 202–4, 216–17, 230n8; Five Gray Years (El Quinquenio Gris), 31, 39, 225n21, 226n26, 226n31; function of as a society's conscience, 10, 30, 41, 105, 202, 216–17, 225n23, 230n8, 233n16; great Cuban, 10, 29, 40; influence and outstanding quality of Cuban, 15, 27, 29, 41, 218; internationalist mission experiences as an inspiration to Cuban, 111–12, 125–26, 135, 137–43, 217; island environment of Cuba as an inspiration to its, 65–68; Mark Behr (South African novelist), 214–16; Nancy Alonso on experience of writing, 133, 237n4; short story, 10, 28, 67, 134, 135, 137–43, 217; support and promotion of by Cuban government, 26, 28, 30, 39–40. *See also* art and artists; intellectuals; poets

Yáñez, Mirta, 66, 133
Yemen, 71, 179, 199, 207, 224n17
Yes I Can (Yo sí puedo) literacy program, 152–55, 158, 172, 221, 239nn14–15

Zaire, 72, 73, 74, 190
Zaldívar, Alfredo, 66–67
Zambia: Cuban medical assistance in, 135–37; Maasai tribesmen, 140
Zarza, Rigoberto, 200, 201, 242n8
Zimbabwe, 71, 184